WALCHEREN
1809

WALCHEREN 1809

The Scandalous Destruction of a British Army

Martin Howard

Pen & Sword
MILITARY

First published in Great Britain in 2012
By Pen and Sword Military
an imprint of
Pen and Sword Books Ltd
47 Church Street
Barnsley
South Yorkshire S70 2AS

Copyright © Martin Howard, 2012

ISBN 978 1 84884 468 1

Printed and bound in England by
CPI Group (UK) Ltd, Croydon, CR0 4YY

Typeset in Times New Roman by
Chic Media Ltd

Pen & Sword Books Ltd incorporates the imprints of
Pen & Sword Aviation, Pen & Sword Family History, Pen & Sword Maritime,
Pen & Sword Military, Pen & Sword Discovery, Wharncliffe Local History,
Wharncliffe True Crime, Wharncliffe Transport, Pen & Sword Select,
Pen & Sword Military Classics, Leo Cooper, Remember When,
The Praetorian Press, Seaforth Publishing and Frontline Publishing

For a complete list of Pen and Sword titles please contact
Pen and Sword Books Limited
47 Church Street, Barnsley, South Yorkshire, S70 2AS, England
E-mail: enquiries@pen-and-sword.co.uk
Website: www.pen-and-sword.co.uk

Contents

List of Illustrations

List of Maps

*   *   *   *

Acknowledgements

Staff at the following institutions have given me valuable assistance: Zeeuws Archief, Middelburg; The National Archives, London; The National Archives of Scotland, Edinburgh; The National Army Museum, London. I am most grateful to Peter Blom for his generous hospitality during my visit to Walcheren and for his crucial help with source material. Thanks to Ian Robertson for his support and advice and to Jamie Wilson for giving me the opportunity to tell the little known story of one of the greatest expeditions ever to leave Britain's shores.

Prologue

A Bad Omen

Thomas St Clair and his comrades in the Royal Scots were amused to see nightcaps popping up from behind the windows. It was 5 o'clock in the morning and the drums beating the old favourite *Hey, Johnnie Cope, are ye Waking Yet* had roused the good people of Chelmsford. The soldiers recognised some pretty faces and acknowledged them with a kiss of the hand and a smile. Marching on through London, they had to ask the permission of the Lord Mayor to cross the capital with unfixed bayonets. At Kingston, covered with dust and half-choked with the heat, they were drawn up and reviewed by the Duke of Kent. The Duke carefully inspected the knapsacks, commenting to the younger men that they would feel less heavy if carried high on the shoulders. Arriving at Portsmouth, a camp was made on South Sea Common; all the talk was of a secret expedition.

St Clair knew that troops were being 'brushed up' in all parts of the country. John Green and his fellows in the 68th Durham Light Infantry were also aware that something serious was afoot. His brigade had received orders to march fourteen miles in full military order twice a week. Men sometimes dropped down as if dead from the heat and fatigue. When the order came to make for Portsmouth the marches were forced and extra ammunition was carried. Nearly all the soldiers arrived lame. Green understood that such hardships were necessary preparation for what might be to come; he had recently shared his barracks with the devastated remnants of the 50th Regiment returned from the Corunna Campaign. Whatever their doubts, most officers and men put on a brave face. On the march to Deal, twenty-two year old John Kincaid of the 95th Rifles was determined to impress the natives. In addition to the numerous pistols in his belt he screwed up his usually placid features to appear as ferocious as possible.[1]

After the unpleasantness of the march, reaching the coast was a welcome respite. The sleepy towns of Ramsgate and Deal had been transformed overnight, suddenly full of thousands of soldiers and excited locals. An army doctor saw the shops filled with more people than on the busiest market day and the streets packed with troops of all ranks and descriptions moving about with 'all the bustle of the stock exchange'. Another officer thought Ramsgate to be like a 'country lady in a London rout'; everything was bustle, agitation and running backwards and forwards. Around the town and along the shore the fields were speckled with the white of the army's tents. Regimental bands played from morning till night. William Keep of the 77th was pleased with the appearance of so many troops in one place and was much impressed by the regiments of Highlanders with their black plumes, tartans, and bagpipes. He messed with three or four of his fellow officers. The cold meat and bottle of porter under the canvas canopy were, he insisted, better than the finest dinner he had ever sat down to. The number of visitors grew by the day. Keep's regimental comrade Robert Blakeney saw 'thousands' of superbly dressed women crowding on to the beach near Deal to the airs of the National Anthem. Blakeney was much affected; 'the show was august, the pageant splendid, the music enchanting'.[2]

If events on land left any doubt, then the scale of the force gathering offshore was proof that this was to be a 'Grand Expedition'. The chalk cliffs were crowded with sightseers staring in astonishment. St Clair thought the fleet to be magnificent and prodigious; it covered the whole surface of the water as far as he could see. A Scottish soldier imagined that the sea must be groaning under the weight of so many vessels. All agreed with Commissary Richard Henegan that this was the finest armada ever sent by England from her shores. He counted upwards of 100 pennants fluttering in the breeze on the navy's finest. The masts of the smaller transport ships, designed to carry the troops, appeared as a distant forest.[3]

On their march, St Clair and his friends had convinced themselves that the object of the expedition was Paris and the dethroning of Napoleon. Now, on the eve of departure, he had to admit that he was entirely ignorant of their destination. He was not alone. John Green heard various reports; 'some said it was one place, and some for another.' The medical officer was keen to get underway, irked by the fact that he was oblivious of where they were headed. He did, however, hear a growing rumour that the force was destined for Holland. An officer of the 81st wrote home that this was 'one of our secret expeditions, the precise object of which is known to all the world'. William Keep was in agreement that they were going to Flushing, a heavily fortified town on the island of Walcheren in the Scheldt Estuary.[4]

Following the bitter experience of the retreat to Corunna where the army's women had been abandoned, it had been decided that very few wives should accompany the troops. Rifleman Benjamin Harris heard a terrible outcry among the women on the beach as the time of departure approached. Some of them clung to their men so resolutely that the officers had to issue orders that they be separated by force. 'Even as we were in the boats and fairly pushed off, the screaming and howling of their farewells rang in our ears far out at sea.' In St Clair's regiment, no women were allowed to march from Chelmsford but many of them now congregated on the shore with their children. He also heard the lamenting cries as husbands and fathers stepped into the boats. Not all were so sympathetic. James Hale of the 9th only saw women with watery eyes who were deprived of their 'fancy men'. Another was reminded of Sir John Moore's maxim that a soldier should have nothing to do with a wife. He thought it a shame, however, to give them all up to non-military gentlemen.[5]

Officers and men were not immune to the pain of parting. St Clair's family were still in mourning for his brother William, killed in Martinique, and his mother had become hysterical when he had announced his orders. He talked her round and his sisters made up his kit in secret. William Dyott, an experienced campaigner, was in command of a brigade. This was the third time in eighteen months that he had been forced to take leave of his young family. These separations were hard to endure but as the moment of embarkation grew ever closer, dismal thoughts were replaced by excitement. Our anonymous doctor felt privileged to be part of such a momentous event. Watching the Rifle Corps and the mercenaries of the King's German Legion embarking and hearing the hurrahs of the men in response to the cheering of the watching crowd, he became elated. William Wheeler and his comrades in the 51st were gleeful at the turn of events and even St Clair, torn from the heart of his grieving family, rejoiced at the order to board the ships. He and his men stepped into the boats full of 'ardour and activity'. Lady Georgina Nugent, wife of a serving Lieutenant General, wrote in her diary.

> The Downs full of ships and altogether magnificent. The poor fellows cheering as they embarked, and I don't know why, but I could scarcely refrain from shedding tears at their joy; it seemed indeed so thoughtless when they were so soon to meet an enemy & c. But soldiers, I believe, never think, and perhaps it is fortunate for them that they do not.

Her husband had no doubt that the expedition would be successful and anticipated good news as early as the following week. William Keep expected to be back in a fortnight but John Gunn of the Black Watch was not so sure. During a heavy downpour at Ramsgate, a large ball of fire had appeared near the fleet. Soldiers and sailors who witnessed it thought it a bad omen. Many years later, Gunn wrote in his memoirs, 'the sequel will tell whether they were prophets or not.'[6]

Notes

1. St Clair, Lt Col T., *A soldier's recollections of the West Indies and America with a narrative of the expedition to the Island of Walcheren*, Vol. II, pp. 253–67; Green, J., *The Vicissitudes of a Soldier's Life*, pp. 23–4; Kincaid, J., *Adventures in the Rifle Brigade*, p. 1.
2. *The Walcheren Expedition. The Experiences of a British Officer of the 81st Regiment,* pp. 9–16; Keep, W. T., *In the Service of the King*, p. 36; Blakeney, R., *A Boy in the Peninsular War*, p. 128; Cooke, J., *A True Soldier Gentleman*, p. 51; *The Walcheren Expedition by a Medical Officer*, p. 112.
3. St Clair, Vol. II, pp. 278–82; *Vicissitudes of a Scottish Soldier*, p. 86; Henegan, R. D., *Seven Years Campaigning in the Peninsula and the Netherlands*, Vol. I, p. 71.
4. St Clair, Vol. II, pp. 260, 277; Green, p. 24; *The Walcheren Expedition by a Medical Officer*, pp. 111–12; *The Walcheren Expedition. The Experiences of a British Officer of the 81st Regiment*, pp. 11–2; Keep, pp. 38–43.
5. Harris, B., *Recollections of Rifleman Harris*, p. 172; St Clair, Vol. II, pp. 272–3; Hale, J., *The Journal of James Hale*, pp. 45–6; *The Walcheren Expedition. The Experiences of a British Officer of the 81st Regiment*, pp. 9–10, 17.
6. St Clair, Vol. II, pp. 255, 271; Dyott, W., *Dyott's Diary 1781–1845*, Vol. I, pp. 275, 285; *The Walcheren Expedition by a Medical Officer*, p. 112; Wheeler, W., *The Letters of Private Wheeler 1809–1828*, p. 23; *Lady Nugent's Journal*, July 21; NAS, GD 364/1/1188; Keep, p. 38; Gunn, J., *The Memoirs of Private James Gunn*, p. 103.

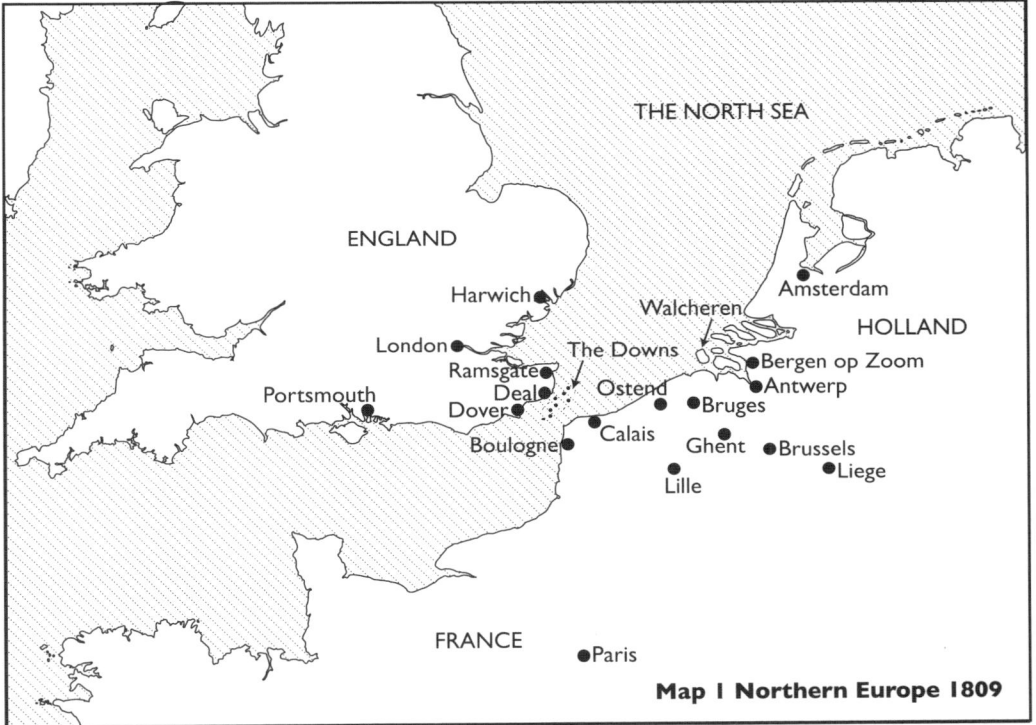

Map 1 Northern Europe 1809

THE NORTH SEA

ENGLAND

Harwich

London

Ramsgate

Portsmouth

Deal

Dover

Boulogne

The Downs

Ostend

Calais

Walcheren

Amsterdam

HOLLAND

Bergen op Zoom

Antwerp

Bruges

Ghent

Brussels

Liege

Lille

FRANCE

Paris

Map 2 The Scheldt 1809

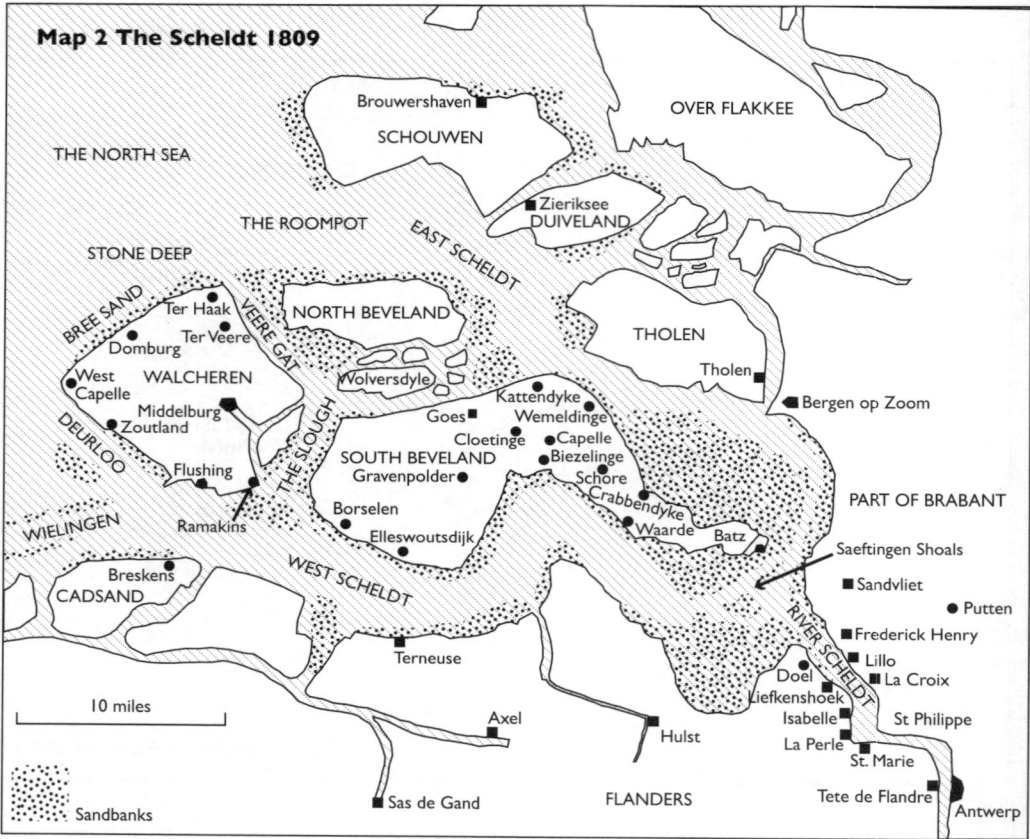

THE NORTH SEA

Brouwershaven

SCHOUWEN

OVER FLAKKEE

Zieriksee
DUIVELAND

THE ROOMPOT

EAST SCHELDT

STONE DEEP

BREE SAND

Ter Haak

Ter Veere

Domburg

VEERE GAT

NORTH BEVELAND

THOLEN

Wolversdyke

Tholen

West
Capelle

WALCHEREN

Bergen op Zoom

Middelburg

Zoutland

Goes

Kattendyke

Wemeldinge

Cloetinge

Capelle

DEURLOO

Flushing

THE SLOUGH

SOUTH BEVELAND

Biezelinge

Gravenpolder

Schore

PART OF BRABANT

Ramakins

Borselen

Crabbendyke

Elleswoutsdijk

Waarde

Batz

Saeftingen Shoals

WIELINGEN

WEST SCHELDT

Sandvliet

Breskens

Putten

CADSAND

Frederick Henry

RIVER SCHELDT

Lillo

Terneuse

Doel

La Croix

Liefkenshoek

Isabelle

St Philippe

Axel

La Perle

St. Marie

Hulst

FLANDERS

Tete de Flandre

Antwerp

Sas de Gand

10 miles

Sandbanks

Map 3 The British Landing on Walcheren and advance on Flushing
30 July-1 August, 1809

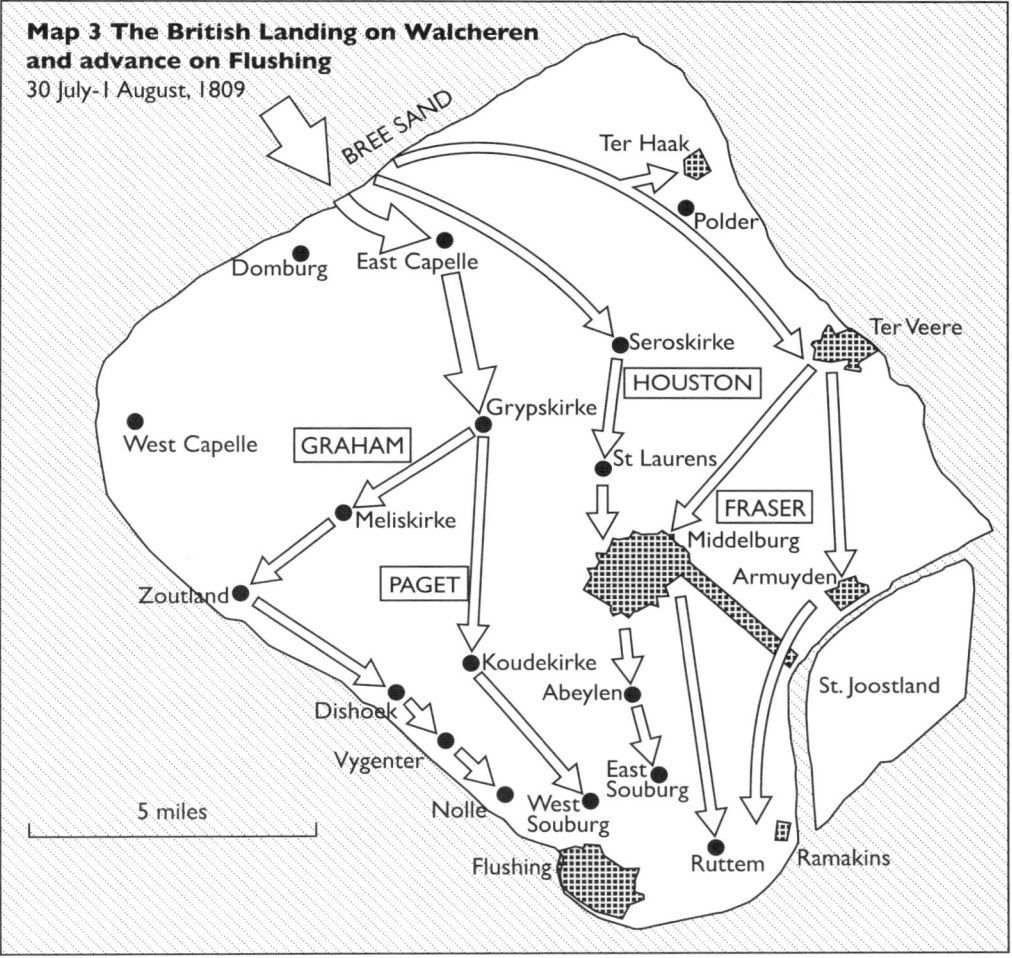

BREE SAND

Ter Haak

Polder

Domburg

East Capelle

Seroskirke

HOUSTON

Ter Veere

West Capelle

Grypskirke

GRAHAM

St Laurens

FRASER

Meliskirke

Middelburg

Armuyden

PAGET

Zoutland

Koudekirke

St. Joostland

Abeylen

Dishoek

Vygenter

East Souburg

5 miles

Nolle

West Souburg

Ruttem

Ramakins

Flushing

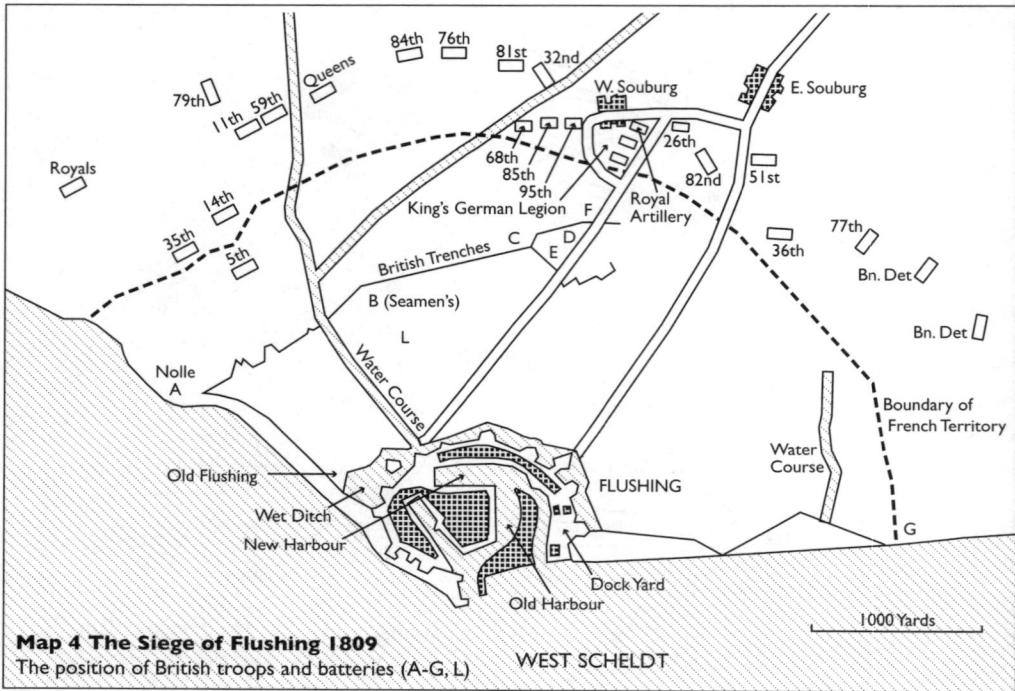

79th 11th 59th Queens 84th 76th 81st 32nd

Royals

W. Souburg E. Souburg

14th 68th 85th 26th 82nd 51st

35th 5th 95th 77th

King's German Legion F Royal Artillery 36th

British Trenches C D E Bn. Det

B (Seamen's) Bn. Det

Nolle L Boundary of French Territory

A

Water Course

Old Flushing Water Course

Wet Ditch FLUSHING

New Harbour G

Dock Yard

Old Harbour 1000 Yards

Map 4 The Siege of Flushing 1809
The position of British troops and batteries (A-G, L) WEST SCHELDT

CHAPTER 1

Generals and Admirals

The 1809 expedition to the Scheldt Estuary and the Island of Walcheren was in a long tradition of British amphibious assaults. The combined efforts of the Nation's army and navy since the Age of Elizabeth did not, in truth, justify much optimism. The attacks on Lisbon in 1589, Cadiz in 1595 and 1626, Toulon in 1707, Lorient in 1746, and Rochefort in 1777 were all 'brilliant in conception but lamentable in execution'. One notable exception to this catalogue of mediocrity was the Quebec campaign of 1759, where the young and supremely talented Major General James Wolfe snatched an improbable victory at the cost of his own life. Quebec was noteworthy for the high level of cooperation between the two services. Wolfe's naval colleague, Admiral Sir Charles Saunders, was content not to fight battles himself but to support the army by every means in his power. The admiral later wrote that 'during this tedious campaign there had continued a perfect good understanding between Army and Navy'. The writer of the military despatch, Field Marshal George Townshend, agreed:

> I should be wanting in paying my due respects to the Admiral and the Naval Service if I neglected this occasion to acknowledge how much we are indebted for our success to the constant assistance and support we have received and to the perfect harmony and immediate correspondence which has prevailed throughout our operations ...

In all the diaries and memoirs of the campaign there is no mention of friction between the services.

In the combined operations at the end of the eighteenth century and the early Napoleonic era, the challenge for British military and naval commanders, and indeed their political masters, was to reproduce the brilliance of Wolfe and Saunders and to maintain good relations between soldiers and sailors. This would be no mean achievement, there remaining the constant threat of fall-out between the services and a return to the more longstanding precedent of failure. Antagonism was potentially increased by the perceived ascendancy of the British Navy over the country's land forces.

1

Though the mutinies of 1797 were a serious setback, this memory was quickly erased by the naval victories of the Nile in 1798 and of Trafalgar in 1805. In contrast, the reputation of the British soldier was on the wane. Marlborough's campaigns were receding into the past and the purely military exploits of the 1790s were well summed up by Arthur Wellesley, the future Duke of Wellington, whose participation in the Flanders campaign of 1793–5 inspired the typically acerbic comment that he 'had learnt what one ought not to do, and that is always something'.

The care taken to try and paper over the cracks between the services is well illustrated by the Minorca expedition of 1798 where the naval commander, Commodore Sir John Duckworth, was advised to preserve the 'strictest harmony' with his military comrade, Lieutenant General Sir Charles Stuart. The latter was a very capable soldier and the British overwhelmed the Spanish garrison despite being outnumbered and lacking siege equipment. Stuart was grateful to the seamen who had helped him ashore, giving them sincere thanks. Unfortunately, the rancour between the services was never far below the surface and Duckworth bridled when Stuart refused to let him share in the capitulation, accusing the general of being a man who 'would sacrifice everything, the navy in particular, to military aggrandisement'. Despite these angry words, Duckworth later wrote to a superior that the two men had 'kissed and are friends again'.

The Helder expedition of 1799 was relatively small-scale in the context of the Second Coalition's uprising against France but it was a qualified success for British combined forces with an unopposed landing, the capture of a fleet, and the avoidance of disaster in two pitched battles. The army returned mostly intact. A year later, the uneasy relationship re-emerged in an abortive attempt to take Cadiz. The two commanders, General Sir Ralph Abercromby and Admiral Lord Keith, avoided any public recriminations but the whole enterprise was marked by hesitation and dissension. Abercromby believed Keith to have urged military action whilst evading responsibility. When the general was later appointed to command the British Army in Egypt in 1800, the Admiralty went so far as to suggest that Keith, apparently an automatic choice to lead the naval force, should instead send his second-in-command. The letter from the First Lord left no doubt as to the motivation for this change: 'there is a rumour that you and Sir Ralph Abercromby are not upon those terms of cordiality and good understanding which are essential to the conducting with energy and effect any conjunct operation'.

Such insights were no protection against further failures. Perhaps the greatest bungle was the expedition to South America in 1806 which was

2

accompanied by grandiose plans to conquer the whole continent. After an inauspicious start, things got considerably worse when Lieutenant General Whitelock's attack on Buenos Aires was such a disaster that he was forced to withdraw all his troops in return for an exchange of prisoners. On his return home, Whitelock was cashiered whilst the chief protagonist of the expedition, Captain Sir Home Popham of the Royal Navy, a man of whom we will hear more, escaped with a reprimand and was soon re-employed by the government. British morale was somewhat restored by the capture of Copenhagen in the summer of 1807. The operation was not universally popular among military officers, the Danes protesting their neutrality, but it was a complete success, giving the British control of the Baltic for the remainder of the war. Even such straightforward operations did, however, provide reminders of the pitfalls of amphibious warfare. The landing of troops in Denmark was unopposed but it still took a week to complete. Setting ashore 9,000 men at Mondego Bay on the Portuguese coast in 1808 took four days. The practical difficulties of moving large numbers of men and horses across the water and disembarking them on a hostile land were much increased by the vagaries of the weather and the lack of proper military intelligence.[1]

At the start of 1809, the British government, apparently undaunted by this rather mixed history of expeditionary success and mishap, was considering a new continental adventure for its combined armed forces. The Tory Prime Minister, the Duke of Portland, had previously held the post in 1794 but fifteen years later he was almost seventy years old and ill. He was often absent from cabinet, rarely spoke in the House of Lords and his leadership was of a nominal nature. Much more influential were a group of younger ministers including men such as Castlereagh, Canning, Hawkesbury (the Earl of Liverpool) and Perceval. On the whole, the cabinet functioned efficiently with ministers willing to accept the collective view and none individually powerful enough to threaten the status quo. However, two key politicians were incompatible. Viscount Castlereagh, originally Robert Stewart, was very experienced in high office. Entering the House of Commons when only twenty-one years of age, he acted as Secretary for Ireland before becoming an elected member. A determined opponent of France, he was Secretary of State for War and the Colonies from 1805 until the fall of the ministry after Pitt's death and he then occupied that post again under Portland in 1807. He gave such strong support to the Peninsular War effort that Wellington later said that a brother could not have done more to help him. George Canning had entered politics as a Member of Parliament in 1793 and then served as

3

Undersecretary in the Foreign Office, Joint Paymaster of the Forces, and as Treasurer to the Navy before becoming Foreign Secretary in Portland's cabinet. The great historian of the British Army, Fortescue, summarises the chasm between the Secretary for War and the Foreign Secretary.

> Canning's talents were brilliant, Castlereagh's were less conspicuous but more solid; Canning based his judgement chiefly upon intuition, often, but not always, amazingly true, Castlereagh upon laborious comparison of facts; Canning was witty, fluent, and eloquent in speech and writing, Castlereagh ponderous, clumsy, and inarticulate; Canning was tricky, vain, and consumed by egoism, Castlereagh was straightforward and thought first of his country; finally, Castlereagh was a gentleman and Canning was not.

Canning's personality invoked either admiration or loathing and he was often at odds with his more senior colleagues. Castlereagh was rather unpopular, his introversion often interpreted as arrogance and his poor public speaking losing him respect. Canning was thought more vital to the government's survival but Castlereagh had hidden depths.

The antagonism which was natural between two such different political animals was exacerbated by a lack of clarity as to the relative roles of the Secretary of State for War and the Foreign Secretary in wartime. In 1794, Pitt created the new post of Secretary of State for War from the previous separate posts of Secretary of State for Foreign Affairs (who planned campaigns in Europe) and the Colonial Secretary (who planned them elsewhere). The post, re-united with the Colonial Office in 1798, was undermined by its essentially part-time nature and it fitted awkwardly with the prestigious post of Foreign Secretary. The incumbent of the latter post, particularly if a forceful personality such as Canning, was also likely to take a keen interest in military strategy and would expect to be closely involved in the deployment of troops. In a sense, there was even less of a chance of unity than before, as the Foreign Secretary maintained the power to influence strategy but no longer had responsibility for its successful inception. It was all too easy to resolve different views between these two senior cabinet ministers with flaccid compromise, perhaps agreeing to military initiatives but not following them through. This was keenly felt in the Peninsula in 1809 when Wellington was denied enough men and specie to fully exploit his opportunities. The rift between Castlereagh and Canning was worsened by differences over military policy. Castlereagh sought to defend General John Moore's actions in Spain whereas Canning disliked

Moore and was always more likely to criticise senior military staff for shortcomings.

With such political discord, the more military post of Commander-in-Chief of the Army might have helped to stabilise the situation and, indeed, in 1809 it had been held for fourteen years by George III's second son Frederick, Duke of York. The Duke had almost single-handedly improved the army but now he was embroiled in scandal, an ex-mistress accusing him of using her as a channel for the receipt of bribes for promotion. It was unlikely that he played any part in this but he was censured and forced to resign. The Duke was popular with the rank and file and widely known as the soldiers' friend. In contrast, the government was often derided by military men. One officer, no doubt remembering Canning's lack of support for his generals in the Peninsula, wrote home from campaign that 'nothing is more cruel and more unjust than party attacks on the military'. The political gossip of the day was that the government was divided and its opponents were on the attack. William Cobbet, an ex-sergeant major and publisher of the famous *Weekly Political Register*, referred to the House of Commons as 'infamous and corrupted'.[2]

The cabinet, lacking strong leadership and distracted by scandal, had to make some difficult strategic decisions. There was a desperate need for a coherent vision. The military situation in early 1809 was dominated by a dramatic campaign in the Peninsula which can be traced back to the interplay of politics and military events of the previous year. It is important to appreciate that the contemporary perspective was quite different from our retrospective view. Whereas we now see the events of 1808–9 as simply the precursor to even greater drama and ultimate British, Spanish and Portuguese success in the Peninsular War, the politicians and generals at the outset of 1809 were confronted with unsurpassed difficulties and dangers. The first intervention in Portugal in August 1808, where British troops were led by the young Wellesley, was a qualified success with a decisive triumph over the French at the Battle of Vimeiro rather undone by the subsequent unpopular Convention of Cintra. The French were allowed to return home in British vessels carrying their loot, a concession which infuriated the Spanish. Despite its notoriety, the Convention was still a significant strategic victory with the French cleared from Portugal.

It was then resolved that an army of 30,000 infantry and 5,000 cavalry was to be employed in northern Spain under the command of Sir John Moore. British forces were to cooperate with the Spanish armies to drive the French back across the Pyrenees. By December, Madrid was under French occupation and Napoleon personally led a thrust at the rear and flank of the

British army. Moore executed a carefully planned escape and commenced the famed retreat from Sahagun to Corunna. A combination of appalling climate, difficult terrain, inadequate supplies and low morale took an increasing toll on the men. Corunna was finally reached on 11 January and a defeat inflicted on Marshal Soult's pursuing army four days later. Moore was killed but the army was able to embark unmolested. Despite the avoidance of a catastrophic defeat in battle, 6,000 British troops were lost; around 2,000 were sent as prisoners to France and the remaining 4,000 perished by the roadside or in hospital. The British papers trumpeted the victory at Corunna but the disembarkation of the remaining 28,000 filthy, exhausted soldiers on the south coast of England caused consternation and appeared more like an unprecedented disaster.

The government still hoped for ultimate success in the Peninsula. The Spanish people were unanimous in their resistance to the French invader. It was the only instance since the French revolution in which a whole nation had taken up arms in their own defence. In April 1809, the rising star, Arthur Wellesley, returned to Portugal at the head of 23,000 men.

Although providing staunch support to her Iberian allies, Britain's record of help to her other continental friends in the years since 1792 was patchy at best. To many continental observers, she appeared to stand aloof behind her ocean barrier, playing little part in the actual fighting against Napoleonic France. The returning army after Corunna was a small and isolated reminder of the realities of land warfare. Austria's request for help in the campaign of 1800 led to a British broken promise and again in 1805, the year of Austerlitz, Britain appeared to stand apart, spurning the opportunity to invade north Germany. During the Polish campaign of 1807, marked by the battles of Eylau and Friedland, British help was limited to the supply of arms. As 1809 unfolded, the government, already committed to Iberia, sensed a strategic opportunity created by a new Austrian war. This would be the only year of the Napoleonic era when two British armies, each of around 40,000 men, would march on the continent at the same time.[3]

Austria's latest conflict with Napoleon was catalysed by the creation of a 'war party' in Vienna in late 1808. Chief proponents of this new war were the Emperor Francis's wife, Ludovica, and Prince von Metternich, the Austrian Ambassador to France. Seeing that Napoleon would be weakened by the 'bleeding ulcer' of the Peninsula, they urged the Emperor to strike whilst France's forces in central Europe were limited to less than 200,000. Further encouragement was derived from Tsar Alexander's assurance of Russian neutrality and an alliance with Great Britain concluded in April 1809.

The Archduke Charles commenced hostilities without a declaration of war with a surprise attack in southern Germany. After initial Austrian successes, the superior French military machine gained the ascendency and the *Grande Armée* entered Vienna in May. It had been Austria's assumption that once the fighting started, Britain would come to her help. As was traditional in transactions between powerful European allies, Austria sought both huge financial support and direct military action. Any tardiness on Britain's part to comply with these demands was likely to be interpreted as more shilly-shallying and an unwillingness to endanger British specie and lives in the common cause. Resentment at Britain's substantial colonial and maritime power would be increased. Thus, when the first supplications were made, Britain was motivated to try and comply both by a need to pander to Austrian sensibilities and a strong desire to keep her continental friend fighting.

The demands were considerable. Austria asked for a subsidy of £5 million a year for her 400,000 men in the field as well as half that sum for equipment. The negotiations were undertaken in Malta by the diplomat Benjamin Bathurst who was permitted to proceed to Vienna as necessary, and also in London. The choice of Bathurst, a relatively minor player, probably reflected practical difficulties – he could leave the country unnoticed – rather than indifference. British ministers welcomed the approach but decided the amount was too much. They were already making a hefty financial commitment to the war in Spain. Negotiations continued and, by early July 1809, the temporary collapse of the Continental system, Napoleon's trade embargo, and a surge in British exports allowed the British to provide Austria with almost £1.2 million in subsidies. It was less than had been asked for but it was a laudable effort in the circumstances and the money was sorely missed elsewhere.

This left the question as to how Britain could aid Austria by military action. Vienna made proposals for expansion of British operations in the Peninsula, a possible landing in South Italy, and for an expedition to northern Germany to exploit anti-French feeling in the region. The British government had already taken some of this action. In the Peninsula, Wellington was leading an army in Portugal, and operations, albeit limited, were afoot in the Mediterranean. Admiral Collingwood coordinated naval sorties in the Adriatic and Sir John Stuart mounted an attack in the Bay of Naples. In reality, these southern initiatives could only make a small contribution to the Austrian cause compared with the more serious prospect of a diversionary attack in the mouth of the Weser in Germany.[4]

It is worth dwelling on the reasons for the rejection of the German option as it was the only major alternative to an attack on the Dutch coast and it was not only the Austrians who were lobbying for it. Ludwig van Kleist, a Prussian agent who claimed to represent the insurrectionary committee in Berlin, made his way to London and stated that the whole country between the Rhine and the Elbe was ready to rise up against the French without waiting for Prussia to declare war. This opinion was treated with caution, not least as Kleist's credentials were doubtful. He probably lacked the official support of his government; he has been described as being a 'mere adventurer' and also as a man 'wholly devoid of patriotic feeling'. Austria persisted with more conventional diplomatic pressure, also arguing that a British landing in the Elbe or Weser Rivers would incite a popular uprising. The cabinet remained unconvinced. They were reluctant to gamble on Prussian patriots – earlier spontaneous insurgency had not been sustained as it had been in Spain – and they were not disposed to send a large force to the north of Germany without Russia first declaring war on France.

Fortescue concludes that the rejection of the German expedition was the correct decision. Three great German patriots – Stein, Scharnhorst and Gneisenau – were plotting their country's freedom but the King, Frederic William, showed no inclination to take up arms. Any British expedition to Germany would depend much on the success of its continental allies. Ministers had fresh memories of the expedition to Bremen in 1805 which had been forced to turn back upon receiving news of the catastrophic defeat at Austerlitz. It was equally true in 1809 that if Napoleon defeated the allies, the French Emperor would then be able to turn on his greatest enemy with overpowering force leading to another inglorious evacuation.

The rejection of the German option brought another scheme, also previously considered by British governments, into sharp focus. This was an attack on Napoleon's great naval base at Antwerp on the River Scheldt, also referred to as the 'Walcheren expedition' as the capture of Walcheren, an island in the river, was a vital first step. There were purely practical considerations making Holland a more attractive target than Germany. Firstly, it was cheaper. This was significant as Britain's military and pecuniary resources were being drained by the number of troops maintained in Portugal, Sicily, and in her colonial possessions round the globe, and also by the subsidies to Spain and Austria. Castlereagh believed that a Scheldt expedition would enable the country to employ a higher proportion of its disposable force against the enemy than it could attempt to do so in any other way. William Huskisson, Secretary to the Treasury (but remembered as the first man to die in a railway accident), was equally confident that Britain could not afford the expedition to Germany. A campaign in Hanover would be on friendly soil and all local supplies would have to be paid for.[5]

The second consideration favouring the Scheldt was its proximity. This not only reduced cost but also allowed ministers greater control than would be the case for a more distant or protracted operation. It was difficult to send bodies of more than 5–10,000 men abroad because of the problems of supply and coordination. Chaotic events at the end of 1807 in the Mediterranean, where ministers completely lost the plot and Sicily was very nearly garrisoned twice over, was a reminder of how, in an age of rudimentary communications technology, control of the armed forces was tenuous. An assault across the North Sea on the Dutch Coast was therefore an attractive proposition. Thirdly, once disembarked in Holland, the army would be less vulnerable than in Germany. Intelligence (imperfect, as we will see) suggested that the entire northern coast of France had been denuded of troops to support Napoleon's effort against Austria. There appeared to be less risk of the expeditionary force becoming isolated and having to fight to escape a tight corner, or just dwindling away to no purpose or, worst of all, being trapped with no safe point of re-embarkation.

The fourth consideration was that an attack on the Scheldt would serve as a useful diversion for the Austrian cause as it would prevent all French troops in Holland marching east to the Danube and would also distract Napoleon's reserves around Strasbourg. Castlereagh believed that the French defence effort which would be required to frustrate the British attack on Antwerp would have to be on a scale which 'cannot fail to relieve our allies on the continent from much of the pressure to which they must otherwise be exposed in their present struggle for independence'. If the expedition was a success, then, with a garrison in place on the island of Walcheren, the remainder of the troops might be employed in some other part of Europe. Canning reassured his Austrian peers that the government would still consider the sending of British troops to Prussia, but only if the King had declared war against France and there was a regular allied army the British troops could join at disembarkation.[6]

When Castlereagh referred to the 'powerful' diversionary potential provided by the expedition to the Scheldt he also noted, cryptically, that this was in addition to the 'immediate pursuit of objectives of the utmost value in themselves'. The major reason for the British decision to target the Scheldt and the French naval forces of Antwerp was a self-serving one – the opportunity to extinguish the growing threat to British security and shipping. There is a modern perception that, during the Napoleonic period, Britain's pre-eminence on the seas was unchallenged and that the French Navy was a pale imitation of Albion's mighty armada. The truth is that the period was a renaissance of French sea power. When France conquered Belgium and Holland in 1794–5 it rid itself of one of its ancient weaknesses. Previously, it had no useful naval stronghold north and east of Brest but after 1794 there was Antwerp which Napoleon developed into a greater base than Brest itself. With another new base at Cherbourg and the traditional French naval facilities at Brest, Rochefort and Toulon, Napoleon was positioned to use the men and material from all the subject nations of his empire to out-build the Royal Navy. The French objective was a fleet of 150 line of battle ships. Not even the British victory at Trafalgar in 1805 stifled this ambition. Captain Edward Brenton, a naval veteran and historian, declared that after Trafalgar, 'another French navy, as if by magic, sprang forth from the forests to the seashore, manned by a maritime conscription exactly similar in principle to that edict by which the trees were appropriated to the building of ships'.

This danger persisted throughout the war; Britain could never hope to match Napoleon's capacity for the building and manning of ships. In 1809, with British naval superiority so parlous, the government was likely to take any opportunity to diminish France's naval might. Antwerp was an attractive target as its destruction, and that of the twin port of Flushing on Walcheren, would both reduce the enemy's shipbuilding capacity and also diminish the threat of a French invasion of Britain. The Scheldt had become France's second largest naval arsenal. It was well placed for the delivery of timber and other naval supplies via the Meuse and the Rhine and the French were able to build around twenty sail of the line each year, possibly as many as twenty-five. Once constructed, these vessels were sheltered behind the fortifications of Antwerp and the difficult navigation of the Scheldt estuary. Flushing was less well protected but ships could put to sea quickly and it was difficult to blockade because of the surrounding sandbanks.

Britain was nervous of Napoleon's growing naval strength and acutely anxious as to how it might be used against her. Antwerp was a 'pistol cocked and pointed at the head of England'. French control of the Low Countries posed a direct threat to the east coast. This was especially vulnerable being flat and with sea conditions and winds making defence difficult. A French invasion force might land in the Thames in less than a day. The estuaries of the Scheldt, Rhine and Meuse could shelter the large number of transport ships required for the invasion of Napoleon's greatest foe. The Emperor's forces on the Dutch coast held the initiative. That this threat was real, and not simply a theoretical difficulty for the government, can be discerned from the tone of contemporary memoirs and political commentaries. The diarist Charles Greville agreed with Lord Melville's analysis that if Antwerp was left untouched then Napoleon would have such a powerful fleet that 'our navy must have eventually been destroyed'. Melville was later to be First Lord of the Admiralty and was conversant with the latest intelligence from across the North Sea. Castlereagh, writing after the recapture of Copenhagen in 1807, warned that 'with the possession of Cartagena, Cadiz, Corunna, Ferrol and various other Spanish ports in addition to the ports of France, Holland, and likewise in possession of Copenhagen, the power of Bonaparte will be almost irresistible'. This palpable fear of French hegemony, and especially the threat of invasion from the Low Countries, makes Fortescue's allegation that ministers sent men to war in 1809 because 'when they chanced to have troops at their disposal [they] could never be easy until they employed them somewhere' appear unfair and overly reliant on hindsight.

Castlereagh used the above considerations to rationalise the case for the expedition; this was in essence a mixture of pragmatic decisions based on disposable forces and finance, and the more aspirational objectives of the stunting of French naval power and the support of Britain's allies. All agreed that there was little room for error. Captain Sir Home Popham of the Royal Navy commented that,

> In general, expeditions are so hurried off at the last, and with such little previous arrangement and attention to equipment, that it is the occupation of a long voyage to get all the appointments perfect; but here everything must be perfect before it moves: every man must know his duty and every implement its place; for it is more than possible that the whole armament may be in action before it has time to sleep after quitting the shores of England.[7]

The responsibility for this planning weighed heavily on Castlereagh's shoulders. He, more than any other, had recognised the growing menace of the Scheldt and had forcibly made the case for an attack; Gordon Bond refers to the 1809 assault as 'Castlereagh's Expedition' and this is apt. Castlereagh had qualities which made him suitable for this onerous task. We have already briefly compared him with the more exuberant Canning but it is worth analysing his strengths in more detail. He worked extremely hard and took a great deal of time to master the detail of any situation, characteristics he shared with both Napoleon and Wellington. Despite his seniority and influence, he was a modest man who readily sought advice. He was logical and capable of foresight, strengths which allowed him to bring consistency to his country's wartime strategy. As early as his first month in office, he wrote to the Duke of York that Britain must be ready 'to menace or attack the enemy on their maritime frontier and, by compelling them to continue in force on the coast and in Holland [to] weaken their efforts proportionally in other areas'. Although hardly profound, this suggests that Castlereagh's initiatives in early 1809 were part of a wider vision. He married a global perspective to sound methodology, bringing his intellect to bear on the nuts and bolts of fighting such as the training, placement, transport and make up of armies and the gathering of military intelligence. In Richard Glover's words, 'He did not fail to do the obvious things'. Fortescue lauded him as 'the ablest minister who has ever presided at the War Office'.

Castlereagh was widely admired for his diplomatic efforts later in the wars. The Prussians paid tribute to his calmness and firmness; he was a moderating influence in the fraught discussions of 1813–15. Men with whom he disagreed, including the Russian Tsar, still had respect for his judgement. Frederick Robinson, a friend of Castlereagh, who accompanied him on a diplomatic mission, described him in action.

> The suavity and dignity of his manners, his habitual patience and self-command, his considerable tolerance of difference of opinion in others, all fitted him for such a task; whilst his firmness, when he knew he was right, in no degree detracted from the influence of his conciliatory demeanour.

Castlereagh was not so appreciated in 1809 and he was vulnerable to political attack. In March, Canning began scheming to have him replaced by his political ally Richard Wellesley, the elder brother of the Duke of Wellington. Threatening his own resignation, he persuaded the weakening Duke of Portland to remove his rival. The Duke, who was to suffer a stroke only a few months later, procrastinated, hoping to put off the unpleasant decision until the summer. At this time, Lord Wellesley would take over at the War Office and, in the meantime, Castlereagh was to be kept in ignorance as to his fate. The Prime Minister communicated the plan to several confidants and, by April, the secret was so ill-kept that English travellers in Spain spoke openly of Canning's machinations. The saga played out in June, the Duke of Portland sending for Spencer Perceval, the devout leader of the House of Commons, and informing him of the agreement made with Canning for the removal of Castlereagh. The Prime Minister now understood the difficulty of disposing of a Secretary for War who had been working for weeks and months on a major expedition which was just about to come to fruition and for which he would be held responsible. Perceval, horrified at the whole affair, immediately wrote to Canning protesting at the deliberate concealment from Castlereagh. An awkward compromise was reached which left Castlereagh in post, pending the outcome of the expedition, and still ignorant of the conspiracy against him. Perceval was deeply troubled by his own role in the 'cursed business'. Canning, knowing that Portland's health would soon force him from office, was probably playing for higher stakes than the demotion of the Secretary for War.[8]

Whilst his nemesis continued his intrigues, Castlereagh spent the first half of 1809 in deliberation, consultation and planning. Time was crucial. The best part of the campaigning season was slipping by and the military situations in central Europe and in the Peninsula were in constant flux. The Archduke Charles of Austria and Napoleon were facing up to a major battle on the Danube and, if Britain was to have any impact on the outcome, decisive action was necessary. British victory over the French at Oporto on 12 May was heartening but was not in itself likely to satisfy Vienna. Castlereagh did at least have the advantage that Britain had been considering an attack on the Scheldt for many years. A document drawn up for Pitt in December 1797, and brought to Castlereagh's attention by Robert Dundas in June 1808, suggested Walcheren as the natural target for a combined army and navy operation against the French.

> As we can no longer divide the armies of France by continental wars, we ought to attempt the destruction of the armaments in the havens where they are preparing for invasions and thus oblige the French Directory either to find new plunder from their own subjects, or from among their oppressed allies, to support their armies or to run the risk of those armies turning on the upstart rulers of their devoted country.

The idea surfaced again in 1803 when Robert Hobart expressed a wish to attack Walcheren which was tempered by the need to concentrate on 'defensive measures'. In 1805, Castlereagh himself wrote to Lord Harrowby that the 'insulated and consequently apparently defensible situation of Walcheren strongly incline us to attempt its reduction'. A month later, again writing to Harrowby, he acknowledged that any plan for an immediate attack on Walcheren had been abandoned. The potential assault on the Dutch coast was judged 'a hasty effusion of zeal and vigour which would not bear the test of sober examination, more especially at this season, and in the present position of the armies'. However, the pressure on Britain to intervene in the Scheldt was relentless. As the war in Poland intensified, the Tsar pleaded for 'a diversion of the enemy in the north of Europe by a powerful expedition to the coast of France or Holland'.

Thus, when Castlereagh wrote his memoranda for a possible Walcheren expedition for the attention of the cabinet in early 1809 – curiously, these are not dated but as there is a reference to a possible role for Sir John Moore they must have preceded mid-January – he was rehearsing arguments which had exercised his mind for years rather than weeks or months. In the earliest memorandum, Castlereagh appears cautious of a full scale assault on the Scheldt, suggesting a limited attack on Walcheren prior to the landing of a larger force in north Germany. He refers to the poor cantonments on Walcheren, the possible outbreak of disease in the troops, and the difficulties in the subsequent forward movement of the army to a secondary theatre of operations.

> Under the circumstances, it may perhaps be prudent to confine the operation against Walcheren, in the first instance, to such an amount of force as may be deemed fully equal to its reduction and subsequent defence, which number may be accommodated on the island, with a due attention to their health ...

In a later note, the attack on Walcheren takes centre stage as he considers first the naval difficulties of effecting a landing and secondly the obstacles likely to be met by the troops after disembarkation. He concludes that he needs military advice as to the feasibility of carrying Walcheren and the relative benefits of such an endeavour compared with an attack on north Germany, still the major alternative.

Castlereagh was the chief exponent of the Scheldt expedition but it is equally obvious that he only gradually came to regard this as the best option. The Secretary for War was probably influenced by Admiralty reports received in early 1809 that the French naval force in the river was increasing significantly. This growing naval threat to England was apparently combined with French military vulnerability, a powerful incentive to make a pre-emptive strike. According to spies, Walcheren was poorly defended and unarmed ships of the line were being fitted out at Flushing. The locals were reported to be strongly pro-British. The Admiralty was supportive and by March 1809, it seems that it was more a question of when the expedition would set sail rather than if it would. On the 24th, David Dundas, the new commander-in-chief of the army, was summoned to a meeting with ministers and asked if he could provide a force of 15,000 men. He replied that this was not possible, referring to the well-known 'shattered situation' of the army following the recent Corunna expedition. Apart from the general poor health of the troops, there were also shortages of clothing, arms and other equipment. The commander-in-chief later recalled that his opinion was received with 'no debate or discussion'. A delay was enforced but, on 8 May, Castlereagh again approached Dundas asking the state of the infantry in England and the date by which each battalion might be considered fit for service. By 21 May, a plan was in place for an army of 25,000 infantry and 5,000 cavalry but with no available reserve. Within a few weeks, a total force of around 35,000 infantry and 2,000 cavalry was being prepared for embarkation.

Whilst driving the military build-up, Castlereagh simultaneously sought the necessary approval to make the final preparations and plans.

Lord Castlereagh to the King

St James Square, June 14th, 1809

Lord Castlereagh begs leave to acquaint your Majesty that your Majesty's confidential servants, having considered the information which has been collected relative to an operation against the enemy's naval resources in the Scheldt, are humbly of opinion that, by employing an adequate force of not less than 35,000 men, the attempt may be made with every prospect of success, provided the practicability of a landing at Sandfleet [Sandvliet] can be assured. Till this point can be further investigated, they are desirous to postpone receiving your Majesty's final commands upon the measure, requesting, in the meantime, your Majesty's permission to proceed, with as much *secrecy* and *expedition* as possible, with all the preliminary arrangements, which, when completed, will contribute to render the troops equally applicable to any other service. Your Majesty's servants are desirous of humbly submitting to your Majesty that the conduct of the proposed expedition should be entrusted to the Earl of Chatham.

The obtuse reference to Sandvliet, a small village and potential landing place in the upper Scheldt, reflects the lack of either definitive intelligence or a specific plan at this time. Despite this uncertainty, the King replied on 16 June approving the preparations.[9]

Notes

1. Cresswell, J., *Generals and Admirals*, pp. 82–4, 95–103; Howard, M. E., *The Causes of War*, p. 186; Hall, C. D., *British Strategy in the Napoleonic War 1803–15*, p. 45; Muir, R., *Britain and the Defeat of Napoleon 1807–1815*, pp. 6–8, 16, 23–5; Glover, R., *Peninsular Preparation*, pp. 24–5.

2. Muir, pp. 9–11; Hall, pp. 53–5, 210–11; Fortescue, J. W., *History of the British Army*, Vol. VII, pp. 44–5; Glover, pp. 15–16, 40–1; *The Walcheren Expedition. The Experiences of a British Officer of the 81st Regiment*, pp. 15–16, 130–1; Creevey, T., *Thomas Creevey's Papers*, p. 57.

3. Fortescue, Vol. VII, pp. 28–9, 44, 50; Glover, R., *Britain at Bay*, pp. 23–4, 28–9; Muir, pp. 86, 103–4; Hall, pp. 9, 67, 168–74; Howard, M. R., *Medical Aspects of Sir John Moore's Corunna Campaign*; Glover, R., *Peninsular Preparation*, pp. 4–5.

4. Fortescue, Vol. VII, pp. 36–8; Bond, G., *The Grand Expedition*, p. 7; Hall, pp. 80–1; Fleischman, T., *L'Expedition Anglaise sur le Continent en 1809*, pp. 11–12; Muir, pp. Xxiii, 87–8.

5. Fortescue, Vol. VII, pp. 48–9; Muir, p. 89; Bond, p. 8.

6. Hall, pp. 75–6, 176–7; Bond, pp. 8, 12, 145; Parliamentary Papers 1810, Vol. XV, pp. ccccxxxii, ccccxxviii; Fortescue, Vol. VII, pp. 49–52.

7. Glover, R., *Britain at Bay*, pp. 19–20; Hall, pp. 12–13, 83–6; Glover, R., *Peninsular Preparation*, p. 8; Bond, pp. 9–10, 13; Fortescue, Vol. VII, p. 53; Castlereagh, Viscount, *Memoirs and Correspondence of Viscount Castlereagh*, Vol. VI, pp. 300–1; Parliamentary Papers, p. ccxxxviii.

8. Glover, R., *Peninsular Preparation*, pp. 32–4, 247, 254; Fortescue, J., *The County Lieutenancies and the Army 1803–1814*, p. 177; Muir, p. 314; Hall, p. 67; Fortescue, J. W., *A History of the British Army*, Vol. VII, pp. 46–54.

9. Fortescue, J. W., *History of the British Army*, Vol. VII, pp. 45–55; Castlereagh, Vol. VI, pp. 44–5, 82–3, 245–54, 275–6; Parliamentary Papers, pp. ccxxvii, lxxxv, xcii, 5xxi, ccxxxvi; Hall, pp. 105, 136–7; Bond, pp. 8–20.

CHAPTER 2

Soldiers and Sailors

To be successful, the imminent expedition would require the cooperation of Britain's land and sea forces and excellent military and naval command. At the start of 1809, the effective strength of the British regular army was 234,000 men. The official return shows 183,000 infantry, 27,000 cavalry, and 23,500 for the artillery and engineers. These impressive numbers reflect a significant increase in the size of the army since the early 1790s when fewer than 40,000 men could be mustered. General Antoine Henri Jomini, who served on Napoleon's staff and was one of the most influential of all military theorists, believed that the Egyptian Campaign of 1800–1801 marked the start of regeneration in the British Army with the growth in its strength matched by improvements in training and discipline. This was fortunate as in 1809 the army was thinly spread with, in the early months of the year, rather more than half of the troops already abroad. There was a force of 25,000 in the East Indies and Ceylon (Sri Lanka), 21,000 in the West Indies, 22,000 in the Mediterranean, 8,000 in North America, and 9,000 in the Cape and other minor garrisons. In the Peninsula, there were around 15,000 men in Lisbon, a mixture of the original force sent to Portugal and the remains of Sir John Moore's army.

In addition to this dispersion around the globe, the actual offensive power of the army was considerably less than the numbers shown in the returns; even counting on the able men in Lisbon and Sicily, and reinforcement by the mercenaries of the King's German Legion, the army fit for an immediate European campaign was no larger than 30,000. The troops who had just returned from Corunna were battle tested but such were the hardships of the retreat and the ravages of disease that many were not likely to be able to re-enter the field until later in the year. Indeed, disease was a constant threat to the army and there was 'wastage' of about 17,000 men per annum between 1803 and 1808. In the year prior to the Walcheren expedition, there were only 13,000 new recruits, including 2,000 boys, meaning a net deficit of at least 4,000 active soldiers. As more campaigns were being planned in the pestilential West Indies, it was unlikely that the army's losses were going to be any less in the foreseeable future.

The solution to this chronic manpower problem was to draw men into the army from the Regular Militia, a force created largely at the instigation of Castlereagh and numbering close to 80,000 in 1809. The militia, one of several layers of home defence forces, could not be sent overseas or, until 1811, even to Ireland. Men were conscripted although compulsion was often avoided by the use of substitutes; balloted men were allowed to pay for another to serve in their place. The Volunteers were a further force of part-time soldiers who served in local units, partly out of patriotism and from a fear of French invasion, and partly to avoid conscription into the regular army. This mixed force of militiamen and volunteers, in total around 300,000 men, was not expected to stand up to the *Grande Armée* but it did provide a convenient pool of men to top up the regulars in time of need. Castlereagh shrank from a formal merging of the militia into the regular second battalions but, in 1807, he introduced a bill to permit men from the militia to more easily enlist into the Line thereby boosting the army's operational strength in future years.[1]

The command of the regular army was in the hands of a number of senior officers. Since 1794, the Secretary for War had been responsible for the direction of military strategy; part of his role was to select the Commander in Chief of the Army who in turn was responsible for the training and discipline of the infantry and cavalry of the Line, the appointment and promotion of officers in those regiments, and also the appointment of general officers to all posts except for those of Commander in Chief overseas. The Master General of the Ordnance was, in effect, a second commander in chief controlling the Royal Artillery, Royal Engineers, and supporting services. His influence was considerable as he was a member of the government and its principal military advisor. In practice, many government ministers believed themselves to be key players in Britain's military plans, not least the Prime Minister who was ultimately responsible for the government's decisions, the Chancellor of the Exchequer who was responsible for the commissariat, the Home Secretary who was the head of the home defence forces, and the Foreign Secretary who was bound to be interested in the choice of destination for any expedition. The creation and launch of a new expeditionary force required an intricate interplay of individuals and departments well described by Michael Glover.

> The Commander in Chief and the Master General had to detail troops from their respective armies. The Treasury had to appoint a

Commissariat staff and provide them with cash or credit for the purchase of supplies. The Sovereign had to give any orders necessary to get the Household Troops in motion. The movement of all troops to their port of embarkation required the warrant of the Secretary for War and their movement by sea was the charge of the Transport Board, a semi-independent offshoot of the Admiralty. The Joint Paymasters General, junior members of the government, had to find cash to pay the troops; the Medical Board provided hospital staff; the Apothecary General medicines and hospital supplies. Tentage came from a thinly disguised commercial firm, operating under the title of the Storekeeper General's Department. Intelligence about the theatre of war must come from the Foreign Office and the Admiralty had to provide escort for the troop convoy.

At lower levels, all administration centred on the regiment. The infantry, the most numerous part of the army, was divided into Foot Guards, line and light infantry and rifle corps, but the regimental organisation remained standard with one or two battalions. Each battalion was made up of ten companies including two flank companies comprised of grenadiers, often the largest most determined men, and light infantry. In theory, each company was 100 men but, in practice, the size of battalions varied greatly and during active service their strength could quickly melt away. The second battalion, traditionally kept at home, was usually weaker than the first but this was also inconsistent; Wellington commented that many of the fittest men were in the second units.

On campaign, it was usual to divide the army into brigades, each consisting of two to three battalions. The term 'division' was vaguely used to describe a larger subdivision of the force. In the Copenhagen expedition of 1807, there were four divisions each under a lieutenant general and composed of two to four weak brigades of around two battalions. A similar arrangement was to be used in the attack on the Scheldt.

The cavalry was split into three basic types: Household and heavy and light dragoons. Heavy cavalry, including the Householders, was used for 'shock' whilst their lighter compatriots were skirmishers and outpost men. Regiments were divided into squadrons subdivided into ten troops. As for the infantry, their number was often less than establishment and in the campaigns of 1808–09 the average regimental strength was about 400. The cavalry made up a smaller part of the British army than was the case for most other European armies who favoured vast masses of horsemen on the battlefield. The artillery was not officially part of the regular army but a department of the Ordnance overseen by the Master General. As the Royal Artillery, it was organised into battalions of ten companies with each company forming an autonomous artillery 'brigade' (now generally referred to as a 'battery') with six pieces of ordnance, most commonly five guns and a howitzer. The size of the guns varied according to need with the heaviest, often difficult to move, used almost exclusively for the defence of or the assault on fortifications.[2]

Each infantry regiment was a complex assemblage of parts: officers, staff, sergeants, rank and file, and musicians. Infantry battalions and cavalry regiments were usually commanded by a lieutenant colonel. There were few full colonels with the army and almost the only ones who commanded a unit were in the brigade of Guards. In addition to these senior officers, the infantry battalion at full strength had two majors, ten captains and around twenty subalterns. It is tempting to think of these men as aloof aristocrats but this is far from the reality. There were sons of Dukes but, in the heat of Napoleonic warfare and with the constant need to refill posts, the choice of officers was more determined by literacy than wealth or land. The basic ability to read and write was vital for a commission. Many officers came from the untitled landed gentry or were sons of clerics, lawyers, doctors, naval officers and ordinary soldiers. Most were unified only by their lack of knowledge of their new profession. Promotion was by purchase, seniority or patronage. In retrospect, promotion by purchase appears unjust although, on occasions, it allowed very able men, Wellington being one example, to rise rapidly through the ranks. Without money, promotion was often a lottery with seniority usually more important than merit. At the end of the wars there were unlucky men who were still only lieutenants after service in six campaigns. Charles Oman, author of a famous history of the Peninsular War, refers to this stagnation among those who lacked either wealth or influence as 'appalling and monstrous'.[3]

In contrast to the popular view of the blue-blooded officer, the rank and file of Britain's Napoleonic army are most commonly defined by Wellington's description of them as 'the very scum of the earth'. He also suggested that most enlisted because they had got 'bastard children' or to avoid punishment for minor offences or simply to get an abundant supply of drink. Certainly, the ranker's life was unlikely to be attractive to decent working-class men. If a man did leave the heart of his family to enlist he immediately increased his chance of dying of disease. Much depended on where he was posted as the prevailing maladies were determined by geography and climate. The enormous loss of European troops in the West

Indies is well documented. In the Leeward and Windward Islands between 1796 and 1805, 25,000 troops died, effectively destroying the garrison twice over; the overwhelming number of deaths were from malaria and yellow fever. Soldiers bound for the region feared these diseases more than the enemy. George Pinckard, an army physician, describes their demoralisation.

> The fearful farewell of desponding friends is every day, and hour, either heedlessly, or artfully sounded in their ears. People walking about the camp, attending a review, or a parade, or merely upon seeing parties of soldiers in the streets, are heard to exclaim – 'ah, poor fellows! You are going to your last home! What a pity such brave men should go to their West India grave! – to that hateful climate to be killed by the plague! Poor fellow, good bye, farewell! We shall never see you again!'

European campaigning was not so dreaded but between the years 1808 and 1814 in Spain and Portugal it has been estimated that nearly three times as many British soldiers died from disease than in battle. In the Corunna campaign, a fresh memory in 1809, 20 per cent of the returning force was sick enough to need medical attention with dysentery and typhus the main afflictions.

The soldier with a tough constitution still had to survive wretched poverty. Army pay rarely kept up with remuneration in civilian life; in 1806, the weekly wage of a man in the ranks with less than seven years of service was 7s 7d (the same as in 1800) whilst an 'artisan' could expect to take home 28s. So the soldier was earning only about a quarter as much as a worker at the lower end of society. If a man with some education entered the ranks he was generally despised by his comrades. In the words of Sergeant Joseph Donaldson of the 94th:

> If he did not join with his neighbours in their ribald obscenity and nonsense, he was a Methodist – if he did not curse and swear he was a Quaker – and if he did not drink the most of his pay, he was called a miser, a mean scrub, and the generality of his comrades would join in execrating him.

Donaldson says that even the youngest were led into drunkenness and debauchery and that their officers did little to protect them. On campaign, the end result was often robbery and murder, most commonly perpetrated against the local population. Such behaviour was not limited to the British Army of the period. George Washington commented that hardened American soldiers had become so inured to punishment that some would accept a further dose of the cat-o'-nine tails in return for a bottle of rum. The unrelenting severity of army life at the beginning of the nineteenth century has to be seen in the context of a toughness of the rank and file difficult for the modern mind to comprehend.

If serving men were rugged and delinquent in equal degree, then the army's women were simply to be pitied. Matrimony was discouraged. The regulations urged officers to explain to their charges 'the many miseries that women are exposed to and, by every sort of persuasion, they must prevent their marrying if possible'. Women following the army on campaign were particularly vulnerable. To survive they needed all the qualities attributed to them by Charles Oman; to be 'as hard as nails, expert plunderers ... and much given to fighting'. As their presence impeded the movement of the troops, their number was strictly limited – perhaps four to six per company. Those left at home received no allowance and had to fend for themselves.[4]

Although Wellington had no illusion as to the nature of his soldiers, by the end of the wars he was able to applaud their collective achievement: 'it really is wonderful that we should have made them the fine fellows they are'. This rings true after the hard fought victories of the Peninsular War and Waterloo but we must remember the lack of confidence in Britain's land forces in 1809. Despite the beneficial reforms initiated by the Duke of York, including the culling of useless officers and the standardisation of training, there was still a general view that the army was incompetent. As recently as 1807, a senior minister, indeed an ex-Secretary for War, declared it absurd to think of British soldiers fighting beside Russians and Prussians in the Friedland campaign. Wellington's victory over the French at Vimeiro did not change this widespread sentiment. This was in stark contrast to the obvious power of the country's navy which was at its peak during the Napoleonic age of sail. Not that the Royal Navy was a perfect service. Manpower was equally a challenge as it was for the army and the navy had to resort to several different methods to recruit crews. Some were attracted by signing-on bounties and were effectively volunteers whilst others joined up to avoid incarceration in jail. The latter were mostly accused of petty misdemeanours and were not hardened criminals. The most notorious recruitment device was impressment, a form of legalised kidnapping carried out by highly organised pressgangs. Despite all these strategies, the navy struggled to enlist enough men and this shortfall was a reminder to ministers of the fragile nature of Britain's naval superiority. Nelson's flagship at Trafalgar, the *Victory*, was more than 100 men short of a full crew. Desertions exacerbated the problem, there being over 12,000 in the period 1803–05. One factor in the navy's favour was the improving health of sailors: between 1806 and 1811, there were only a quarter of the number of sick seen in the years 1793–98. In 1809 there were 142,000 seamen and marines listed in the navy's rolls.

Keeping their warships seaworthy was also a challenge for the naval authorities. Vessels required constant repairs and the limited dockyard capacity meant that there were always a significant number of ships, probably about 20 per cent of the total, out of commission. Timber was in short supply and the use of inferior insufficiently matured wood exacerbated the problem as vessels rotted more quickly, sometimes having to be removed from service after only a few years. By 1807 the navy was showing signs of strain and the government embarked on a major round of building and refitting with the result that by 1809 the total fleet numbered over 1,000 vessels including 108 ships of the line, 150 frigates and 424 sloops.

The movement of troops abroad was the responsibility of the Transport Board who had to procure the necessary additional shipping. This was not requisitioned but hired for periods of time, often for three to six months, from private ship-owners. This reliance on civilian shipping was far from ideal and the converted merchant ships were often too small and poorly maintained. One possible solution was the creation of an Admiralty controlled transport service with the conversion of some warships into military transports but this would inevitably reduce the navy's offensive power. In 1808 a compromise was reached with the conversion of various naval vessels into transports each designed to carry 150–550 soldiers. Amphibious operations required soldiers to be transferred from transports to the shore in flat-bottomed rowing boats. Their capacity was limited and this meant that only a relatively small number of troops could be landed in one wave.

The global employment of the Royal Navy was in the hands of a small number of men at the Admiralty. The most senior officer, the First Lord of the Admiralty, was assisted by the Admiralty Board which was composed of the first, second and third sea lords, the civil lords, and the secretaries. The First Lord would expect to be a prime mover in military strategy as only he could get troops to their destination and support them after their arrival. In charge of the navy's ships were the captains, men as socially distinct from their crews as the army's officers were from the rank and file. Most were gentry and around forty years old. They had usually served in the navy since the age of eleven or twelve years when they had been sent to sea as nominal servants of a captain who was a relative or family friend. Very few rose to the post from humble origins. The navy's sailors were mostly much younger;

the average age of the crew of the *Victory* was twenty-two years. The majority were British but there was a sprinkling of Americans and other foreigners. David Howarth points out that because authentic accounts written by these men are so sparse, contradictory views of them have persisted over the last 200 years, ' ... at one extreme, the Jolly Jack tars, brave, patriotic and devil may care; and at the other, the victims of a cruel system, press-ganged, starved, flogged, and ill-treated to the point of mutiny.' The truth probably lies somewhere between the two.[5]

To survive on campaign the army required its support services. There were seven civil departments attached to military headquarters: the Medical Department, the Purveyor's Department, the Paymaster General, the Commissariat, the Store-keeper General, the Controller of Army Accounts and the Press where general orders and other documents were printed. The most important of these were the Commissariat, tested to the limit in 1809, and the Medical Department. The organisation of the latter will be outlined as it is ignored in most military accounts of the period and it was to play a crucial role in the Walcheren expedition. At the beginning of the Napoleonic era, the British Army Medical Department was broadly divided into three parts: the administrative officers, the hospital and medical 'staff', and the regimental surgeons. For most of the wars, the department's administrative affairs were overseen by the Army Medical Board made up of three senior doctors. Even after a careful study of relevant documents it is difficult to comprehend the role of the individual members. It would be hard to improve on Arnold Chaplin's masterly resume of the idiosyncratic functioning of the Board.

> Surely it is impossible to imagine a more clumsy and impossible arrangement ... The position, so far as can be ascertained, was as follows: Collectively the Board was supposed to meet if questions were submitted to it. It was to obey orders, but it was no part of its business to make representations, and when it did the Physician General took the chair. In their individual capacities the members were assigned special duties, but the conduct of these duties could not be brought under the criticism of the Board as a whole. The Physician General [Lucas Pepys in 1809], with a salary of 40s. [i.e. £2], was responsible for the choice of physicians, for the supervision of medical drugs, and for the examination of candidates for the post of physician in the army. The Surgeon General [Thomas Keate], with a salary of 40s. per diem, and also an extra £800 per annum as the holder of the sinecure post of surgeon to the Chelsea Hospital,

24

appointed the surgeons for the army and provided surgical drugs and appliances. He occupied a seat on the Court of Examiners at the College of Surgeons for granting a certificate to hospital mates [junior hospital doctors]. He consulted with the authorities on medical matters while the troops were on foreign service and he received the returns of the sick and wounded. The Inspector General [Francis Knight] was entrusted with the duty of providing Inspectors of Hospitals and hospital mates. He had charge of regimental hospitals, and had the position of surgeon to the staff of the Commander in Chief. In addition to his salary of 40s. a day, he received an equivalent amount on account of his position of Controller of Army Hospital Accounts. Finally, he was responsible for the provision of drugs for the Guards regiments and superintended the education of cadets for hospital mates.

To complete this description of this edifice of inconsistencies, it remains to be said that the Guards chose their own surgeons, that the medical department of the Ordnance was a separate concern under the control of an Inspector General, and that the medical comforts were under the control of the Commissary General.

Chaplin could also have included the Apothecary General who controlled the supply of medicines, dressings, and surgical instruments from civil firms, and the Purveyor in Chief who directed the provision of hospital equipment.

In early 1809 the Board's members were working on borrowed time as the 1807 Commission of Military Enquiry had recommended their replacement by men with more active service. Neither Pepys nor Keate had significant military experience and Knight's regimental service was limited to the Helder in 1799. The evidence suggests that these senior doctors were less than fully committed to their duties; their office hours extended from 12 o'clock to 2 o'clock daily and during this time they were not invariably to be found at their desks. When they did meet it was mostly to argue with each other. In April, the Secretary for War was forced to write to the Treasury: 'The divisions which exist among the principal members of the Army Medical Board is productive of very serious inconvenience to the public service'. No immediate solution was found and, in August, Huskisson replied that no more time should be lost in tackling the 'dissension'. The three men survived until the following year.

The second major division of the medical department was that of the medical staff. Wellington referred to them as the 'medical gentlemen', which was strictly correct as they were members of a civil organisation and only held relative military rank. They included, inspectors, physicians, staff surgeons, hospital mates, apothecaries, and purveyors. The aristocratic physicians were men of high academic qualifications and the undoubted elite of the army medical profession. They were few in number and often totally unused to the rigours of army life where their Cambridge education, knowledge of Greek, and refined habits were of little relevance. The hospital mates, who served as drudges in the army's hospitals, were equally unsuited to campaigning. At the bottom of the pile, most had little education and they were left to fend for themselves. They were generally held in contempt; when a captain of a transport was asked what he had on board he replied 'horses and hospital mates for the army'.

The third and largest part of the medical department was the regimental organisation. These were the surgeons who provided the routine medical care for the soldiers and who followed them into battle. For most of the wars each battalion of infantry and regiment of cavalry had a surgeon and two assistants. In the infantry the surgeon held the relative rank of captain and the assistant surgeon of subaltern. The professional attainments of most of the regimental surgeons were modest but some were very well educated and achieved great things. All the eminent British army doctors of the period, men such as James McGrigor and George Guthrie, started their careers as surgeons attached to regiments. The medical challenges facing these men were daunting. After a large battle, there were likely to be several thousand casualties on and around the field and many regiments entered the fighting with less than their full complement of doctors. The pervasive influence of disease has already been alluded to. The medical department had been stretched to the limit during the Corunna campaign. James McGrigor, the Deputy Inspector of Hospitals at Portsmouth was forced to take exceptional measures to accommodate the unprecedented influx of ill soldiers. Extra medical officers were enrolled from the militia and the Household Troops and medical students were requested to leave the capital to attend the sick. Despite the reopening of military and naval hospitals and the employment of barracks as temporary medical facilities, McGrigor still had to use transport and prison ships as floating hospitals. He acknowledged that these were wholly unsatisfactory.[6]

In the spring of 1809, with the Walcheren initiative definitely decided upon, Castlereagh and his ministers were more intent on looking forward than over their shoulders at the perceived failure in Spain. However, this misadventure had deprived the army of a rare talent; had Sir John Moore not fallen at Corunna, he would very likely have been selected to lead the new expedition. In his absence, and with Arthur Wellesley in the Peninsula, the responsibility fell upon John Pitt, second Earl of Chatham, the older brother of William Pitt. Chatham had commanded a brigade in the expedition to Holland in 1799. At the time of his appointment to the Walcheren command, he was still Master General of the Ordnance, a post he had held between 1801 and 1806 and again since 1807. He was apparently considered for the command of the Peninsular army in 1808 but, for obscure reasons, possibly his own reluctance to sail for Spain at short notice, Sir Hew Dalrymple was selected instead. His assumption of command in 1809 surprised many – John Barrow in the Admiralty says that the news was announced 'to the astonishment of all' – and also divided opinion. There were conspiracy theories, the favourite being that Canning had connived to appoint Chatham with the expectation that the expedition would succeed and that he would subsequently be able to elevate the general to first place in the government (in place of the ageing Duke of Portland) where he would be able to manipulate him to his own ends. It is unclear that there is any truth in this; contemporary gossip suggests that Canning actually opposed the appointment whilst Castlereagh, his arch-rival, approved of it. There is also little evidence to support another popular theory that Chatham had benefited from his personal friendship with George III. The simplest explanation for the choice of Chatham is that he was the best senior military officer available. David Dundas, the Commander in Chief, later defended the decision.

> Lord Chatham's services were well known to everybody as well as to the Commander in Chief; he was a man of very high military rank, and who had always conducted himself well in his situation in Holland; indeed, I knew him; he served more particularly in the division of the army I was in, and I saw everything that was proper, very much so at that time, in Lord Chatham; he was afterwards under my command in Kent, and I always consulted him and found him a very excellent officer.

Chatham's supporters admitted that he had a weakness. His laziness was so widely known that he was nicknamed 'the late earl' because of his difficulty in rising from bed in the morning. In the words of one British officer, he was 'a veteran accustomed to the routine of official duty but without experience as a leader and without the qualities necessary to the success of an enterprise which demands decision of character and activity of mind and body'. This view may have benefited from hindsight, but another officer wrote of Chatham at the outset of the Walcheren expedition, 'If his activity were but equal to his talents, he would be inferior to none of our most celebrated generals'. Chatham's record at the Office of Ordnance was that of a man capable of good judgement – his administration much improved the department – but flawed by indolence and unpunctuality. Richard Glover, in his superb monograph on the reform of the British Army, gives examples of Chatham's 'sheer laziness'. He was often to be found at his country home when he ought to have been in London and he left remarkably few documents to mark his presence; among them was a small notebook containing lists of garden flowers suggesting that his mind was frequently elsewhere. Fortescue pointedly comments that Chatham could 'when he took the trouble', both think and write.[7]

At around the same time that Chatham accepted his new appointment, in early June, the Admiralty gave the naval command of the expedition to Rear Admiral Sir Richard Strachan. This appointment has been less criticised than that of Chatham. Strachan had a well established reputation as a competent and gallant seaman and had achieved some fame in an action in the Bay of Biscay two weeks after Trafalgar in which he captured four French ships of the line. He was less experienced in amphibious operations but when he raised this with the First Lord at the time of his appointment, the latter is said to have replied, 'Oh! Never mind, we have great reliance upon you and you must command the naval force', whilst another in the Admiralty retorted, 'Go on, I dare say you will do very well'. The sailors who served under Strachan grew to respect him. William Richardson, who had seen the admiral at close quarters in 1805, remembered that he referred to the ship's company as 'damned mutinous rascals'.

> Yet the sailors liked him for all that, as they knew he had a kind heart, and thought no more of it when his passion was over. They gave him the name of 'Mad Dick' and said that when he swore he meant no harm, and when he prayed he meant no good.

Captain Graham Moore, brother of Sir John, was keen to serve with Strachan as he believed him to be 'extremely brave and full of zeal and ardour and an excellent seaman'. Moore had to admit that he was also an 'irregular impetuous fellow'. Like Chatham, Strachan was a decent man with a major flaw. His senior naval colleague, Admiral Sir William Hotham, noted that Strachan was 'intemperate at times aboard ship and headstrong in his zeal'. Sir William Maynard Gomm agreed that the naval commander was capable and a fine fellow but 'all heart and energy' and 'too hasty for anything that requires much combination'. This impetuosity had led Strachan into scrapes. During the action in the Bay of Biscay, he had ordered the firing of guns at a friendly consort to remind them to get into action.[8]

Serving directly under this strange pairing of an indolent general and an impulsive admiral was a tier of senior army and naval officers. Chatham's second-in-command was Sir Eyre Coote. He had served with distinction in Egypt but an illness in the West Indies had left him exhausted and his behaviour in the coming campaign was well meaning but eccentric. Robert Brownrigg was appointed quartermaster general to the army, responsible for the marches and quartering of troops. Fortescue says dismissively that he was selected because he had declared a surprise attack on Antwerp to be a possibility but he was an able officer with a good service record. Other senior army men included Henry William (Lord) Paget, Sir John Hope, George Gordon (The Marquis of Huntley), Thomas Grosvenor, Sir James St Clair Erskine (The Earl of Rosslyn) and Alexander Mackenzie Fraser.

Strachan had a number of excellent men under his command. Rear Admiral Sir Richard Keates was highly capable, probably more so than Strachan himself, whilst Rear Admiral Lord Gardner and Edward Otway were both solid appointments. The Captain of the Fleet, Sir Home Popham, was undoubtedly the most influential and controversial member of this naval elite. From a remarkably large family (his mother's twenty-first child), the forty seven-year-old Popham had an unusual talent for getting the attention of ministers and an extensive experience of amphibious expeditions. He had some knowledge of the Scheldt as he had visited Antwerp in 1794. His most recent exploit had been the unauthorised attack on Buenos Aires which led to his court martial for being absent without permission from the Cape. The court sentenced him to be severely reprimanded but, by 1809, he had sufficiently recovered from this setback to be a Member of Parliament and a captain of a line of battle ship. An army captain who accompanied him to the Cape commented that Popham had 'led a miscellaneous life ... he possesses a great deal of what the Scotch call cleverality'. It was widely acknowledged that he was liked by the sailors and that he was very conversant with the details of landing and embarking troops. William Maynard Gomm described Popham as being much more capable than Strachan but he also believed him to be not universally popular with his naval colleagues:

He is what they call too meddling, by which they mean to imply (without being aware of it) that he makes himself very useful upon all occasions and in all ways; he is so used to be actively employed, and is besides naturally so bustling, that what is evidently an exertion with most men is reduced to a habit with him.

Such a man with knowledge of the theatre of operations was likely to be useful and Popham appeared to have the confidence of Castlereagh and Lord

Mulgrave, First Lord of the Admiralty, as well of that of the expedition's leaders. Indeed, as the expedition took shape, Popham met regularly with Chatham even after Strachan's appointment, doing virtually all of the naval side of the combined planning. Strachan was later to comment that '... he [Strachan] did not attend any of the discussions because he was perfectly ignorant of every part of the country as well of the navigation of the East and the West Scheldt'. He was satisfied that Chatham and Home Popham should make the arrangements allowing him to attend to his 'naval duties'.[9]

Popham was not the only senior figure to be consulted as to the optimal approach and likely chance of success of the forthcoming venture. In the last week of May, Castlereagh solicited opinions from the country's leading military minds. The resulting correspondence is strikingly pessimistic, in stark contrast to the unbridled optimism of the ordinary soldiers and sailors assembling on the Kent coast. In addition to making specific suggestions for the plan of attack, to which we will return, officers strained to highlight the risks of what was proposed. Castlereagh received five discouraging memoranda from the Horseguards which could not easily be dismissed. The Commander in Chief of the Army, David Dundas, left no doubt as to his reservations: 'In whatever way Antwerp is to be approached or taken, the service is one of very great risk, and which the safe return of the army so employed may be very precarious ...'. Major General Harry Calvert was also in no mood to mix his words: '...the service would be arduous, and the troops employed on it must unavoidably be exposed to considerable risk'. He did not, however, believe the difficulties to be insuperable. Robert Brownrigg warned that if the wrong plan was adopted there was a real chance of losing the whole force and Lieutenant Colonel James Gordon thought even the best plan to be a 'desperate enterprise' with a 'very large proportion of our naval and military means put to imminent hazard'. Major General John Hope preceded his advice by stressing the need to accept that any such undertaking required very careful consideration of the difficulties of landing and equipping an army on a hostile coast. He pointed out that the country had little recent experience of sustaining an army on the continent. These were 'primary but indispensible considerations'.

This negativity was not limited to the corridors of power. Those who were to lead the troops on the ground were uncharacteristically nervous. Unlike the memoranda to Castlereagh in early June, some of these comments were made later and may have benefited from hindsight. Coote stated that he always thought the outcome of the expedition to be doubtful and the attempt to be 'hazardous'. In similar vein, Sir Thomas Picton, was later to write:

> You know my sentiments respecting the undertaking. The object (which was the capture of a few ships) was in every respect paltry and most unworthy of the national exertions made on the occasion; and besides the risqué [sic] to the Fleet and army employed was great, and the probability of ultimate success very little. It would have been more possible to have marched to Paris than to have seized Antwerp ...

The expedition's commanders can hardly have been ignorant of this scepticism. Strachan later remembered that prior to the departure of the expedition he had been approached by Sir William Erskine at Deal. Erskine warned the admiral that the attack upon the Scheldt, and particularly Antwerp, was likely to fail; this opinion Strachan freely admitted 'made a great impression upon my mind'. Chatham was eventually to admit that he had 'entertained great doubts' as to the practicability of the undertaking entrusted to him. He was, however, somewhat reassured by the more optimistic attitude of the Admiralty.[10]

We cannot know what Chatham and Strachan actually said to Castlereagh. When the admiral was later asked whether he had communicated Erskine's damning assessment to the Secretary for War, he was rather vague: 'I think I did some parts. If not the whole of it ... I did not consider it exactly as an official communication'. Castlereagh did have the official communications from the Horseguards – all appear in sequence in his published correspondence. So why did he and the government push on with the Walcheren expedition despite this widespread and informed pessimism? The reasons can be broadly divided into two. Firstly, there were political considerations and, secondly, new military intelligence.

The political reasons for the assault on the Scheldt have already been discussed; the propitious news of the Austrian victory over Napoleon at Aspern-Essling was received in the first week of June, just when Castlereagh was receiving the negative opinions from his military commanders, and this encouraged the government to take prompt action to support an apparently successful ally. The Walcheren expedition was the only immediate option. Furthermore, evolving military intelligence from the Scheldt, not available to the Secretary for War's military advisors, seemed to support the timing of such an attack. From mid-March until June, numerous reports indicated that the French garrisons in Zealand, the Dutch province through which the Scheldt River opened into the North Sea, were being weakened, the troops being directed to the *Grand Armée*. The quality of soldiers left behind was poor. On the island of Walcheren there were about 3,500 men, mostly foreign and many sick. At Flushing, there were only four battalions composed mainly of Dutch, Germans, Spanish and Irish. There was friction between Dutch and French forces and the local population was rumoured to be strongly pro-English. At Antwerp, there were no soldiers at all and the citizens were obliged to keep watch and guard the city. Sailors reconnoitring the Scheldt believed the French defences to be vulnerable to attack.

When Castlereagh was later questioned regarding the pessimistic stance of his senior military men, he immediately pointed out that they were not in possession of all the facts:

> I may say the principal share of the information describing the weak state of the enemy's force in the Netherlands and in countries adjacent was received subsequently to the opinions of the officers alluded to... I perfectly understood from those opinions and the communications with those officers that they did not feel they had sufficient information to form a conclusive opinion upon the subject.

Castlereagh wrote to Chatham in June, the exact date of the letter is unclear, stating that the possibility of the failure of the expedition had been considered but that 'Whatever may be the risk of it [failure] occurring, that it is one of those contingencies in contemplation of which his Majesty's confidential servants have nevertheless felt themselves called on to recommend that the enterprise should be undertaken'. This was not an inspiring call to arms.[11]

The expedition may have developed an unstoppable political momentum but the ponderous pace of the military preparations was also causing anxiety. As weeks slipped by in June without a definite date for the sailing of the fleet, many believed that the chance of ultimate success was being compromised. Castlereagh himself stressed the importance of a speedy departure and execution, referring to the expedition as a *coup de main*, literally an attack achieving complete surprise. The scale of the project – ultimately to involve 70,000 soldiers and sailors with their equipment and stores – militated against this. Dundas toiled to assemble the necessary force, later insisting that he did not believe that 'such great exertions ever were made' with respect to the embarkation of an army. Senior naval officers were especially fretful. Keates emphasised the importance of 'celerity'. Home Popham wrote to Castlereagh on 13 June, six weeks before the eventual departure date.

> I see the season advancing fast and if we are imperceptibly led on till the Midsummer fine weather is past, we shall have the most dreadful

of all difficulties, the elements, to encounter ... I again venture to press on your Lordship how important it is to save even an hour.

In the same letter he urges the Secretary for War to 'seize the favourable moment'. The normally languid Chatham agreed with his naval peers that 'every day lost is a loss of much valuable time. I think we should get on faster ...'[12]

Notes

1. Glover, R., *Peninsular Preparation*, p. 6; Fortescue, J. W., *History of the British Army*, Vol. VII, pp. 33–4; Fortescue, J., *The County Lieutenancies and the Army 1803– 1814*, pp. 233–4, 291, 293–4; Muir, R., *Britain and the Defeat of Napoleon 1807– 1815*, p.14.
2. Glover, R., p. 44; Glover, M., *Wellington's Army*, pp. 14–18; Haythornthwaite, P. J., *The Armies of Wellington*, pp. 17–18, 75–7, 100–1, 108–9; Oman, C., *Wellington's Army*, pp. 163–6..
3. Oman, pp. 195–6, 198–200; Glover, M., pp. 36–7, 44, 76, 88–9.
4. Brereton, J. M., *The British Soldier*, p. 44; Howard, M., *Wellington's Doctors*, pp. 155–67; Glover, R., pp. 175–6, 220–1; Donaldson, J., *The Eventful Life of a Soldier*, pp. 70–2; Glover, M., p. 16.
5. Hall, C. D, *British Strategy in the Napoleonic War 1803– 15*, pp. 10–12, 29–31, 41–6; Lloyd, C., and Coulter, J. L. S., *Medicine and the Navy 1200– 1900*, Vol. III, p. 169; Muir, p. 17; Glover, R., *Britain at Bay*, pp. 55–6, 65–6; Glover, M., p. 19; Howarth, D., *Trafalgar*, pp. 23–35; Glover, R., *Peninsular Preparation*, pp. 5–6.
6. Oman, pp. 160–2; Howard, M., *Wellington's Doctors*, pp. 2–31; Chaplin, A., *Medicine in England during the reign of George III*, pp. 78–84; Crowe, K. E., *The Walcheren Expedition and the new Army Medical Board*, pp. 771–81; Howard, M., *Medical Aspects of Sir John Moore's Corunna Campaign 1808– 1809*.
7. General Orders for the Army July 11, TNA, WO28/352; Haythornthwaite, P. J., *Who was Who in the Napoleonic Wars*, p. 68; Glover, R., *Peninsular Preparation*, pp. 37–9; Muir, pp. 44–6; Barrow, J., *An autobiographical memoir of Sir John Barrow Bart*, p. 304; Fortescue, Vol. VII, pp. 54–5; Bond, G., *The Grand Expedition*, p. 18; Parliamentary Papers 1810, Vol. XV, p. xcix; *The Walcheren Expedition. The Experiences of a British Officer of the 81st Regiment*, p. 10; Verner, W., *History and Campaigns of the Rifle Brigade*, Vol. II, p. 40; Fortescue, J., *The County Lieutenancies and the Army*, p. 162.
8. Haythornthwaite, P. J., *Who was Who in the Napoleonic Wars*, p. 312; Christie, C. A., *The Royal Navy and the Walcheren Expedition of 1809*, pp. 192–3; Cresswell, J., *Generals and Admirals*, pp. 105–6; Richardson, W., *A Mariner of England*, p. 220; Gomm, W. M., *Letters and Journals of Sir William M Gomm*, p. 131; Creevey, T., *Thomas Creevey's Papers 1793– 1838*, pp. 58, 81; Fortescue, Vol. VII, p. 86.
9. Fortescue, Vol. VII, pp. 57–9; Bond, pp. 19–21; McGuffie, T. H., *The Walcheren Expedition and the Walcheren Fever*, p. 200; Glover, R., *Peninsular Preparation*, p.

153; Parliamentary Papers, Vol. XV, pp. 5lxiv, clxxviii; Cresswell, pp. 106–9; Gomm, pp. 131–2; Barrow, p. 306.

10. Castlereagh, Viscount, *Memoirs and Correspondence of Viscount Castlereagh*, Vol. VI, pp. 261–3; Bond, pp. 13–16; Parliamentary Papers, Vol. XV, pp. ccccxv, ccxxxix, ccxlv, ccclviii, Vol. XVI, p. 1106; NAS, GD364/1/1187; Havard, R., *Wellington's Welsh General*, pp. 101–2.

11. Parliamentary Papers, Vol. XV, pp. ccclxiii, ccccxxviii, 5xxvii; Bond, pp. 16–17.

12. Bond, p. 24; Parliamentary Papers, Vol. XV, pp. 5xv, ci, clxii, cclxxxiv, ccxviii, clxxvii: Castlereagh, Vol. VI, p. 275; Fortescue, Vol. VII, p. 58.

CHAPTER 3

Coup de Main

On 21 June Castlereagh wrote to the King that there was still some uncertainty as to the practicability of landing a force in the Scheldt. Nevertheless, he continued:

> your Majesty's confidential servants, not disguising from themselves the general difficulties of the enterprise, but deeply impressed with its importance, feel it their duty humbly to recommend to your Majesty that the operation should be undertaken.

King George quickly acquiesced but he was unable to resist pointing out that it was regrettable that the information upon which the expedition was based was so 'imperfect'. Despite their reservations, both men clearly believed that the die was cast. Three weeks later, the King issued instructions to Chatham including his major objectives.

> You will consider that this conjoint expedition has for its object the capture or destruction of the enemy's ships either building at Antwerp and Flushing, or afloat in the Scheldt, the destruction of the arsenals and dock-yards at Antwerp, Terneuse [on the south bank of the river], and Flushing, the reduction of the Island of Walcheren, and the rendering, if possible, of the Scheldt no longer navigable for ships of war.

If this were to prove impossible, then Chatham was to use his 'utmost endeavours' in concert with the navy to secure as many objects as feasible before returning to England and leaving a garrison on Walcheren.

As would be expected, Castlereagh and Chatham were in frequent correspondence through late June and early July. The Secretary for War emphasised the objectives to his military commander and added that the army was not yet equipped on a scale to extend operations beyond these specific goals.

> The expedition must therefore be considered as not, in the first instance, assuming any other character than that of a *coup de main*.

In other words, there was little prospect of a successful initial assault on the Scheldt being followed by an advance into northern Germany. Chatham was allowed some leverage; Castlereagh acknowledged that the details of execution would 'more correctly suggest themselves to your lordship's military observations on the spot'. He also allowed that once the expedition was underway, new developments might change the view of the government as to its ultimate scale. Chatham sought clarification, complaining that his instructions were in turn restrictive and vague.

Strachan received the expedition objectives from the Admiralty. The Sea Lords stressed the importance of occupying the islands of Cadsand and South Beveland whilst Walcheren was being attacked; this would allow safe passage up the West Scheldt. Popham went so far as to state that Cadsand was effectively the first object of the expedition. All were keen to encourage close cooperation between the two services. Castlereagh informed Chatham that the King was assured that his army and navy 'will vie with each other ... that the utmost spirit of concert and harmony will prevail.' Strachan was reminded that 'cordial cooperation' with his army colleague was essential.[1]

With the objectives set and the commanders briefed, it was now crucial to agree a detailed and workable plan for the attack on the Scheldt. This was a considerable challenge. It required knowledge of the geography of the campaign theatre and of the enemy's land and sea forces. Castlereagh had been influenced by the information he received from the Scheldt but this was not the product of a proper military intelligence service. Unlike her French foe, Britain had no formal organisation, either independent or attached to the army, for the collection and analysis of information. In peacetime, there was reliance on the reports of diplomats stationed abroad but by 1807 much of Europe was hostile and most of these men had been necessarily recalled home. Britain's Napoleonic secret service was a 'Cyclops designed to become useless at the moment of greatest need'. In the early months of the year there was thus dependence on a combination of sporadic naval reports and the opportunistic use of spies for up to date information on the topography and defences of the Scheldt.

We get a flavour of the nature of this intelligence from the myriad correspondence later included in the parliamentary papers. In January, Vice Admiral Campbell passes on news of French shipping and batteries in the estuary obtained from a 'confidential person' whom Campbell believed to be trustworthy as his answers were 'very readily and circumstantially given'. Two months later, another unidentified informant, quite possibly a French deserter, tells Campbell that 'he supposes there are about 5,000 troops in the

Island [Walcheren] but they are very young; that the batteries around Campveer [Ter Veere]are in a very bad state and that the drawbridges are every night drawn up'. Locals were used as British spies; Thomas St Clair later makes reference to 'a little Dutchman in the English service' who was allowed to pass back through the lines. Professional smugglers, with their intimate knowledge of the coastline and talent for subterfuge, were natural intelligence gatherers. The notorious Captain Tom Johnson proved so valuable that Castlereagh pardoned him for previous offences and recommended him to Chatham. This memorandum from the Secretary for War, probably written in July, suggests that such men could be surprisingly influential.

> Mr Johnson having represented that he has a plan, which he has undertaken to carry into execution in person, by which he conceives Flushing can be taken by a 'coup de main', upon Lord Chatham and Sir R. Strachan certifying that this object has been accomplished by Mr Johnson's means, he will receive full pay at the above rate, or the value of it, for life. For any other extraordinary service Mr Johnson may render of less importance, he will receive such reward as his services may appear to Lord Chatham and Sir R. Strachan to merit.

Johnson was later involved in a fanciful plot to rescue Napoleon from St Helena using a primitive submarine.

This variety of sources of information – to which we might add neutral merchantmen and French newspapers – was often inconsistent and contradictory. Double-agents were a constant threat; in April, the captain of a sloop writes to Strachan that he believes an anonymous individual to be 'upon our side of the question' but that he will take care that he has no opportunity of contacting the enemy. The more official naval reports were probably the most reliable but sailors were often poor judges of what troops could achieve ashore. There was no professional staff to sift through all this information, to crosscheck it, make specific enquiries, and to ensure that it was more than idle rumour. The soldiers were aware that their view of the Scheldt would be obscured by more than sea fog. The anonymous officer of the 81st wrote home at the outset of the expedition that there were few provinces in Europe as little known as Zealand and its islands. He was later to conclude that the attack on the Scheldt was based upon 'bad information', a view shared by Engineer John Squire who complained of the profound ignorance of those planning the expedition; they knew nothing of the country, its soil, its climate, its defences or its basic geography. William Stewart of the 95th concurred, stating that the government was unaware of the risks of entering the Scheldt estuary.

The most significant result of these intelligence reports of early 1809 was the perception of the British government and its officers that the French defences of the Scheldt River and Antwerp were weak. We have seen that Castlereagh was encouraged to ignore negative opinion by his interpretation of the fragmented information which filtered through to him. He believed this intelligence to be from 'persons entitled to confidence'. Popham had the impression, after talking with government ministers, that Antwerp was in a defenceless state and that there were very few enemy troops in the Low Countries. Not all were so convinced of French vulnerability. Brownrigg, having seen Antwerp in 1794, held the majority view but he admitted that Sir John Hope had more respect for the city's defences. Hope was pragmatic.

> The details of execution it is acknowledged must finally rest upon the accuracy and truth of the information on which the success or destruction of an Army may depend – still it is useful previously to plan as we thereby separate parts – become aware of possible contingencies – and frequently obtain just conclusions as to the nature and extent of the resources which are required.

It would be unfair to imply that Castlereagh and Chatham naively swallowed all the intelligence available to them. In late July, the Secretary for War wrote to his commander acknowledging that that the latest news of French troop dispositions was imprecise at best. Chatham was uncertain whether to believe it.[2]

Ignorance of geography was not limited to far-flung theatres of war. If Napoleon had invaded England in 1803, British troops would not have fought with a confident knowledge of their own land. There was no dependable map of Kent and the whole coastline from The Wash to Land's End was not fully mapped until 1837. The geography of the Scheldt estuary was particularly challenging (see map II). The River Scheldt entered the North Sea through the province of Zealand which was made up of the islands of Walcheren, North and South Beveland, and Schouwen, in addition to other smaller tracts of land. There were more than a hundred towns and villages, the largest on Walcheren, including the provincial capital Middelburg and the key port of Flushing. Walcheren divided the mouth of the river into two main channels, the East and West Scheldt; command of both entrances gave the island its strategic importance. The East Scheldt itself had two branches, the northern leading up to Willemstadt which was to be of limited importance and the southern which was navigable for over forty miles and ended at the fortress of Bergen-op-Zoom. The West Scheldt flowed between Walcheren to the north and the island of Cadsand to the south. It in turn had two main channels, the northern called the Deurloo which was commanded by the guns of Flushing and the southern, the Wielingen Channel, which was swept by batteries at Breskens on Cadsand. In 1809, the two channels merged under the gaze of these defences and then formed a single waterway practically all the way to Antwerp. Opposite Elleswoutsdijk, there was a further parting into two channels with the southern defended by the fort of Terneuse and the northern by redoubts on the southern shore of South Beveland. Heading further east along the river, the sailor eventually encountered the fort of Batz where there was a strong battery of guns. Significant defences were also in place on the north bank of the river at Fort Lillo and on the south at Fort Liefkenshoek and then there were some smaller forts to pass before the citadel of Antwerp was finally reached. From Flushing to Terneuse, the distance by water was twelve to fifteen miles, from Terneuse to Batz twenty to twenty-five miles, from Batz to Lillo around nine miles, and from Lillo to Antwerp ten to twelve miles. Whichever branch of the Scheldt was used, the occupation of both Walcheren and South Beveland was imperative and for unimpeded access to the West Scheldt, control of Cadsand was also crucial.

This daunting geography was further complicated by the vulnerability of the land to flooding. Many of the islands of Zealand lay below sea level and were only preserved by large numbers of dykes erected by locals fighting an endless battle with the elements. A British officer described Walcheren as 'a round basin or a deep soup-plate floating in the sea'. Most of the islands were flat; the same officer noted that a billiard ball rolled from one side would pass without impediment to the other. He presumably forgot the numerous canals which intersected the countryside: 'A Dutchman will almost dig a canal for the conveyance of the dung from his stable to his garden'.[3]

Whereas the canals were easy to navigate, this was not true of the Scheldt. The West Scheldt was a sizeable river, three and a half miles wide between Cadsand and Flushing, but it was intricate with frequent sandbanks and shoals. The East Scheldt was shallower and probably even more difficult. Strachan and his colleagues were well aware of the challenge they faced. The naval commander freely admitted that he had no personal knowledge of the river and that he was reliant on a French survey provided by the Admiralty and the expertise of Home Popham who, in Strachan's words, had a 'general notion of the Scheldt'. Popham, in memoranda drawn up prior to the departure of the expedition, stressed that beyond Flushing he would also be dependent on the French chart and that it would be necessary to get local pilots to mark out the crucial channels: 'From 60 to 80 buoys will be wanted, sloop's buoys and frigate's buoys, one half painted black the other red; small anchors for each, with hawsers, leads and lines ...'. This detailed plan to render the Scheldt navigable hinged on finding willing and reliable local pilots in Flushing. Sir Richard Keats described naval pilots as the men 'least to be trusted' in the service.[4]

There was also the uncertainty as to the strength of French and Dutch forces in Holland. Between March and May, the Walcheren garrison was variously reported to be anything from 1,400 to 5,000 men. Estimates of enemy troops in the wider area were even more erratic; one report announced 10,000 in Cadsand with as many more on the way to Walcheren whilst another claimed that there were only 8,400 soldiers in the whole of Holland. The early French response to the expedition will be described in more detail in the next chapter but, at this point, it is sufficient to say that the reality was that, by July, the enemy had around 6,000 troops immediately available to meet Chatham and that this number could be increased threefold within a few days. There were about 4,000 men in Flushing, a further 2,000 on Cadsand, and the additional troops, many of them French National Guard, could be called up from around Ghent and Antwerp and from the north of France.[5]

It was on the foundation of this patchy intelligence of the theatre of operations and enemy forces that the British authorities tried to develop a workable plan for the Grand Expedition. Home Popham, writing in June, again emphasised the need for meticulous preparation.

> This is a force of such magnitude, and the point of operation at so short a distance from England, that it is absolutely necessary every arrangement should be made before a single man is embarked; and the commanding officers of the several brigades and divisions should be so perfectly acquainted with the duty assigned to them, as to make them feel satisfied of success.

This philosophy, added to the lack of an immediately available land force, explained the cabinet's summary rejection of Canning's proposal for a quick strike against the Scheldt in late March. In the following months, consultation between senior ministers and army and navy officers led to the formulation of two possible plans for the expedition. These are most explicitly stated in a memorandum of Lieutenant Colonel Gordon, Secretary to the Commander in Chief of the Army, dated 3 May, but others, notably John Hope and Popham, reached the same conclusion. The first plan was to land the army

40

on the coast, most likely at Ostend, and then to secure the south bank of the Scheldt whilst the navy controlled the river. The army would then invade the surrounding country and ultimately take possession of Antwerp. This city was sixty miles inland by the most direct route and there were a number of objections to this amphibious operation well summarised by Hope on 1 June.

> In a landing on the coast of Flanders is to be observed the absence of any port adequate to receive and give security to a large armament; next, the difficulty of the country through which the military operation is to be conducted, and the facility with which the enemy would improve its natural obstacles. Lastly – the time which would be afforded him for this purpose, as also to collect his force, by the delay necessarily attending the equipment (after landing) of a large army – It will also immediately occur to any military man, that an army which had once made its point upon the coast of Flanders would be exposed to the accumulated force, not only of the enemy in the Netherlands [Belgium] and French Flanders but also to the army in Holland which would be conveyed across the islands of Zealand, or through the different channels which divide them, to the left bank of the Scheldt.

Others agreed that this approach would leave the army vulnerable to the vagaries of the local countryside – a land of marshes, canals and fortified villages – and the wider threat of a growing enemy force drawing on the full resources of the French dominated continent.

The second plan proposed by Gordon was a more purely maritime operation whereby a large naval and military force would be launched directly against the islands of the Scheldt. Following an initial landing on Walcheren, Cadsand or South Beveland, troops would provide the necessary protection for the fleet's advance upriver to the village of Sandvliet where the main military force would disembark to march on Antwerp, twenty miles away. This plan was more favourably received, albeit with the reservations already discussed, and it was to be essentially that adopted for the expedition. Hope noted that the capture of Flushing would provide a port of sufficient capacity for the army's armament, the occupation of Walcheren and South Beveland would yield valuable resources for the deployment of the army, and by securing the river, troops could be brought close to Antwerp at lesser risk. Furthermore, enemy forces would initially be limited to the Army of Holland, that of Flanders requiring a circuitous movement via Malines or Antwerp to bring it into play. There would still be the need for a second embarkation for the main attempt on Antwerp but, should the worst happen and the army be forced to retreat, then the close proximity of the navy would give some security. In contrast, the rejected first option was more an 'all or nothing' venture: 'it is presumed that the more brilliant but more precarious plan of landing in Flanders will give way to the different considerations which favour the occupation of the islands in Zealand'.

The favoured approach still required exact timing as any delay would allow the French and Dutch to quickly concentrate their forces in and around the Scheldt. By early July, the plan had been refined and it was decided that there would be three broad theatres of operation necessitating the division of the expeditionary force into three parts. The first, a naval force under the command of Sir Richard Keats and the Reserve of the army under Sir John Hope, was to seize the island of Schouwen on the north shore of the East Scheldt so as to free up the navigation of this part of the river and to ensure the safety of the anchorage known as the Roompot off the north shores of Walcheren and North Beveland. Once this was achieved, troops were either to land on North Beveland or to descend the Veere Gat (dividing North and South Beveland from Walcheren), before disembarking on South Beveland and capturing the fort of Goes and other local defences, By traversing the island, marching south and east, they would give protection to British forces coming up the West Scheldt and would be ultimately able to combine with these forces in the advance to Sandvliet.

The second part, the naval contingent under the command of Commodore Edward Owen and the 2nd Division of the army under the Marquis of Huntley, was entrusted with the capture of Cadsand. This required the disembarkation of a force sufficient to overpower the riverside batteries. Once Cadsand was under British control, the mastery of the Wielingen channel would allow a rapid advance up the West Scheldt.

The third part of this complicated equation was the capture of Walcheren and Flushing. This vital task was given to a naval force under the command of Admiral Edward Otway and to the Left Wing of the army, or the 'Grand Division', under Sir Eyre Coote. The principal choice for a landing site was Zoutland Bay on the southwest of the island. This had good beaches and was close to the ultimate target, Flushing. As south-westerly winds might make this untenable, another possible landing place was selected to the north between Domburg and East Capelle (see map III). A second simultaneous disembarkation was to be made on the north-east of Walcheren near the fort of Ter Haak. With this fort in British hands, gunboats would be able to enter the waters of the Veere Gat and facilitate a further attack upon the town of

Ter Veere. When these operations in the north of the island had been successfully completed, troops could then march south to join those already advancing from Zoutland (or Domburg) to invest Flushing. The navy would meanwhile sail down the Veere Gat into The Slough to complete the investment of Walcheren. The French garrison in Flushing would, as necessary, be distracted by a demonstration near the town, possibly involving the landing of some part of the Right Wing of the army.

After these various actions had been taken, the remaining two divisions of the army, the Earl of Rosslyn's Light Division and Lieutenant General Thomas Grosvenor's 3rd Division, would be summoned from The Downs to join the expeditionary force. By this stage, Coote should be in charge of Walcheren and Chatham should be able to advance with all available troops to Sandvliet for the final push on Antwerp. In contrast to the initial dispositions, this last part of the plan was a little vague, not least because of a lack of firm intelligence. Was it even possible to land an army at Sandvliet? Brownrigg believed Antwerp close enough to this landing site for the city to be taken by a *coup de main*, a term which was very freely used.

Chatham was later to admit that 'no plan in detail was ever concerted for the attack on Antwerp. It must have depended entirely on circumstances after we had landed on the continent'. The Admiralty had initially expressed doubts as to the wisdom of a combined assault directed against the Scheldt. In a memorandum of 18 May, it is noted that the obstacles to carrying the army up the river are 'very material' with the risk of significant delays and exposure to the shoreline batteries. Although not explicitly stated, the Admiralty appears to favour the rejected option of a landing at Ostend. Whatever the final approach, the Sea Lords viewed Cadsand as the key. Its possession would give the fleet a safe anchorage and, if the army captured batteries along the south bank of the West Scheldt, permit the ships to move slowly upstream while maintaining contact with the land forces. In a submission of 9 June, the Sea Lords agree that Walcheren should be taken first. They also emphasise the importance of control of the right (north) bank of the river and add that once Batz was secured:

> The naval force would be capable of protecting and conveying the whole Army in a very short space of time to Sandvliet, or any other point below the narrow part of the Scheldt at which the General may think it proper to land. An arrangement may be made for putting on shore about 14,000 men at the first trip, by flat boats ... and the remainder of the army could follow from ships to be anchored close to the shore.

The navy could also re-embark the army from Sandvliet but it was warned that the fleet could not enter into the narrowest part of the Scheldt unless the army was in control of both banks of the river. All details would have to be settled between Strachan and the army's commander. Strachan agreed with Popham that, because of the 'unavoidable complicated nature of the undertaking', exhaustive planning was vital. Writing to Otway on 16 July, regarding the latter's role in the seizure of Walcheren, he speaks of the expedition's 'extensive and minute combinations' and exhorts that 'every part of our proceedings should be clearly understood before we sail'.[6]

Whilst the plan of campaign was being finalised, Castlereagh continued his efforts to assemble and equip a proper force. He shared responsibility for the onerous task with the Commander in Chief of the army, the Master General of the Ordnance, and the First Lord of the Admiralty. In the third week of June, Chatham remained concerned that his army would be insufficient, writing to Castlereagh that he thought the number of available troops to have been exaggerated and that disease, such as the eye disorder ophthalmia, may reduce this number even more. Soldiers were struggling to recover from the effects of the Corunna Campaign. Subaltern Robert Dallas of the 9th was judged unfit by his regimental surgeon but he managed to find another doctor who passed him for active service, whereupon he joined his comrades at Deal. Compromises were also required at regimental level. Certain battalions, for instance the 2/8th and the 2/23rd, embarked with the expeditionary force made up of only two or four companies rather than the normal ten.

More unusual was the creation of a detachment battalion, officially entitled the Corps of Embodied Detachments, an initiative more associated with the early months of the Peninsular War. Dundas noted that there were more than 3,000 remaining at the Army Depot; these were drawn upon to create a provisional battalion of around 800 rank and file for service with Chatham. This last-minute measure, first documented on 3 July, demonstrates that the authorities were prepared to think laterally to expedite the departure of the expedition. Similarly, the Admiralty were calling upon all possible resources, particularly for the transport of the troops. In a memorandum of 9 June, it is stated that it would be proper 'to collect as many revenue vessels as possible; and when the expedition is about to sail, we should lay hold of all Folkestone and Deal cutters, all Berwick smacks that may be on the river, and such Harwich packets and vessels of that description as can be procured'.[7]

Thanks to his exhaustive efforts and the recovery of men who had served in Spain, Dundas was able, on 22 June, to send Castlereagh a more detailed state of the force ready to proceed on foreign service. The final returns towards the end of July suggest a total strength of 36,500 infantry and 3,500 cavalry (see Appendix I). It was, in Fortescue's words, 'incomparably the greatest armament that had ever left the shores of England'. The infantry was made up of three battalions of Foot Guards, just under 3,000 men, and thirty-nine battalions of the line and the single corps of embodied detachments. The size of 'full strength' battalions varied widely; at the two extremes were the first battalion of the 1st Foot Guards with 1,239 bayonets and the second battalion of the 63rd Regiment with only 400.

The whole force was nominally arranged into two wings and actually into six divisions (numbered 1st to 4th with the Light Division and the Reserve). The cavalry was incorporated into the Light Infantry Corps in each wing. Under orders to attack Walcheren, the Left Wing of the Army numbered just over 13,000 men. It was commanded by Sir Eyre Coote and was composed of the 1st Division under the command of Major General Thomas Graham (and not Craddock as stated by Fortescue), the 4th Division led by Lieutenant General Mackenzie Fraser, and Lieutenant General Lord Paget's light infantry. The remainder of the army, the 'Right Wing', was divided into four parts. The Reserve, under Sir John Hope, was detailed for the landing on South Beveland, whilst the 2nd Division, commanded by the Marquis of Huntley, was assigned the attack on Cadsand. The remaining two divisions, The Earl of Rosslyn's Light Division and Lieutenant General Thomas Grosvenor's 3rd Division, were to wait in The Downs during the initial operations in accordance with the plan described earlier.

The artillery, separately organised by the Board of Ordnance – Brownrigg later had to admit that he could not recollect the 'particulars' of its organisation – was commanded by Brigadier General John Macleod and was made up of 3,234 men (of which almost a third were drivers) and 1,813 horses. This included one troop of horse artillery and sixteen companies of foot artillery. The siege train included seventy cannon, seventy-four mortars, and Congreve's rockets. The wagon train, nominally attached to the cavalry contingent, had over 300 wagons and carts. Over 6,000 horses were to be embarked.

Castlereagh wrote to the Admiralty on 11 July asking for details of the naval contingent and the maximum number of troops who could be accommodated in the ships of war. Strachan had at his disposal forty-two ships of the line and eighteen frigates. To this principal force was added a veritable armada of other vessels; thirty-three sloops of war, five bomb vessels, twenty-three gun brigs, seventeen hired cutters, fourteen revenue cutters, five tenders, eighty-two gunboats, 150 flat bottomed boats, all the dock-yard lighters, all the fast sailing smuggling vessels which could be procured, and every rowing galley at Deal and Folkestone. There were also the transports to convey military stores and provisions. The hired shipping amounted to almost 100,000 tons. Each ship of the line was upwards of 200 feet long, fifty in beam, and carried between 600 and 800 men. The frigates were smaller, faster, and more manoeuvrable and were used mostly for communication and observation together with the sloops and other craft smaller still. With respect to firepower, the ships of the line generally carried seventy-four guns, the frigates between twenty-four and forty-four guns and the sloops fourteen to eighteen guns.

We will also consider the medical provision for the expedition. It has already been noted that this oft forgotten department was to be sorely tested. There was little proper consultation with the Medical Board prior to sailing. At the end of May, Pepys, Keate, and Knight were requested to provide medical staff suitable for a force of 30,000 men – these were the non-regimental medical officers and this establishment was listed as six physicians, twenty staff surgeons, three apothecaries, one purveyor of hospitals, three deputy purveyors, and sixty hospital mates. In the event, only thirty-three medical staff and thirty hospital mates were attached to the significantly larger force. Even with the addition of an extra seven medical staff and eight hospital mates in September, the medical staffing was considerably below strength. To make matters worse, some regiments were without surgeons or assistant surgeons. The senior doctor with the expedition, Inspector of Hospitals John Webb, put on record that he thought the means granted to him were 'very inadequate to the services expected to be performed'.

Medicines supplied to the expedition were calculated to be sufficient for an army of 40,000 men for six months and the hospital stores – bedding, hospital clothing, marquees and tents – were furnished on a similar scale. The latter were enough to provide 4,000 hospital beds or for 10 per cent of the total force. Keate agitated for the provision of hospital ships but Castlereagh informed Gordon that as transports were few and the distance short, there was no need for these. Eventually, one ship, the *Asia*, and two transports were made available. The closeness of the Scheldt to England and the perception that the campaign would be short led to complacency in the medical arrangements.[8]

The momentum of preparation was not seriously slowed by the depressing news, received in London on 21 July, of Napoleon's defeat of the Austrian army at Wagram. An armistice had been signed but ministers still hoped that

Austria would resume hostilities and that the expedition would give her encouragement. It might at least weaken Napoleon's negotiating position. However, changes in the specific plan of campaign arose out of a series of meetings in the last week of July. On the 24th, a conversation between Strachan, Popham, Hope and Brownrigg led to a number of new conclusions. The first part of the memorandum from this meeting is worth quoting in full as it casts light on contemporary thinking regarding the crucial landing on Walcheren.

> According to the plan at present arranged for the attack on Walcheren which provides for the landing of the principal corps in Zoutland Bay or the north side of the island near <u>Domburg</u> as the state of the wind will allow, and a division of 5,000 men under General Fraser to the east end of Domburg or in the Veere Channel, it appears that the boats of the fleet will not be able to land more than 3,000 men of the principal corps at one time, & that an interval of one hour and a half will take place between each disembarkation, and that in regards to General Fraser's corps not more than 700 men can be put ashore at one time by the boats attending that division.
>
> The means of landing being thus so inadequate – it would be highly imprudent to risk landing the Irish [sic] Division so small in number, ... & as it is so important to the secrecy of the operation that the greatest number of troops within the power of the boats of the fleet should be landed in one operation, it is [sic] that the separate disembarkation intended under Lt General Fraser should be abandoned & that the whole of the left wing of the army destined to act against Walcheren should land at one point where 5,000 men can at once be sent ashore.

Thus, the first decision was that the entire left wing of the army would be landed on Walcheren in a single operation. Secondly, it was judged that it would take two days to transport Sir John Hope's division along the East Scheldt to land near Goes on the north coast of South Beveland and it was decided that it would be better for Hope to wait until Ter Veere (on the north east of Walcheren) had fallen before proceeding down the Veere Gat to land on South Beveland's west coast. Finally, the capture of the southwest point of Schouwen island was necessary to ensure the safety of the anchorage in the Roompot. The corps landed there was to be taken from Grosvenor's division and was to be commanded by 'an officer of intelligence'. Chatham was absent from this discussion but he approved the alterations.

Later on the 24th, Strachan received news that the French fleet, eleven sail of the line under the command of Admiral Missiessy, had dropped down the river to Flushing. The British admiral became excited by the possibility of defeating the enemy fleet in the open sea or cutting off its retreat by the rapid occupation of South Beveland. He soon 'subsided into soberness' and he simply ordered Lord Gardner's squadron, stationed off Walcheren to observe the French, to be reinforced with four additional ships of the line under Sir Richard Keats.

More significantly, the proximity of the French fleet to Flushing persuaded Chatham and Strachan to abandon their original plan of a landing at Zoutland Bay or another location close to Flushing and to instead land the left wing of the army on the north side of the island. Strachan confirmed this in his orders of 26 July to Otway who, we will recall, had naval responsibility for the assault. Otway was informed that, dependent on wind and weather, the troops would now disembark on the northeast side, to the east of Domburg if the beach was smooth but, if not, near Ter Haak. Chatham agreed to the change despite the fact that the army would now be landed at a point on the island most distant from its ultimate target, Flushing. Any transient hope of trapping the French fleet faded when Missiessy withdrew his ships back up the Scheldt just before the expedition sailed.[9]

The embarkation of the army had commenced on 16 July. Because of the shortage of transports, most of the troops, around 25,000, had to be embarked on Strachan's vessels. The admiral was advised that he might remove the lower gun decks from the ships of the line for their more convenient accommodation. That part of the army destined for the reduction of Walcheren, 15,000 soldiers, came aboard at Spithead off Portsmouth and Gosport. Here, most of the larger vessels were used as they would be exposed as little as possible to the intricate navigation of the Scheldt. The remaining men were embarked at the towns of Ramsgate, Deal, Harwich, Deptford, Dover and Chatham (see Appendix I). The Downs, a sheltered anchorage or roadstead off the Kent coast, was to serve as the final rendezvous for the fleet.

This initial embarkation was performed with few problems; William Keep says that at Spithead the men were transferred to the ships with 'astonishing expedition'. Castlereagh wrote to the King on the 17th to inform him that, with the sole exception of the cavalry at Ramsgate, all would be on board that evening. Unfortunately, the weather now caused a significant delay. The unfavourable easterly wind prevented the division embarked at Portsmouth from reaching The Downs until the 27th. This caused grumbling among the soldiers confined on board. Keep and his fellow officers made the best of the situation – 'We are like a hive of bees in this floating habitation' – but all were in a constant state of suspense. Probably not fully understanding the navy's reliance on the elements, Keep noted in his journal, 'It is very strange what can detain us so long. I fear Bonaparte will have received information of our intentions'. This enforced wait caused more than psychological damage. The officer of the 81st, who was fortunate to defer his own boarding until near departure, found his men to have already enough of the sea and to be 'panting for breath' on the crowded decks. In General Orders for the 26th, Chatham expressed his 'surprise and concern' that many officers at Deal had not boarded the ships as instructed. The commander reminded the whole army that the success of the expedition would depend in large part upon their discipline and their conduct towards the local inhabitants. He expected his officers to set an example.

It was a great relief to all when, at dawn on 28 July, the *Venerable*, carrying Strachan's flag and with the Earl of Chatham and his staff on board, led the bulk of the ships away from The Downs towards the Dutch coast. Rosslyn's Light Division and Grosvenor's 3rd Division, and the cavalry and ordnance were to follow on within twenty-four hours. A Captain Taylor wrote to Castlereagh from Windsor that His Majesty was persuaded that there had not been any delay except that attributable to the elements. 'God grant that wind and weather may continue favourable and that our anxiety may soon be relieved by the most satisfactory reports!' The departure of the expedition had been stalled by the weather but there were also manpower problems. A shortage of pilots meant that Otway, who admitted that he was unacquainted with the local navigation, had to leave some of his ships behind. At the highest levels, some of the pessimism of the Horse Guards memoranda persisted. Brownrigg wrote to Hope from the *Venerable* that he wished that he was more confident of success. Enemy resistance was unlikely to be 'so trifling as has been supposed in Downing Street'.[10]

A helpful breeze from the southwest carried the *Venerable* and the vanguard across the North Sea in fourteen hours. Many of the troops had not been on saltwater before and, whether they sailed in transports or ships of war, they found conditions difficult. Captain John Cooke of the 43rd occupied a quiet corner in the cockpit but he was still affected by seasickness and cockchafers crawled over his face and under his blanket. The ship had just returned from a passage to the West Indies. Most military officers respected their naval peers. William Keep commented that the regulations and arrangements that existed in a man-of-war were admirable. Respect was not reciprocated at all levels and the ordinary soldiers were often the butt of sailors' jokes. These 'hard, stubborn, jealous, mischievous sons of the ocean' contrived to let ropes and yard-arms swing alarmingly thereby knocking down dozens of soldiers and discouraging others from getting in the way. Another effective and less violent device was the false forecasting of a gale. This announcement cleared the open decks in record time, the troops making a rapid retreat below. Not all the miseries of the voyage were caused by the ships and their crew; Captain John Patterson of the 50th bemoaned having to listen to the 'eternal droning sound' of the bagpipes.

The low-lying coast of Holland was barely visible until the last moment. When seen at a distance the sea seemed to overhang it. The tops of the trees were first spotted and the land then appeared as if it were rising out of the ocean. The coastline was sterile, a great stretch of sand with only scattered villages. There was not much activity. St Clair was unable to spot any Frenchmen through his spyglass. Corporal John Douglas of the Royals at first thought he saw a long line of infantry drawn up on the sand-hills but then realised that they were large wooden posts designed to break the surf and protect the precious land.[11]

On the evening of the 28th, the vanguard, including Strachan's flagship, anchored in the Stone Deep, a waterway about nine miles to the northwest of Walcheren (see map II). Twenty-four miles to the south, Owen and Lord Huntley's 2nd Division dropped anchor off Blankenberge a few miles west of Cadsand at the mouth of the Wielingen Channel. Strachan despatched some skilled pilots in Deal boats to find an entrance to the Roompot. This anchorage at the mouth of the East Scheldt had been identified as a potential 'safe-haven' in the event of bad weather. Early on the following morning, Strachan was joined by Sir John Hope's Reserve and by Sir Richard Keats; the naval officer had left the command of the blockading squadron to Lord Gardner to resume his planned charge of Hope's force. Sir Home Popham took responsibility for leading Hope's division into the Roompot where it was well placed to commence operations against Schouwen and South Beveland.

Admiral Otway, carrying Eyre Coote's left wing of the army for the assault on Walcheren, arrived an hour or so later. The weather now intervened again. William Richardson, a press-ganged sailor on the *Caesar*, made the following diary entry for the 29th.

At half-past three this morning we all got underway with the third division [the left wing of the army] and, having a fine wind in our favour, saw the island of Walcheren at five in the afternoon. Our first and second divisions were at anchor near the Stone Deep [the 2nd

Division was actually off Cadsand]. We soon came to anchor near them in eight fathoms, and about four miles from the land; but it blew so strong towards the shore, and raised such a surf, that no attempt was made to land, and most of the troops were seasick.

With the wind growing stronger, Strachan was informed by Keats that there was sufficient room in the Roompot for the ships of the left wing. He therefore ordered Otway to also proceed to the anchorage, to be led in by the *Venerable*. In his account of this manoeuvre, Strachan simply states that 'they all came in safely' but Richardson's version serves as a reminder that all such movements around the Scheldt were perilous.

Next morning [30th] we all got underway, and ran through the Veere Gat on the north side of the island, and came to anchor in the Roompot, Flushing being on the south side of Walcheren. In going through the Gat our ship took the ground, broached to, and struck so heavily on the sandy bottom that she nearly shook the lower masts out of the steps, and yet for all this she leaked none. The after guns were run forward, and other things had recourse to be in order to bring her more on an even keel, and when the tide rose we got her over the Braak or bar, and soon after came to anchor among the others in the Roompot, about two miles from the shore.

This meant that there was no longer any possibility of landing Coote's part of the army to the west of Domburg or at West Capelle on the northwest of Walcheren. Instead, an attempt would have to be made to the east on the more protected sands near East Capelle or Ter Haak.

The severe weather led to a second enforced change of plan. The divisions of Rosslyn and Grosvenor also arrived off Walcheren and were, in turn, also directed into the Roompot. The original intention had been for the two divisions to anchor in the West Scheldt from where they would make the advance on Antwerp. There is little doubt that Strachan's hand had been forced; he later claimed that the move to the Roompot was 'highly approved of' by Chatham, all the naval officers and most of the officers of the army. In his despatch to Castlereagh, Chatham agreed that the change of anchorage was 'expedient'. He had himself seen the strength of the waves on the beaches at Zoutland and Domburg. The expedition's leaders nevertheless now faced an even greater challenge. The left wing of the army had to land on Walcheren at the furthermost point from Flushing and the Antwerp-bound divisions were sheltering in the East Scheldt. Walcheren would have to be traversed and a new route to Antwerp would have to be found.[12]

Notes

1. Castlereagh, Viscount, *Memoirs and Correspondence of Viscount Castlereagh*, Vol. VI, pp. 281–2, 285–6; Parliamentary Papers 1810, Vol. XV, pp. ii, ccccxxiv–vi, ccxlviii, ccxxvii, clxxxiii; Bond, G., *The Grand Expedition*, pp. 23–4; Fortescue, J. W., *A History of the British Army*, Vol. VII, p. 62; Brenton, E.P., *The Naval History of Great Britain*, Vol. II, p. 293; Christie, C.A., *The Royal Navy and the Walcheren Expedition*, p. 193.
2. Glover, R., *Peninsular Preparation*, pp. 20–2; Hall, C. D., *British Strategy in the Napoleonic War 1803–1815*, pp. 47–8; Christie, pp. 190–1; *A Collection of Papers Relating to the Expedition to the Scheldt*, pp. 232–4, 241, 264, 291; Castlereagh, Vol. VI, pp. 298–9; St Clair, Lt Col, *A Soldier's recollections of the West Indies and America with a narrative of the expedition to the Island of Walcheren*, Vol. II, p. 299; Parliamentary Papers, Vol. XV, pp. clxxx, 5xxix, cccxxv, clxxxvi, 6vii, cccliv, cccxciii; *The Walcheren Expedition. The Experiences of a British Officer of the 81st Regiment*, pp. 40, 107–8; Squire, J., *A Short Narrative of the Late Campaign of the British Army*, pp. 38–9; Verner, W., *History and Campaigns of the Rifle Brigade*, Vol. II, p. 40; NAS, GD364/1/187.
3. Glover, R., pp. 19–20, 80; Fortescue, Vol. VII, pp. 60–1; Bond, pp. 37–8; *The Walcheren Expedition*, pp. 27–30, 54, 100.
4. Brenton, Vol. II, pp. 292, 303; Fischer, A, *Napoléon et Anvers*, p. 165; Bond, p. 38; Parliamentary Papers, Vol. XV, pp. ccxlix, ccxl, ccxxxiii, cclxxiv; Fortescue, Vol. VII, p.59.
5. Hall, p. 48; Fortescue, Vol. VII, p. 65.
6. Parliamentary papers, Vol. XV, pp. ccxxxviii, cccxlviii, cxcvii, ccxiv, clxv, cxcvi, ccclii, ccxlviii; Christie, pp. 190–2; Fortescue, Vol. VII, pp. 45–6, 61–2; Bond, pp. 13–14, 38–41, 24–5; Fischer, p. 158; Castlereagh, Vol. VI, pp. 261–3, 279; *A Collection of Papers*, pp. 313–4, 377–8; Brenton, Vol. II, p.294.
7. Parliamentary Papers, Vol. XV, pp. 6xviii, xc–xci; Castlereagh, Vol. VI, pp. 282–3, 278–9; Dallas, R. W., *A Subaltern of the 9th in the Peninsula and at Walcheren*, pp. 62–3; Bamford, A., *The Corps of Embodied Detachments 1809*; Fortescue, Vol. VII, p. 55.
8. Fortescue, Vol. VII, pp. 56–8; *A Collection of Papers*, pp. 24–7, 32–3, 349–51, 546–7, 635–40; *Papers Ordered by the House to be Printed Relating to the Expedition to the Scheldt 1810*, Vol. VII, pp. 59–63; General Orders for the Army July 10, TNA, WO 28/352; Bond, pp. 167–72; Jones, Sir J. T., *Journal of Sieges carried on by the Army*, Vol. II, pp. 363–4; Brenton, Vol. II, pp. 289–91; TNA, WO 6/27:19; Howarth, D., *Trafalgar*, pp. 20–1; McGuffie, T. H., *The Walcheren Expedition and the Walcheren Fever*, pp. 193–4; Cantlie, N., *A History of the Army Medical Department*, Vol. I, p. 396; Parliamentary Papers, Vol. XV, pp. ccclvi, cxi, cvi.
9. Muir, R., *Britain and the Defeat of Napoleon 1807–1815*, p. 102; Christie, p. 193; NAS, GD364/1/1188; Enthoven, V, *Een Haven Te Ver*, pp. 283–4; Bond, pp. 42–3; *A Collection of Papers*, pp. 381–2, 402; Fortescue, Vol. VII, pp. 65–6.
10. *A Collection of Papers*, pp. 342–4, 348, 336–40; Keep, W., *In the Service of the*

King, pp. 37−40; Castlereagh, Vol. VI, pp. 286, 297; General Orders for the Army July 25 and 26; Dyott, W., *Dyott's Diary 1781−1845*, Vol. I, pp. 277−8; *The Walcheren Expedition*, p. 18; Bond, pp. 41−4; *British Minor Expeditions 1746 to 1814*, pp. 58−9; NAS, GD364/1/1188.

11. Brett-James, A., *The Walcheren Failure*, p. 812; Cooke, Lt J., *A True Soldier Gentleman*, pp. 52−3; Keep, p. 43; *The Walcheren Expedition*, pp. 18−19; Patterson, J., *Camp and Quarters*, Vol. I, p. 325; *The Walcheren Expedition by a Medical Officer*, p. 125; St Clair, Vol. II, p. 284; Douglas, J., *Douglas's tale of the Peninsula and Waterloo 1808−1815*, p. 6.

12. Bond, pp. 44−5, 52; Fortescue, Vol. VII, pp. 66−7; Parliamentary Papers, Vol. XV, pp. cclxv, xxiii, 6xiii; Journal of the Army pp. 1−4, TNA, WO 1/190; Richardson, W., *A Mariner of England*, pp. 262−3.

CHAPTER 4

Brothers in Arms

The Minister of War in Paris was suddenly receiving a large number of semaphore telegraphs from the north coast of France and the Scheldt. On 26 July, General Louis-Claude Monnet, commander at Flushing, warned of increasing British naval activity around the island of Walcheren. He was nervous that there would soon be ships of war on the horizon. Monnet's frame of mind was not helped by a false report, received by the Dutch General, Stewart Bruce, that there had actually been an enemy landing on the island. Three days later, General Saint-Suzanne, Commander at Boulogne, telegraphed that he had received news from Flushing that around sixty British ships were moored around twenty miles to the northwest of Walcheren and that there were soldiers aboard. In the evening, he sent a despatch announcing that the ships had moved further to the north and were approaching land. That there was a significant British fleet on the move was confirmed by General Chambarlhac at Ghent and General Lamorlière at Le Havre. Wherever the enemy were to land, all were determined to do their duty. Chambarlhac, suspecting disembarkation at Blankenberge to the south of Walcheren, vowed to repel any attack, and Saint-Suzanne, despite his poor health, meant to hold his post to the last.

The locals were also aware of a breaking storm. Jacob Hendrik Schorer, burgomaster of Middelburg, was walking with his family on the dunes at Domburg on 28 July when he spotted English ships. He counted sixteen. By the next day, he could see considerably more to the west from his vantage point on the Bree Sand. Neither Schorer nor the French generals, nor indeed the Minister of War, were entirely surprised at this turn of events. The British expedition to the Scheldt was one of the worst kept secrets of the wars. The spies of Joseph Fouché, Napoleon's Minister of Police, had been working hard, although it hardly required Fouché's 'furious partiality for clandestine operations' to guess British intent. The vast build-up of armaments in England since the beginning of 1809 and the incessant reconnoitring of the Scheldt River by British frigates kept the war administration in Paris on its toes. In April, it was already known by the French that, in the first plan for the campaign developed by Castlereagh, Zoutland was the favoured landing site on Walcheren. Lord Cochrane's brilliant attack on the French fleet in Aix Roads later the same month did deflect French attention, albeit temporarily, to the Atlantic coast.

Any doubts which the enemy might have harboured as to Britain's plans were resolved by the popular press. By mid-July, most newspapers on the continent were publishing extracts from English newspapers detailing the military build-up and quoting the Scheldt as the expedition's most likely destination. Details of armaments were available; it was reported that the new rockets invented by General William Congreve were to be carried by the force. At the end of the month, Napoleon informed Fouché that 'for the last two months, the Continent has been kept in a fright about the great British expedition'.[1]

That the Emperor had long expected just such an attack is clear from his correspondence with his brother Louis whom he had placed on the throne of Holland. In late February 1809 he wrote to Louis from Paris.

> Please send me the state of your troops, so that, in the general arrangements I make, I can see what you have to fear from an English attack this summer, and your means to repulse it.

Napoleon urges his brother to put 26,000 men under arms for the defence of his realm. He warns that war is imminent, that he can spare Louis no troops from his own armies and that Holland will surely be attacked in June or September. A few days later, Napoleon puts pen to paper again; Louis is once more reminded of the inevitability of war and is harangued for allowing his own army to become weak.

> I repeat that nothing is finished in Europe and that, whilst you have disarmed, I have raised new conscriptions and reinforcements of 150,000 men. You will feel the effects of your imprudent measures and the dangerous results they might have for your country and for the whole world.

In mid-April, the Emperor is losing patience with his sibling. Another demand for the raising of extra troops for the defence of Holland is followed by a warning that time is running out.[2]

Louis's realm had been overrun by the French during the Revolutionary Wars and had acquired the label of the Batavian Republic. In 1806, Napoleon revised the constitution and renamed the republic the Kingdom of Holland. The elevation of his brother to the Dutch throne was just one part of the Emperor's great scheme to create a dynasty of French princes out of his immediate family. Joseph, the eldest, to whom Napoleon gave a modicum of respect, received the Kingdom of Naples confiscated from the Bourbons in 1806 and then replaced Charles IV on the throne of Spain. Jerome, who had a stormy relationship with Napoleon, became King of Westphalia and only Lucien, the most intelligent, failed to receive a kingdom. The Emperor's sisters were also honoured: Elisa was Princess of Lucca and Piombino and later Grand Duchess of Tuscany; Pauline, the most beautiful, married the Prince Borghese; finally, Caroline, màrried to the flamboyant Murat, became Grand Duchess of Berg and Queen of Naples.

As kings, Napoleon's brothers were mere instruments of his politics. It was not the Emperor's intention that they should act autonomously. They were placed in an impossible situation, pretending to reign as independent sovereigns whilst, in reality, they were imitation royalty who owed everything to their brother's military genius and over-ambitious foreign policy. Proclaimed King of Holland in June 1806, Louis entered The Hague three weeks later accompanied by Queen Hortense. The Emperor had informed him that it was better to die on a throne than live as a prince. Louis either misunderstood his role or was incapable of meeting Napoleon's expectations, particularly the exacting requirements of the Continental System designed to block Britain's trade with the continent. Holland depended on its maritime trade and was obliged to tolerate English contraband to escape ruination. Louis was a victim of his own generous nature. In Jean Tulard's words, 'An excellent sovereign, he took to heart the interests of his state, stricken as it was by the Continental blockade; from then onwards a conflict with his brother was inevitable'. Rather than acting as Napoleon's vassal, the kind-hearted king was determined to be a good and popular ruler of Holland, loved by his subjects. He took lessons in Dutch, set up a lavish court, recruited a royal bodyguard, founded new orders of chivalry, and introduced new senior ranks into the army and navy. Surrounded by Dutchmen rather than the usual French advisors and hangers on, his popularity with the local population grew such that he was referred to as 'Good King Louis'. Queen Hortense added to the bonhomie by emptying much of the royal coffers into the hands of Amsterdam's diamond merchants.

The Emperor was annoyed and he rejected Louis's attempts to adapt his civil code to local law. 'A nation of 1,800,000 inhabitants cannot have a separate legislation. Rome gave her laws to her allies; why should the laws of France not be adopted in Holland?' Louis did not have the force of character or intellect to win a war of words with his brother; few could have done so. Also at odds with his Queen, he suffered from poor health and depression. He was not an inspiring military leader. Late in 1806, after Napoleon's triumph at Jena, he undertook a half-hearted invasion of Hesse and East Friedland. The fighting was limited to a cavalry skirmish and Louis was constantly criticised by Napoleon for his negotiations with the enemy, for taking territory in his own name (and hoisting the Dutch flag rather than the French), and for disobeying the Emperor's orders. When the King was gifted the opportunity to capture an almost defenceless Hanover, he refused to advance without reinforcements. A disgusted Napoleon, determined to save the family honour, quoted ill health as the reason for Louis's subsequent withdrawal.[3]

A further cause of tension between the brothers was Louis's apparent inability to raise the requisite number of troops for either the *Grande Armée* or for the defence of Holland. The Dutch Army was made up of sixteen battalions but the Emperor's demands for reinforcements for Germany and the Iberian Peninsula meant that only six remained on Dutch soil. These men were mostly encamped along the coast and, according to Louis, over half were sick and in the hospitals. He replied to his brother's demands in April pointing out the weakness of Holland and asking for the return of the Dutch troops. He was both indignant and apprehensive.

> I request from Your Majesty my divisions in Germany and Spain ... I understand that Your Majesty ordered me to raise 20,000 more men; believe me that I have done everything humanly possible and I do not blame myself for anything.

Nervous of a British attack, he wrote to his brother later in the month vowing that, if necessary, he would send his few spare troops to Monnet in Flushing and keep only the minimum necessary to protect Amsterdam.

As was suspected by the British, the physical defences of the Scheldt were also weak. At Antwerp, the rapid expansion of the shipbuilding facility had been at the expense of the fortifications. Parts of the front were encumbered with piles of earth from the recent enlargement of the docks and the batteries were rudimentary. The numerous forts on the banks of the Scheldt protecting the approach to Antwerp (see map II) were in no better repair. Two of the more substantial of these, Lillo and Liefkenshoek, were first constructed in the late sixteenth century and were incomplete and poorly manned. St Marie and Frederick Henry had no armament at all, whilst La Croix, St Philippe and La Perle had all but disappeared. The fort of Batz on the eastern extremity of South Beveland was in better repair and was manned by a small Dutch garrison. Louis's men were also defending much of the island of Walcheren but not the port of Flushing which had been ceded to France in the Treaty of Fontainebleau in November 1807 and was garrisoned by French troops. Napoleon had ordered the strengthening of defences but these works were continuing and until they were completed it was unlikely that the city would be able to withstand a siege.[4]

The Emperor did not entirely ignore his brother's supplications. Throughout April, he gave detailed instruction to his Minister of War in Paris, Clarke (the Duke of Feltre), for the raising of seventeen provisional demi-brigades as a reserve for the French army on the Rhine but also for the defence of the coast. The bulk of the troops in the north were in camps at Boulogne, St Omer and Ghent; the former two places were only two to three days from Antwerp. Napoleon also gave explicit directions for the leadership of these units. General Saint-Suzanne was to command at Boulogne, General Chambarlhac at Ghent, and General Antoine-Alexandre Rousseau at St Omer. An additional 6,000 men of the National Guard were added to the camp at St Omer under the command of General Antoine-Guillame Rampon.

On 13 April, Napoleon urged Clarke to expedite the formation of the new demi-brigades which were 'necessary for the defence of the Scheldt' but the reality was that, at the same time, troops were being ordered from the coastal areas of Holland and Northern France to reinforce the *Grande Armée* in Germany. The Emperor was giving with one hand and taking with the other. In early May, Louis left Amsterdam for a tour of inspection of the Scheldt. He wished to see for himself the state of his men and defences. This was good for morale – cheering crowds greeted him at Middelburg – but the King was dismayed. As he later related to his brother, Flushing was weak and its garrison poorly led. There was, he complained, 'no firmness or unity in the command, and the soldiers do not have the necessary harmony or spirit'. Very likely believing that Louis's concerns were in part due to his rancour at the cession of Flushing to France, Napoleon paid little attention.[5]

These various forces around the Scheldt needed a proper command structure. This was crucial to ensure the coordination of the disparate French units and to gain the full cooperation of the Dutch. Napoleon barked orders at Clarke, first from Paris and then from the Austrian Campaign, but it was not clear who was in local control of the defence of the region. Problems in the French high command were common when the Emperor was not personally on the scene. In the Scheldt, Louis controlled the Dutch troops but had no jurisdiction over the French. As a result, when Minister Clarke in Paris received news of the sighting of British ships on 30 July he immediately ordered General Rampon to take charge of French troops on the left bank of the Scheldt and also of the 6,000 National Guard, who by this stage had been despatched from St Omer to the island of Cadsand. No doubt nervous at taking such a decision, he gave Rampon the command on a temporary basis and immediately wrote to Napoleon requesting further instructions. Rampon appears a sensible choice. Entering the army at seventeen years of age, his courage and leadership qualities led to rapid promotion. He came to Bonaparte's attention at the Battle of Montenotte in 1796 and, after glorious service throughout the Italian Campaign and in Egypt, he was promoted to *général de division* in 1800. He then undertook a number of more administrative roles before being appointed as the commander of the National Guard in the *department du Nord*. This brilliant career was in stark contrast to his co-commander Louis Bonaparte who, as his brother was quick to remind Clarke, had not led as much as a regiment during the wars. Interestingly, Napoleon also makes a carping comment regarding Rampon – 'even General Rampon would have been better' – when later discussing the command of his troops.

The Emperor set high standards but the best officers struggled with the tenuous French chain of command. Napoleon tried to influence events from Austria whilst Clarke made cautious contributions from Paris, and there was a divided command of French and Dutch troops on the ground. General Jean-Louis Fauconnet, Commander of Antwerp, a further link in this hierarchy, was uncertain of his seniority relative to Rampon. The assertion of General Jean Jacques Pelet that 'the greatest harmony reigned' between all the French commanders of the land and sea forces should not be entirely dismissed; perhaps there were examples of good cooperation. Others saw only chaos. Sous-Lieutenant Albert Jean Michel de Rocca of the 2nd Hussars had recently come to the Scheldt after service in the Corunna Campaign. He was soon under the command of the two French generals, Chambarlhac and Dallemagne.

> Their arrival doubled the confusion. Each wanted to have at least an entire division under their orders, something difficult to achieve since all our detachments brought together in a single corps might scarcely form a brigade. Our generals were equal in grade and, neither wanting to cede to the other, the shared command of troops was bound to cause great difficulties. Not having taken the precaution to bring with them chefs d'état major, they were at first reduced to transmitting their multiple orders verbally; these were nearly always contradictory and gave place to endless misunderstandings.

Competition between French and Dutch commanders was also a source of friction. Napoleon was forced to instruct Clarke on the subject.

> When you write to Holland, make it known to the King that the defences of Zealand [the Scheldt] would be improved if rivalry between the Dutch and French commander had been avoided; if it is necessary that one of them commands then it is more natural that it is the Frenchman who commands the Dutchman.

Louis, to his credit, had insight into his own inexperience as a military leader and was also aware of the disunity of command and the real possibility of a Dutch uprising. Within a few days of the British arrival, he wrote to Clarke asking that a French Marshal be sent to direct operations in the Scheldt. On the same day, he also wrote to Jean Jacques Cambacérès, Consul of the Empire, stressing the urgent need for a Marshal to unify the command of the land and sea.

The French garrison on Walcheren was under the command of General Monnet with General Pierre-Jacques Osten his second-in-command. The Dutch troops were led by General Bruce. These three men were responsible for the defence of the island against the imminent British invasion. Monnet was forty-three years of age and in ill health. He had been promoted to general in the Army of Italy and had received the command of Flushing in 1803. We have no definite account of his character but what we do have is against him. Pierre Berthezène, who served in the Scheldt as Colonel of the *10e léger*, believed Flushing's governor to be unprepared and incompetent.

> General Monnet, despite the continued warnings of smugglers, had refused to believe that this expedition threatened him; so it was that he was caught off guard in Flushing. He was man of mediocre ability but he had gained a reputation for great tenacity, a precious quality in an officer, and especially in the commander of a town. He did not keep this reputation and it was claimed that he lost this virtue when he lost his wife from whom he had borrowed it. Entirely occupied with his pleasures and amassing wealth, he put himself in the hands of arrogant men, bringing upon himself the low regard of his troops and, at the same time, the hate of the inhabitants from whom he extracted money.

That there is some truth in this portrayal is suggested by a letter from Napoleon to Clarke in January 1809 in which the Emperor states that he has received serious complaints regarding Monnet and that it was his intention to replace him with a man of probity. For whatever reason, he relented. Savary, the Duke of Rovigo, comments in his memoirs that Napoleon actually had great confidence in Monnet despite 'receiving many reports injurious to his character'.

Monnet did not get on with his immediate subordinate, the fifty-one-year-old General Osten, a man who, according to Berthezène, was 'energetic, intrepid, well liked and held in high esteem in the country'. There was probably snobbery in this dislike; Osten was Flemish and had kept the manners and habits of his birthplace. His appearance resembled more a peasant than a senior officer of the French Empire, a fact well attested by a surviving portrait. He had proved his heroism in the French Revolutionary Wars and had served on Walcheren intermittently since 1795. Apparently more aware of the vulnerability of the island than his senior commander, he had addressed a proclamation to the local population two years earlier, urging them to arm against a possible British attack. General Bruce was reputedly of British origin. He was to emerge from the coming campaign with little distinction.[6]

The French and Dutch forces on Walcheren and across the Scheldt were mostly of poor quality. Napoleon admitted to Clarke that the troops available to Rampon were 'mediocre'. This was due to the best men being removed for service in the *Grande Armée* whilst the worst were sent to the corners of the Empire. This was particularly the case for the Scheldt as it was notoriously unhealthy; the Emperor was too much of a pragmatist to risk his elite in such a place. According to Salomon-Louis Laurillard-Fallot, a Dutch doctor serving in the French army on Walcheren in 1808, a posting to Flushing was regarded as a disgrace in Paris. When it was announced, others immediately asked, 'What has he done?' Under constant threat of deadly disease, most of the troops led a dissolute lifestyle. Ironically, Laurillard-Fallot believed himself to have been saved only by a low grade fever which prevented him joining in the worst excesses of his friends.

De Rocca's account of the march of reinforcements to the front is equally damning.

All the available troops in the towns of Liege and Maastricht, of which we were part, were ordered to Antwerp. We formed a column of 8–9,000 men made up from the depots of 26 different regiments: dragoons, chasseurs, hussars, infantry, all were obliged to leave, even dismounted cavalrymen and workmen. For the first two days of the march, there was no commander in chief; each detachment moved in isolation. Here, a sergeant led ten lazy and undisciplined conscripts; elsewhere, two or three officers fought over the command of about twenty men, and our march towards the border was almost a stampede.

The defence of the Scheldt was in the hands of a polyglot army. Pelet saw uniforms of different eras; the Ancient Regimen, the Republic and the Empire were all represented. Not all were regulars. The National Guard, France's final reserve against her enemies at home and abroad, formed a significant part of the force converging on the region. Its senior officers, men such as Antoine Rampon, were often drawn from military members of the senate who were thought still capable of active service. The National Guards of the major cities of the Rhine and close to the English Channel were put on a war footing as necessary, often to be used to man garrisons or coastal defences. A British prisoner of war, Peter Bussell, described the Arras National Guard marching north to defend Walcheren as a 'motley group'. They seemed a mixture of bakers, barbers and tailors. Those who arrived at Antwerp were intimidated by the sight of so many wounded old soldiers. In the words of de Rocca, 'When they saw the mangled arms and legs of our respected veterans they said to themselves, 'If this is the fate that awaits us, we will probably never return to finish our harvests'.

This was, above all, a multinational force. De Rocca saw a 'confused and strange' mixture of Poles, Spanish, Hanoverians, and 'all the different races of men brought together in the name of France'. In Monnet's command on Walcheren, Irish, Prussian and Colonial troops were joined by deserters and veterans. The *Légion Irlandaise*, formed in 1803, consisted mainly of Irish volunteers and was led by officers inspired by patriotism and politics. Few had seen action. By 1809, the Irish contingent had been joined by significant numbers of Poles and Germans and even some British prisoners of war who usually enlisted with a plan to desert. It was regarded as one of the better of the foreign regiments in French service but morale was often poor. Miles Byrne described his time in the Legion at Flushing as 'irksome and desponding'. Monnet's Prussian troops were a hangover from the 1806 Jena Campaign, made up of prisoners and deserters. The Colonial Battalion at Flushing was composed of men drawn from the French Empire's dependencies whilst the Veterans Battalion was one of a number of units of old soldiers who were used for garrison duty at seaports or in fortified towns, particularly where the local National Guard was weak. The Dutch troops under Louis's direct command were better dressed and equipped than most of the French-led forces but their commitment to the common cause was in doubt. Marshal Victor believed the Dutch soldier to lack the Frenchman's 'love of victory and conquest'.[7]

The French fleet was also afflicted by command issues. Admiral Édouard-Thomas de Burgues, Comte de Missiessy, a veteran sailor and talented officer, took his direct orders from Admiral Decrès, Minister of the Navy in Paris. Louis believed that Missiessy should be under his jurisdiction or that Decrès should personally come to Antwerp to direct matters. The King wrote to Napoleon in mid-May stating that the fleet was well organised but that he was not convinced that it was safe.

> The Admiral does not take real precautions; he waits for the enemy to arrive for fear of appearing frightened of them. It's the same idea that Admiral Bruey had at Aboukir [Nelson's destruction of the French fleet in 1798]. I have recommended that he does not lose a minute ...

Missiessy replied to Louis's request that the fleet should be immediately removed upriver to Antwerp that he required authorisation from Paris. It was this apparent vulnerability of French ships at the mouth of the Scheldt which raised Strachan's hopes, albeit temporarily, of a pre-emptive naval attack. In the event, Missiessy did eventually start to move his fleet to safety on 29 July as British vessels were entering the Roompot. Despite adverse winds, the retreat was orderly and the remaining ships off Flushing – nine ships of the line, a frigate and a brig – were removed within the next forty-eight hours. The majority of the French fleet, including the ships of the line, were placed behind a boom in the river between the forts of Lillo and Liefkenshoek. Louis's comment to Napoleon that Missiessy was expert but 'a little slow' seems justified.[8]

The boom behind which the fleet was sheltering was made up of logs linked by a chain and weighed by anchors. A small gap in the centre permitted the passage of smaller vessels but larger ships would have to break the boom itself. This was one of a number of additional defensive measures taken as the French braced themselves for the British attack. The Emperor had also released funds for the construction of batteries on Cadsand and the strengthening of the fortifications at Flushing and Antwerp. At the latter place, a large lock now protected the inner part of the port. The first brick carried a portrait of Napoleon. The Emperor, sensing the danger, had taken the work out of the hands of the civil authorities and entrusted it to Pierre-Victor Malouet the local *préfet maritime*. Building was on a scale to allow nineteen large ships of the line an apparent safe haven but the French remained nervous. At the end of June, a strike in the dockyards and the depletion of the garrison were reminders of Antwerp's potential vulnerability.[9]

It was crucial that the local Dutch and Belgian populations remained calm and cooperative. At the least, it was necessary to prevent frank insurrection. Both Holland and Belgium had reasons to support a British invasion. French dominance had denied them access to the seas and damaged local trade. De Rocca says that the locals looked forward to the arrival of the British so that their goods could again be exchanged for colonial products. 'They had become used to using tea and coffee to warm themselves and reawaken themselves from the apathy caused by the heavy and nebulous air that they breathed'. The Church was also anti-French, resenting the Emperor's rift with the Pope. Prefect Malouet complained that the priests of Antwerp were 'in a state of continual revolt against the government ... they are fanatics and spread the most absurd rumours about the Pope, religion and the Emperor'. News of the incipient British attack was everywhere in Antwerp and the reception was mixed. The Commissioner of Police wrote to the prefect on 31 July informing him of the gathering of crowds. He noted that some expressed anxiety at the rumours of a British disembarkation whilst others appeared unconcerned. De Rocca arrived in the city a few days later and saw more panic, the fear of a bombardment causing a flight to the surrounding countryside. Louis had previously placed a report in the *Le Moniteur* (9 June), the official newspaper of the Empire, emphasising the 'efficient and elaborate measures' that had been taken to repel any attack. In any case, after the 'disasters' that had befallen the Austrian army, it was unlikely that the English would keep their promises.[10]

In reality, it was clear that Britain was determined to follow through and King Louis's relationship with his subjects was not his only problem. By July, the Emperor was becoming highly critical of his brother's methods, particularly with respect to the execution of the workings of the Continental System. He was especially irritated by Louis's decision to open Dutch ports to American vessels, a measure which made it much easier for British shipping to trade illegally with Holland. France recalled its ambassadors and closed its borders to Louis's realm. Napoleon's preoccupation with Holland was such that he wrote to his brother twice in one day (17 July) from Schönbrunn near Vienna. In the second letter, he informed him that the country was an 'English province' and that the Dutch were 'trumpets' of his greatest enemy. He admitted that this might not be Louis's fault but, as the campaign in the Scheldt progressed, the Emperor's correspondence to his hapless sibling became increasingly antagonistic.

A French historian asserts that Louis had unrealistic expectations.

Did he not persist in his stubbornness as he was sat on the throne, considering himself as King of Holland in the total and unique

64

service of this country, without taking any account of the plans of his brother who had given him this realm? He had never wanted to understand that he was or rather had to be a king sent to Holland by Napoleon ... He did not understand that he had been sent to Holland to cooperate with everything in the war which the Emperor made against England.

Was this simply a misunderstanding or was Louis fundamentally disloyal to his brother? Some around the King thought his attitude to the British attack to be ambivalent. The Dutch General, Dirk Van Hogendorp, stated that Louis 'had only made feeble efforts to repulse this attack, and his conduct was so equivocal that many believed that he was not far short of seizing this opportunity to make an accommodation with the English, to unite with them against his brother'.

Minister of War Clarke had an unenviable task. As news of an enemy incursion in the Scheldt trickled into Paris, he had both to placate the elder Bonaparte brother in Austria and to motivate the dithering younger one on the scene. On 31 July, he wrote to Napoleon informing him of the appearance of the British fleet off Walcheren. News took a day or so to reach the French capital; unbeknown to Clarke, the British were by this time already ashore. It took a further week for the minister's letter to reach Schönbrunn. Napoleon was determined to influence the course of the Scheldt campaign but the distance between Imperial Headquarters in Austria and Paris meant that his opinions were retrospective and his orders often too late. On 6 August, the Emperor instructed Clarke of the need for reinforcements for the Scheldt and the necessity to put Antwerp and other major towns in the region in a state of siege.

> With all the advantages that we have here, I do not suppose that the French will allow themselves to be insulted by 15 or 20,000 English. I do not see what the English can do; they cannot take Flushing as the dykes can be cut: they cannot take the fleet since it can retreat to Antwerp and that place and its port are safe from all attack.[11]

It is not clear that the Minister of War shared this complacent view of the French position. He had already appointed Rampon and had ordered the National Guard from St Omer to Cadsand. This was just the start of a significant reinforcement of forces on the island which the French expected to be a key British objective. The reasons for placing particular emphasis on the defence of Cadsand were threefold. Firstly, the village of Breskens was the most convenient place from which to reinforce Flushing. Secondly, the batteries on Cadsand were vital for control of the Wielingen Channel, the entry to the West Scheldt. Thirdly, the French feared a British landing on the island followed by a combined navy and army operation against their ports to the south. General Rousseau, the senior officer on Cadsand, received a further eight companies of reserve from Ecloo on the 30th and, on the following day, General Chambarlhac arrived to take over the command of what was by this stage close to 6,000 men including 300 cavalry. Chambarlhac's concern regarding an immediate British attack led to the rapid addition of General Jean-André Valletaux's 1,500 men from Louvain. Rampon's 6,000 National Guard arrived on 3 August and were joined by a further 5,500 National Guardsmen from the Department of the North under the command of General Olivier.

Away from the Scheldt, French troop dispositions were designed to protect other possible British targets. At Ostend, Dunkirk and Calais, the National Guard were alerted. Boulogne was reinforced by a mixture of regular and light infantry and by a Colonial battalion. As the destination of the expedition became obvious, some of these men were ordered on to the Scheldt. More movements of troops were made to Lille and Ghent. The 700-man detachment of the Legion of the Vistula in Lille would be able to be rapidly deployed along the Scheldt or on the coast between Cadsand and Boulogne. A number of smaller detachments were mobilised for the defence of the region and all the mayors and sub prefects in the Department of the North were directed to raise men for garrison duties and to expand the National Guard. In Antwerp, General Louis-Joseph Saint-Laurent took control of the artillery and 800 gendarmes were brought in from Brussels.[12]

On Walcheren, there were around 4,000 soldiers of mixed nationality under Monnet's command. According to Osten, this force was as follows: 1er Colonial Battalion 729 men, Battalion of Deserters 982, 1er Prussian Regiment 1,589, 1er Irish Battalion 464, Veterans forty-five, French artillery 117, *Cannonières Vétérans* forty-six, *Cannonières gardes-côtes* 127. The exact strength of the French forces on Walcheren is uncertain as Osten's total figure of 4,099 differs from other primary sources; estimations vary from 3,570 to 4,500 men. Certainly, reinforcements were smuggled into Flushing in the first few days of August. Monnet's troops were supported by around 850 men of the Dutch 5th Infantry Regiment and 250–300 men of the Dutch 3rd Artillery Battalion under the command of Bruce. These forces were in Zoutland, Middelburg, Ter Veere and Fort Ter Haak. In addition to these regular troops, there were just over 1,000 men of the *Burgerwacht*, the Dutch equivalent of the National Guard, divided between Flushing, Middelburg and Ter Veere.

General Osten first became aware of the presence of the British fleet at 8am on 29 July when the arrival of enemy vessels off Walcheren was spotted from the tower in Middelburg. He immediately informed Monnet and was ordered by his superior to return to the village of West Capelle on the west coast of the island where the Irish and Colonial battalions were encamped. On his arrival, he noted that the fleet was now even larger and that it contained around 300 transports which he presumed to be carrying troops. Asking Monnet for more men and artillery, he fired cannon to alert his available forces of the urgent need to ready themselves for action. By two o'clock in the afternoon, around half of the British fleet had raised anchor and was sailing to the north apparently heading for the fort of Ter Haak. Monnet wrote to Abraham Van Doorn, Mayor of Middelburg, warning him of a likely British landing on the Bree Sand possibly as early as that evening. He had just ordered Osten to move on Domburg and Bruce to concentrate at Ter Haak. In the course of writing the letter, Monnet increased his estimate of the number of British ships from fifty to 240. He believed that the first attack would be at or near Ter Veere. A copy of this communication was sent to Bruce. Osten moved his men to the Bree Sand, leaving only a small detachment behind to cover his camp. He could now see enemy ships strung out between the Bree Sand and Ter Haak and soon received news of more vessels in the East Scheldt near the island of Schouwen. Giving instructions to the commander of the 2nd Battalion of the Prussian Regiment, just arrived at Seroskirke to the south, to make patrols to Polder to watch the enemy fleet, Osten returned with his men to West Capelle. The number of ships visible from the village continued to grow and the two battalions spent a nervous night under arms.

Osten recounts the events of the following day, 30 July.

At an early hour, I saw that the fleet had been reinforced by about twenty more ships. At 8.45 am, a large part of it set sail and took the same course as the day before, heading towards the East Scheldt between North Beveland and the Island of Schouwen. Soon a report from the signal at West Capelle informed me that the advance guard had dropped anchor between the fort of Ter Haak and East Capelle. I ordered M. Meunier, my aide-de-camp, to return immediately to Seroskirke, to find out from the commander of the 2nd Prussian Battalion if the enemy had really dropped anchor off Bree Sand (the only point of debarkation), and if this was the case, to move this battalion to Polder to watch the enemy and to inform me of its movements.

I informed General Monnet of these dispositions and set off immediately with the two battalions at the camp in the direction of Polder where I found my aide-de-camp with the 2nd Prussian Battalion. There were about 300 ships at anchor in front of the fort of Ter Haak up to East Capelle. I observed that all the ships of the line were moored off the Bree Sand and that the enemy was putting troops into barges and small sailboats; this action left me in no doubt that they were going to make a landing.[13]

Notes

1. *Archives Parlementaires de 1787 a 1860*, Vol. X, p. 297; Parliamentary Papers 1810, Vol. XV, p. clxxxvii; Schorer, J. H., *Dagboek van Jacob Hendrik Schorer*, p. 1; Fleischman, T., *L'Expedition Anglaise sur le Continent en 1809*, pp. 23–4; Bond, G., *The Grand Expedition*, pp. 28, 34; Loyd, Lady M., *New Letters of Napoleon I*, p. 139.
2. *Correspondance de Napoléon Ier*, Vol. 18, pp. 282, 334, 379, 468.
3. Tulard, J., *The Myth of the Saviour*, pp. 164, 235; Seward, D., *Napoleon's Family*, pp. 34–8; Bond, p. 10; Fleischman, p. 30; Fischer, A., *Napoléon et Anvers*, p.162.
4. Von Pivka, O., *Armies of the Napoleonic Era*, p. 173; Rocquain, F., *Napoléon Ier et le Roi Louis*, pp. 194–5, 197–8; Bond, p. 29; Wauwermans, General, *Napoléon et Carnot*, pp. 69–70; Fischer, p. 159.
5. Bond, pp. 31–5; *Correspondance de Napoléon Ier*, Vol. 18, p. 470; Rocquain, p. 199.
6. Bond, pp. 66, 74–5, 108; Tulard, J., *Dictionnaire Napoléon*, Vol. II, p. 620, 335; Loyd, pp. 148–9; Pelet, Général, *Mémoires sur la Guerre de 1809*, Vol. IV, p. 324; Fleischman, p. 35; De Rocca, Mr, *Campagne de Walcheren et D'Anvers*, pp. 100–1; Wauwermans, p. 79; *Correspondance de Napoléon Ier*, Vol. 18, p. 196; Rovigo, Duc de, *Mémoires du duc de Rovigo*, Vol. II, p. 139; Berthezène, Lt Général, *Souvenirs Militaires par le Baron Berthezène*, pp. 152–3; Osten, Général, *Rapport Circonstancié de ce qui s'est passé dans l'ile de Walcheren*, pp. 1–4.
7. *Correspondance de Napoléon Ier*, Vol. 19, p. 322; De Rocca, pp. 92–102; Laurillard-Fallot, S-L., *Souvenirs d'un Médecin Hollandais sous les Aigles Françaises 1807–1833*, pp. 19–20; Fleischman, pp. 28–9; Pelet, Vol. IV, pp. 323–4; Elting, J. R., *Swords around a Throne*, pp. 356–60, 382, 421–3; Byrne, M., *Memoirs of Miles Byrne*, Vol. II, p. 47; Osten, p. 278; Pigeard, A, *Dictionnaire de la Grande Armée*, p. 327.
8. Tulard, J., *Dictionnaire Napoléon*, Vol. II, p. 317; Rocquain, p. 200; Fischer, pp. 159–60; *Archives Parlementaires*, Vol. X, p. 300; Bond, pp. 32–3, 42–3, 75–6.
9. Bond, pp. 29, 31; Fischer, pp. 153–4, 159–61; Fortescue, J. W., *The History of the British Army*, Vol. VII, p. 64.

10. Fleischman, pp. 28, 71–4; Wauwermans, pp. 86–7; De Rocca, pp. 107–8; Fischer, pp. 160–1; Bond, p. 33.
11. Fischer, pp. 155–6; *Correspondance de Napoléon Ier*, Vol. 19, pp. 261, 311–2; Fleischman, pp. 31–2, 61–2.
12. Bond, pp. 66–9; Fleischman, p. 27; *Archives Parlementaires*, Vol. X, p. 298.
13. Osten, pp. 258–61; ZA, Archieven Der Gewestelijke Besturen van Zeeland 1799–1810: 647; Bond, pp. 53–4; Enthoven, V, *Een Haven Te Ver*, p. 109.

CHAPTER 5

First Landing

The army was well prepared for the assault on Walcheren. General Orders from the *Venerable* on 27 July explained the signals that would be given. The first troops to disembark would be drawn up on the quarter-deck. Each man was to be provided with sixty rounds of ammunition, a good flint in his musket, two spare flints in his pouch, and three days' provisions in his haversack. Once embarked in the boats to the shore, the strictest silence was to be observed. Each boat was to carry forty men. Officers were to maintain order; no man was to move from his seat or stand up and not a musket was to be loaded until ashore. After landing, advanced troops (picquets) were to be thrown out and the commanding officer was to decide whether to go on to the attack or to take cover. Any immediate march into the surrounding country was to only to be undertaken with extreme caution with advanced guards and flanking parties and patrols. The regimental surgeons were to be assisted by musicians, drummers and the men least fit for active service. Orderlies were to carry the cases of surgical instruments.

William Keep had written to his mother a week earlier informing her of the arrangements.

> The officers are recommended to take no more on shore with them than what they can carry. We in consequence intend taking our boat cloaks rolled up and fastened to our backs like the soldiers' knapsacks and carrying our eatables in haversacks etc ... I have no great faith in my own personal strength and don't desire to be encumbered too much lest we should have to scale walls, etc ... what baggage we have is to remain on board for a few days so that we shall probably bivouac (that is, remain in the open field, in such cover as we can form for ourselves with the boughs of trees etc.)... We shall be allowed 8 guineas each on landing, in addition to the £12 10. already received but this, I suppose, only in case of need to purchase animals for conveyance of baggage if it is a protracted campaign. But we must make good our landing.

FIRST LANDING

It had been agreed by Chatham and Coote, whose left wing of the army was charged with the capture of Walcheren, that the troops would land on the Bree Sand on the north of the island. This beach had a number of advantages well described by a mathematically minded observer.

> In front of some dunes of slight elevation is the Bree-Zand which offers the greatest facility for landing. Its form is that of a segment of a circle which has sides 300 m. and an arc 200m. Everywhere a short distance from the shore, even at low tide, there are three, six and eight fathoms water so that frigates and brigs, by placing themselves at the extremity of the chord, flank within their fire a space where 6,000 men can be drawn up. The nearness of the dunes which join the beach besides allow the disembarking force to turn the right and left of any troops drawn up for the defence of the coast.

The Navy Board had provided 159 ships' launches and flat boats to make the short transfer to the shore. Troops were to approach the beach such that the left end of the line made for a beacon or signal post a gunshot's length to the west of the small fort of Ter Haak on the Veere Gat. Avoiding the fort's fire, they were then to wheel around and attack it from the rear. The precise selection of the point of disembarkation was crucial. It had been acknowledged in discussions with the navy that a failed landing and hasty re-embarkation would cost many lives.[1]

At eleven o' clock on the morning of the 30th, a signal was made for the men to get into the boats but the flood tide with a stiff south-westerly gale at its back meant that the small vessels could make no headway. By 5.30pm, the tide was ebbing and gunboats were well positioned to support the landings which were effectively made in four waves. The first troops to enter the flat-bottomed craft were those of Fraser's division under the immediate command of Lord Paget made up of General Gore Brown's brigade (1,695 men) on the right, General Franz Rottenburg's brigade (2,479) on the left, and Captain Marsh's light brigade of artillery. This advanced force is generally termed the 'First Division' although Brown's men were originally part of Fraser's 4th Division and Rottenburg's the light infantry component of the Left Wing; the divisional designations are complicated by a continuing reorganisation of the army which was to culminate the following day. Under the cover of fire from mortar brigs and gunboats, which soon silenced the three French guns in Ter Haak, ships' boats towed the flat-bottomed craft to the shore.

William Wheeler, whose regiment was not to land until later in the day, had every opportunity to observe the work of the 1st Division.

On a signal, the flats advanced. All was now solemn silence, saving the gunboats who were thundering showers of iron on the enemy. Their well directed fire soon drove them to shelter behind the sandbank. The flats had now gained the gunboats, shot through the intervals and gained the shallow water, when the troops leaped out and waded ashore, drove the enemy from behind the hills where they had taken shelter from the destructive fire of the gunboats.

Other eyewitnesses concur with Wheeler although most remember the ringing out of cheers rather than the silence demanded in the General Orders. The first landing was made at 6pm. The boats immediately returned to the ships and brought ashore Graham's division composed of General Houston's brigade (1,509 men), Colonel Hay's brigade (2,491) and Captain Mcffrey's light brigade of artillery. St Clair and his comrades were in the second landing. They had seen the heads of enemy soldiers peeping above the sand hills and they expected stiff resistance. The men of his regiment had become friendly with the sailors of the *Revenge* and their three days' provisions were generously supplemented by the ship's cook. Some also carried ship's pistols.

Armed like an Italian bandit, laden with five plum-puddings besides beef, biscuit, my shaving articles, and clean shirt, with a Scotch plaid hung from my shoulder, I contrived, though with considerable difficulty, to let myself down the walled side of the old *Revenge* into my boat in the stern of which were already seated Major Hill and my two subalterns with 100 men rank and file of my company. Each boat, as it filled with troops, dropped astern, until the last arrived, when Captain [Edward] Paget calling out 'Now boys! Let go!' in an instant our heads were to shore. The ship's company gave us three cheers which were answered by us with a hearty good-will. On nearing the shore, Captain Paget passed us ahead, having with him his brother Lieutenant General Lord Paget, seated by his side ... the next minute all our captains sprang on shore at one and the same moment; so dexterously were the boats kept in line, that we all touched the shore at the same time.

I now leaped from my boat up to my knees in water and stood on the beach, forming my men as they arrived ... already the two bold brothers, the Pagets, had mounted a sand-hill and his Lordship's cap was waving us on ... I dashed on with my company; but, on gaining the heights, saw only a few jägers scouring to a wood without looking behind them. The 71st Regiment, under Colonel Pack, with our flank companies, immediately advanced, and a fire of musketry soon commenced in the wood under the hills, where they made some prisoners, and drove the enemy before them.

John Douglas was in the same boat as St Clair and he confirms the bravery of the Paget brothers. He says that the men had expected to be attacked whilst still in the water. To their relief, most of the British landing force crossed the sands and the three lines of dunes before encountering the enemy. Here, there was a sharp action in the wood referred to by St Clair. A soldier of the 71st remembers that they saw enemy troops 'lurking in a wood' and that two companies engaged them. The French resistance was stubborn and the fighting certainly more intense than the 'slight skirmish' referred to by Fortescue. George Bourne of the 85th, who were among the first to land in Rottenburg's brigade, reports that when reaching the top of the sand hills the British were;

> vigorously attacked by 1,500 Riflemen with four six-pound field pieces and after a smart contest of about two hours the enemy were defeated and driven into the woods being dispersed in all directions with the loss of many killed and wounded and three of the field pieces and about one hundred and fifty men taken.

Bourne's account agrees broadly with the French version of the landing for which we are reliant on Osten's comprehensive report. As the British descended on the Bree Sand, the general had 1,200 men at his disposal. He had posted his three battalions with the Colonials on the left with the two 3-pounders, the Irish battalion in the centre and the 2nd Battalion of the Prussian Regiment on the right maintaining contact with Fort Ter Haak which was garrisoned by the Dutch. The Colonials and Irish were initially on the beach but were soon forced to retire behind the dunes by the ferocity of the gunboat fire. They should have been supported by grenadiers and light infantry from the Prussian battalion but these men remained with their unit behind the dyke.

> At six o'clock, fire commenced along the line; the grenadiers and voltigeurs of the Irish and Colonial battalions, not able to tolerate the fire of the enemy for very long, retired towards me; then the soldiers I had with me fought back against the English; but assaulted by their large numbers and by the murderous fire of their vessels, they started to thin out despite all my efforts to keep them together.

As the Irish and Colonials fell back, two pieces of French artillery were abandoned by the local peasants hired to move them. Osten intervened personally to save one of the 3-pounders. The Prussian battalion, under the leadership of Osten's aide-de-camp, General Meunier, broke and fled to the rear without firing a shot and surrendering two further guns. It would probably have been routed if Chef de Bataillon Petrozelli of the Irish Battalion had not mounted his horse and blocked the road with a handful of picked men.

Osten was also poorly served by the Dutch contingent in the fort of Ter Haak. Prior to the landing, he had sent his aide-de camp to the fort to agree the best plan of defence with General Bruce.

> The general replied that I might do as I thought best but that I should not count on him; that the English were too strong for him to be able to properly oppose their landing and that, in consequence, if he was attacked he would restrict himself to destroying the battery and the fort and then retreating towards Ter Veere; after such a response, I judged it useless to speak to this general.

Bruce at least kept his word. He had aimed a few shots at the gunboats and landing troops but without effect. He was now under fire from the cutter *Idas* and Rottenburg's brigade had orders to take the fort from the rear. The British, having cleared some French sharpshooters from the wood, met no more opposition. The fort was abandoned with four of its seven 24-pounder guns spiked. Colonel Dennis Pack soon occupied it with half of the 71st while Bruce and his men retired to the larger and better fortified town of Ter Veere.

Osten was now forced to retreat. His right flank was exposed by the loss of Ter Haak and his left was also vulnerable as Dutch troops had fallen back from the villages of West Capelle and Zoutland. Bruce had ordered the retreat without consulting his fellow general. The Irish and Colonials had showed courage but could do little more against a superior British force. Accordingly, Osten moved his men back to Seroskirke. This manoeuvre was covered by the Irish company of voltigeurs who, according to Captain William Lawless of the regiment, behaved with 'remarkable sangfroid'. Monnet wrote again to Van Doorn in Middelburg informing him of the British landing and warning him that he had insufficient forces to stop a British advance. Anticipating the fall of the city, he asked that the French sick be well cared for. The mayor replied that he would support the French as best he could. He had raised some troops for Bruce but there was a shortage of horses.[2]

A number of French prisoners were taken on board British ships. William Richardson saw fifty brought aboard the *Caesar*, including three women. Graham's division was ashore by about 7pm. At 10pm Picton's brigade

(2,504 men) and artillery followed and, with the arrival of the remains of Houston's brigade (1,481) during the night, this meant that there were just over 12,000 infantry and three brigades of light artillery on Walcheren. William Keep was helped out of his boat by a 'good natured tar' who then carried the officer on his shoulders to prevent him getting too wet. Keep saw a deep red glow in the sky over the dunes which he thought must be caused by burning buildings. He soon realised that it was only the light of the camp fires of the advance party. Among the soldiers on the beach was a brigade of seamen under the command of Captain Charles Richardson, a naval officer from the *Caesar*. The eighty sailors had been trained to land with the army and were armed with nine pieces of ordnance. Whilst some of their naval comrades reached terra firma on the evening of the 30th, the troops who were not disembarked fretted at their idleness. A private soldier of the 42nd, the proud Royal Highlanders, comments on the unhappiness of the men when no orders arrived to leave the ship for the boats alongside. Captain Charles Kinloch of the 52nd shared the frustration, writing home to his mother that 'our troops seem almost the [only] ones on board'.[3]

At half past ten, Picton was despatched with the 36th to support Pack who was considering a night attack on the town of Ter Veere on the north-east shore of the island. The colonel of the 71st had observed that the garrison sent patrols outside the walls suggesting the possibility that a small force might be able to steal up under the cover of the sand hills and enter the gates left open to readmit the guards. The garrison could then be surprised and overcome. Furthermore, Italian prisoners captured at Ter Haak reported that the town was badly fortified and that the defending force of 500 men was sickly. Captain Joseph Barrailier of the 71st translated the Italians' words and was given the responsibility of reconnoitring the town, taking with him a sergeant, two rank and file, a bugler and one of the prisoners.

Having placed the prisoner between the file of men, I proceeded along the sea dyke. The night was intensely dark, but I had not marched many minutes when I was challenged with 'Qui Vive'. My sergeant (Smith) had a little dog who had followed him, and the animal commenced barking. The French sentinel instantly fired and, by the flash of his musket, I found I was close under a cavalier battery. A guard of about twenty men had turned out, and commenced firing at me, but as I was close to the walls, the whole fire passed over my head; I now desired my men to cover their white belts with their greatcoats and to lay down; but instead of this the sergeant commenced firing. The commanding officer's [Pack's] bugle sounded the advance and it was instantly repeated by all the bugles; but no one came to my aid. The enemy now directed his fire from every part of the ramparts to the place from where the bugles had sounded.

Barrailier fell over some wooden pickets spraining his knee and was forced to limp to the rear. The advance guard of the 71st rushed forward and actually reached one of the town gates with the drawbridge still open before the ferocity of the enemy fire forced them back along the dyke. One of the regiment's soldiers thought that the scene was 'appalling enough'; there was a constant roar of guns and the whistling balls crushed or lopped off the branches of the surrounding trees. He was lucky to be narrowly missed by a musket ball which entered his knapsack but not all were so fortunate. The skirmish had cost the 71st forty rank and file killed and wounded. The regimental surgeon was among the casualties, shot in the head whilst dressing a wounded soldier. Pack later admitted to Barrailier that there had been little chance of forced entry to the town which was better defended than expected. At least one senior officer thought the episode to have been 'ill-judged'.[4]

Poor weather had delayed the disembarkation and diverted it to the part of the island most remote from Flushing but, in Fortescue's words, there had so far been 'no lack of energy'. There was no serious prospect of an advance on the night of the 30th; it was late, at least 7pm before the first 8,000 men were ashore and most were tired and wet having been cooped up on board for several days. There was scant shelter available and soldiers and officers made their bivouacs as best they could. William Keep's experience was probably typical.

> The men piled their arms and laid themselves down on the sloping sand hills in their greatcoats and now the rain began to descend very heavily, which it continued to do with little intermission during the six hours we reposed there. Here I found my boat cloak of the greatest service as I remained coiled up in it with my fur cap on under the hood, as snugly as if I had been under a gilded canopy.

St Clair slept in a hole in the road with his knapsack as a pillow. John Green was denied this luxury as the 68th had left their knapsacks on board, having with them only their haversacks, rolled coats and canteens. The troops were instructed to light no fires and to maintain complete silence. Headquarters were established at Ter Haak.[5]

On the morning of 31 July, Sir Eyre Coote, under Chatham's direction, re-organised the British Army into four divisions made up as follows:

Right Wing. Major General Graham (3,062 men)
Artillery: five light 6-pounders, one 5½ inch howitzer (1 battery)
Light Infantry: 2 companies 68th Light Infantry, 31 of 2/95th [2nd battalion of 95th]
Infantry: Colonel Day, 3/1st, 1/5th, 2/35th, 30 men of Staff Corps
Centre. Lieutenant General Lord Paget (4,055 men)
Artillery: five light 6-pounders, one 5½ inch howitzer (1 battery)
Light Infantry: Brigadier General Rottenburg, 8 companies 68th, 85th, 120 of 2/95th
Infantry: Brigadier General Browne, 2/23rd, 1/26th, 1/32nd, 1/81st
Left Wing. Lieutenant General Mackenzie Fraser (4,090 men)
Artillery: five light 6-pounders, one 5½ inch howitzer (1 battery)
Infantry: Major General Picton, 50 of 2/95th, 1/36th, 2/63rd, 1/71st, 77th, Battalion of Detachments, 20 men of Staff Corps
Reserve. Major General Houston (2,676 men)
Artillery: five 9-pounders, one heavy 5½ inch howitzer (1 battery)
Infantry: 2/14th, 51st, 1/82nd

This reorganisation took up most of the early part of the day and it was around 2pm when the troops moved forward from the Bree Sand in three columns (see map III). The right, led by Graham, marched to the village of Meliskirke throwing out patrols to Zoutland. The centre, under Paget and with Chatham in attendance, moved on Grypskirke and the reserve, under Houston, on St Laurens. Headquarters were at Grypskirke. All were instructed to keep in close communication with each other and Houston was specifically ordered to maintain contact with Fraser on his left before Ter Veere. The official bulletin describes a march through a country of 'entire flats, divided by deep wet ditches into small enclosures highly cultivated, and bearing plentiful crops, the villages neat and habitations comfortable'. The men were mostly impressed by this 'flat fen turned into a garden'. John Patterson of the 50th saw a 'submarine territory' which was 'varied and enlivening from the number of many-coloured windmills and pretty cottages that meet the eye'. Such was its flatness that virtually the whole island was visible from the top of any of the dykes.

There was plenty of opportunity to take in the scenery as the British advance on the 31st was unopposed. In the morning, Osten had found his position at Seroskirke to be untenable. He was not helped by the flight of a significant number of his men to the rear. There was serious concern that the British would cut his line of retreat and he therefore fell back with his remaining force to Middelburg where he made arrangements to meet the enemy's advance south of the city. The 2nd Battalion of the Prussian Regiment was directed to take up a position on the Middelburg to Flushing road (referred to by Osten as Cygne but not on contemporary British maps), the 1st Colonial Battalion was ordered to East Souburg and the 1st Irish Battalion to West Souburg, both these latter villages around one and a half miles to the north of Flushing. Patrols were sent out to the west towards Zoutland, Dishoek and Vygenter. As the Irish were exhausted by their exertions, they returned to Flushing and were replaced in mid morning by the 3rd Battalion of the Prussian Regiment. Finally, Osten sent a detachment of an officer and forty grenadiers from the Colonial Battalion to the village of Koudekirke and later reinforced this important post with a captain and sixty men from the Prussian unit.[6]

It was obvious to Osten that there was no hope of making a stand in Walcheren's capital.

> Middelburg had no fortifications and was absolutely without defence; the Dutch troops had already left for Ter Veere and other places that General Bruce had decided upon without consulting anybody. This town was in the hands of only the National Guard and everybody knows what the bourgeois, these guards who had no training, are capable of ...

Before Osten had entered the city, early on the morning of the 31st, the mayor had sent a four man delegation to the British to negotiate surrender terms. It was agreed that provided the inhabitants conducted themselves peaceably and conformed to British regulations, they would be guaranteed protection. The nine articles of capitulation signed by the four Dutch deputies and Eyre Coote on the heights of Bree Sand also stipulated the protection of property and the free movement of public functionaries to other parts of Holland. It was the last subject which created the most friction between the Dutch authorities and the British, Van Doorn repeatedly asking the new governor, Brigadier General John Sontag, for passports to allow local officials to carry on their normal duties. The troops were to be quartered in barracks with every care taken to minimise the disruption caused to the local people. Jacob Schorer, who had spotted the arrival of the British fleet, was one of the burgomasters entrusted with the negotiations. His house was soon commandeered by Quartermaster General Brownrigg and his very substantial entourage including his adjutant, servants and horses.

The Dutch were astonished at the number of Chatham's staff. The invaders were impressed by the order of Middelburg. William Wheeler described it as a 'neat clean little city'. His regiment, like others, only halted for a short time in the street before moving on towards Flushing. William Keep thought it as fine a sight as could be imagined.

> The houses of considerable height, and canals for the shipping (of which there was none then) running through the street with several small bridges, and broad water on both sides, ornamented with rows of trees, giving it a very fine effect, particularly with so large a body of troops seen defiling through it, lining the walks in dense columns and crossing with their Colours over the different bridges. The Inhabitants were all at the doors and windows, but received us in profound silence. I suppose there was not less than 10 or 12 thousand men passed through the place in this silent procession (for not a drum was beating) ...[7]

At 8 o'clock on the morning of 31 July, General Fraser had called upon Ter Veere to surrender but the garrison commander, Colonel Bogaert, refused. When local dignitaries tried to persuade him to yield, Bogaert flew into a rage and dismissed them. Ter Veere with a 500 man garrison was capable of frustrating the expeditionary force, a fact acknowledged by Picton.

> This place, by our Information, was extremely weak and incapable of offering any resistance but we found it, in fact, more strongly fortified and surrounded with a formidable Rampart and an insufferable wet Ditch of more than 60 feet broad. The Governor might have given us a great deal of trouble had he persisted to defend the place, for we had neither Battery, Cannon, nor Mortars.

The British General might have underestimated his own artillery strength as other sources suggest that Fraser's division was armed with five 9-pounders and a heavy howitzer. Three guns were hauled into place by sailors but the main bombardment came from gunboats in the Veere Gat. Strachan noted that their fire was 'exceedingly well directed' but by early afternoon strong winds and adverse tide forced the boats to retire. Three had been sunk by returned fire from the town. In his report, Strachan gives the credit for the fall of Ter Veere to Captain Richardson of the *Caesar* who fired some rockets from the top of a dyke on the shore. The captain's namesake, sailor William Richardson, gives the best account of this vital action.

> Next morning, an order came for me to land and bring the Congreve's rockets I had on board along with me for the investment of the place CamVeer [Ter Veere]. I was soon landed with the assistance of the

seamen's brigade, who were my shipmates; we cut off the upper part of a small tree and put the rocket ladder for elevation against it, placed and primed the rockets, and began to blaze away at a fine rate, and I was soon covered with volumes of smoke. In a short time, one part of the town was set on fire by the rockets and soon after two other parts ... the rockets terrified them so much (having never seen such things before) that in the evening they sent out a flag of truce to capitulate.

William Congreve invented his rockets in 1804 and they had been used in the bombardment of Copenhagen in 1807. Many traditionalists resisted their wider employment; Wellington had a 'bad opinion' of them and General John Hope described them as 'a most uncertain weapon'. The men firing the rockets at Walcheren often suffered burns to their hands and faces. It is likely that Bogaert was induced to surrender by the combination of the British landing of heavy artillery and the severe damage to the town already caused by the gunboats and rockets. When they entered Ter Veere, the British were shocked by the extent of the destruction. Bodies of women and children lay in smoking piles of bricks. Although there were still forty brass guns on the ramparts, most believed that Bogaert's surrender was honourable and that further resistance would have been futile. An officer went so far as to comment that 'they fought as a British garrison would have fought under similar circumstances'. Certainly the local councillors, in permanent session in the Town Hall cellar, were relieved at their commander's change of heart.

The terms of capitulation were signed at 7pm on 1 August by Bogaert and three British officers; Fraser, his military secretary Lieutenant Colonel Carey, and Charles Richardson, the senior naval officer on the scene. The garrison was allowed to quit the town with all the honours of war and the inhabitants permitted to 'enjoy all their privileges', their property, that which was left intact, to be respected. Whilst the locals were also allowed to leave the town, the Dutch garrison were to be treated as prisoners of war 'to be disposed of as the British Government shall think proper and as is customary on such occasions'. A return of the prisoners compiled by Carey gives a total of 519 men although the three subdivisions of 375 infantry all ranks, ninety-nine artillery all ranks, and thirty-five crew from the French gun brig *Gowlen* suggests only 509.[8]

In their campaign journals and memoirs, British soldiers devoted much space to descriptions of the local population. George Bourne of the 85th found the Walcheren men to be 'slow but constantly employed; naturally easy and good natured and inoffensive' whilst the women were 'industrious'. An officer of the 81st believed the islanders to have a 'peculiar character' which was superimposed on their Dutch traits. On the one hand, they were 'brave and very manly', but, on the other, 'cunning and fraudulent'. He attributed this to them 'being all smugglers'. It was understandable that the locals saw the invasion force as an alternative source of revenue; Huskisson wrote from the Treasury to the Commissary General warning that the inhabitants would take advantage of the army's presence to raise the price of goods. The soldiers responded in kind.

> Some sharpers among us furnished up their own copper coins and, covering them with quicksilver, passed them off for English coins with great ease; nay, sometimes by merely knocking the eye off a button, and flattening it, the workman obtained the value of a shilling.

The multiplicity of coins and currencies encouraged this subterfuge. A General Order gives the equivalent values of *Grols*, *Slivers*, *Florins*, *Ducats*, *Spanish Dollars* and *Pounds Sterling*. Thomas St Clair was unimpressed by the locals' appearance. The men wore coarse garments and hats with large brims. Some of the women were 'not ill-looking' despite 'mighty stout figures and clumsy legs'. Thomas Picton agreed, believing the people to be wearing the same costume that 'Noah's family slept [in] on shore from the Ark'. The women were, in his opinion, extremely plain.

Unsurprisingly, the Walcheren residents were at first nervous of the invading host. St Clair describes them as 'terrified' but also notes that they freely came out of their farmhouses with pails of water for the thirsty soldiers. Most British believed the Dutch to favour them over the French. According to George Bourne;

> All appear happy to be under the English government and say they are heartily tired of the French yoke and would prefer the sight of an English governor in their palace rather than any other.

Henry Light of the Royal Horse Artillery thought that the welcome he received from the country folk was sincere and William Maynard Gomm commented that such was the local attitude to the British that should the French ever retake the island, they would pay for '*leur perfidie*'.

Most on Walcheren did their best to continue their normal occupations; William Keep pointed out that this was possible as they had 'no fear of molestation'. Warfare of the period was rarely this civilised and, in reality, there was some abuse of the local population by British soldiers and sailors. Mayor Van Doorn complained to Sontag of misdemeanours committed by the troops in and around Middelburg. When John Green entered a farmhouse for a drink he found that the place had been looted, that every vessel had been broken, and that he was up to his ankles in buttermilk. A soldier of the 71st and his comrades had to threaten a party of sailors with their bayonets to stop them raping local women and an officer admitted in a letter home that 'plunder is rare; but this personal kind of outrage so common and so general as almost to prevent any efforts to prevent it'.

The British military authorities were determined to minimise the number of incidents. General Orders issued from Middelburg on 3 August expressed displeasure at the complaints and stipulated that no soldier was to leave his brigade without a pass. Officers were to ensure that the men did not wander from their lines and were to accompany parties seeking fresh water or other supplies. Those caught in the act were severely punished. Two men found guilty of 'violent assaults' on local women were sentenced to 500 and 100 lashes respectively. In the Peninsular War such outrages were commonplace. It seems that the British rank and file on Walcheren behaved as well as could be expected.[9]

Notes

1. General Orders for the Army July 27, TNA, WO 28/352; Keep, W., *In the Service of the King*, pp. 39–40; Brett-James, A., *The Walcheren Failure*, p. 814; *A Collection of Papers Relating to the Expedition to the Scheldt*, pp. 357–8, 228; Journal of the Army, pp. 4–8, TNA, WO 1/190; *British Minor Expeditions 1746 to 1814*, p. 59; Fortescue, J. W., A *History of the British Army*, Vol. VII, pp. 67–8.

2. Journal of the Army, pp. 4–8; Brett-James, p. 814; Wheeler, W., *The Letters of Private Wheeler 1809–1828*, pp. 27–8; Richardson, W., *A Mariner of England*, p. 263; St Clair, Lt Col T., *A soldier's recollections of the West Indies and America with a narrative of the expedition to the Island of Walcheren*, Vol. II, pp. 287–91; Douglas, J., *Douglas's Tale of the Peninsula and Waterloo 1808–1815*, pp. 6–7; Light, Captain H., *The Expedition to Walcheren 1809*, pp. 5–6; Gomm, W. M., *Letters and Journal of Sir William M Gomm*, pp. 122–3; Bourne, G., *My Military Career*, pp. 37–8; *Vicissitudes of a Scottish Soldier*, pp. 37–8; Fortescue, Vol. VII, p. 68; Bond, G, *The Grand Expedition*, p. 56; Osten, Général, *Rapport Circonstancié de ce qui s'est passé dans L'Ile de Walcheren*, pp. 261–4; Gallaher, J. G., *Napoleon's Irish Legion*, pp. 99–100; Verner, W., *History and Campaigns of the Rifle Brigade*, Vol. II, pp. 25–6; ZA, De Archieven Der Gewestelijke Besturen van Zeeland 1799–1810: 647.

3. Journal of the Army, pp. 4–8; Bond, p. 56; Keep, p. 45; Green, J., *The Vicissitudes of a Soldier's Life*, p. 28; *A Collection of Papers*, pp. 447–8; Richardson, pp.

261–3; Fortescue, Vol. VII, p. 68; *The Personal Narrative of a Private Soldier in the 42nd Highlanders*, p. 102; Kinlock, Capt C., *A Hellish Business*, p. 43.

4. Henegan, Sir R. D., *Seven Years Campaigning in the Peninsula and the Netherlands 1808–1815*, Vol. I, p. 72; Ross-Lewin, H., *With the Thirty-Second in the Peninsula and Other Campaigns*, pp. 126–9; Barrailier, Capt J., *Recollections of Service at Walcheren*, pp. 489–92; *Vicissitudes*, p. 88; Gomm, p. 123; Enthoven, V., *Een Haven Te Ver*, pp. 92, 130.

5. Fortescue, Vol. VII, p. 69; Keep, p. 45; St Clair, Vol. II, p. 291; Green, pp. 28–9.

6. Journal of the Army, pp. 8–11; Fortescue, Vol. VII, p. 70; Bond, pp. 59–60; Enthoven, p. 287; Patterson, J., *Camp and Quarters*, pp. 330–1; Osten, pp. 264–6.

7. Osten, p. 265; Parliamentary Papers 1810, Vol. XV, pp. xxiv–xxvii; ZA, De Archieven Der Gewestelijke Besturen van Zeeland 1799–1810: 647; Schorer, J. H., *Dagboek van Jacob Hendrik Schorer*, p. 2; Wheeler, p. 29; Keep, p. 47.

8. Journal of the Army, pp. 11–16; Havard, R., *Wellington's Welsh General*, p. 100; Brett-James, p. 816; *A Collection of Papers*, pp. 80, 409–10; Richardson, p. 264; Glover, R., *Peninsular Preparation*, pp. 69–70; Wrangle, J. P., *A Journal of the Walcheren Expedition 1809*, p. 188; *The Walcheren Expedition. The Experiences of a British Officer of the 81st Regiment*, pp. 24–5; Parliamentary Papers, Vol. XV, p. xxvii.

9. Bourne, pp. 51, 56–7; *The Walcheren Expedition*, pp. 56, 65, 67, 91; Castlereagh, Viscount, *Memoirs and Correspondence of Viscount Castlereagh*, Vol. VI, p. 306; *Vicissitudes*, pp. 90–1; St Clair, Vol. II, pp. 297–8; Havard, p. 102; Keep, pp. 50–2; Gomm, p. 135; Light, pp. 9, 37; ZA, De Archieven Der Gewestelijke Besturen van Zeeland 1799–1810: 647; Green, p. 30; General Orders for the Army 3 Aug, 7 Aug, 22 Aug.

CHAPTER 6

Deep Waters

With Ter Veere and Middelburg in his possession and his army poised to advance on Flushing, Chatham could be satisfied. In the General Orders for 2 August he thanked the troops and the seamen for their gallant efforts. However, the attack on Walcheren was only one part of the wider British assault on the Scheldt. There were also the planned attacks on Cadsand and South Beveland.

The responsibility for the capture of Cadsand had been given to Commodore Edward Owen and the Marquis of Huntley. Owen's squadron with Huntley's 2nd Division had anchored in the Wielingen Channel on the afternoon of 29 July. Both commanders arrived on the scene with more questions than answers. The strategic importance of Cadsand has already been discussed but it appears that this was only fully appreciated by the British planners a few weeks before the departure of the expedition. Unfortunately, the orders to both Owen and Huntley given prior to departure were inexact and inconsistent. Strachan wrote to Owen on the 21st detailing the thirteen ships under his command and two brigades, 4,891 men, under Huntley. The tone was optimistic: '[the capture of Cadsand] I hope will be accompanied without much difficulty'. The admiral reminded Owen of the importance of 'hearty cooperation' between army and navy and of the need to cut any enemy communication between Cadsand and Flushing. The importance of Cadsand appears to have been uppermost in Strachan's mind; three days later, he describes it as the 'first objective' of the expedition. On the same day, he issued definitive instructions to Lord Gardner, whose squadron was blockading the entrance to the West Scheldt twelve miles from Owen, to make his launches and sloops of war available for the proposed landing.

Huntley was confused. On 24 July, he had had a meeting with Owen in which the commodore stated that he had only enough landing craft to land 600 men at one time. The general's official orders, received at Ramsgate from Brownrigg on the following day, contained the following:

It would appear that 2,000 men, with three light 6-pounders, one 5½ inch howitzer and the rifle-men attached to the 2nd division will be a sufficient force [to land on Cadsand]...

Huntley interpreted this to mean 2,000 men in a single wave and he immediately sought out Brownrigg to inform him of his earlier conversation with Owen. Nothing was resolved. The quartermaster general only commented that he had been informed by Strachan that 'there would be ample means for landing a great part of my [Huntley's] division'. Unconvinced, Huntley had a second inconclusive conversation with Owen before embarking at Ramsgate on the 27th. In a final attempt to clarify his orders with Chatham, Huntley took a brig at 4 o'clock on the morning of the 28th and drew close to the *Venerable* but he was frustrated by fog and was forced to turn back with his vital questions unanswered.

Strachan added to the uncertainty in correspondence with Owen on the 26th and 27th. The admiral had suddenly become more cautious.

Use your own discretion about landing, I mean if a great naval opposition is offered; and that if you, and the Marquis of Huntley, think it running too much risk to land, you are not to do it till a convenient and safe opportunity should offer, keeping it always in your recollection, that it is of the greatest importance to obtain possession of Cadsand, when it can be done without the risk to which I have alluded.

Thus, when Owen anchored off Cadsand on the 29th, its capture was viewed, at least by Strachan, as important but not urgent. The poor communication continued. Huntley believed that Lord Gardner's squadron was on its way to offer assistance but Gardner later flatly denied that he had ever been ordered to join Owen in the Wielingen. The weather now started to play a role. Strong winds prevented any action on the 29th but the following day was calmer. Owen and Huntley later gave different reasons for not landing on the 30th. The naval commander emphasised the weather, commenting that if it had not been for the wind, a landing would have been made. The general declared that he had not felt it safe to land a force of only 600 men in the face of what appeared to be a significant enemy presence. Huntley was unsure of the exact strength of the French but his best estimate was that there were several thousand troops. Deserters had reported up to 6,000–7,000 men on the island and Huntley himself had made out 'two distinct bodies, amounting together to eighteen hundred men at one time, in two different uniforms'.

The French were making every effort to intimidate the British commanders. Colonel Pierre Berthezène recalls that General Rousseau maximised the apparent number of his troops by keeping them in permanent movement and displaying them in single file at numerous points along the Cadsand shore. Their adversaries on board Owen's ships were becoming restive. William Dyott was irked by the constant state of suspense; preparations were made to land three or four times and each time they were abandoned. A medical officer describes events on the 31st.

> We were all on the alert and in high spirits. Great satisfaction was expressed by the men on being informed that they were to land with their great-coats and haversacks only. At half past nine a.m. we weighed anchor, the transports containing the sixth brigade taking the lead, and these on board of which we were, following in the wake of the *Circe* frigate. About 11, a gun-brig stood in towards the shore, and received some shots from a battery, several of which passed over her. Some shells also were discharged, but they all burst in the air. About 12, we cast anchor. We could see no sign of any steps being taken to land the sixth brigade; orders were, however, given to dine at one, lest we should still land. We spent a long, listless, and dreary afternoon. Everything had been packed up, and our usual occupations laid aside. Our minds had been bent for entering immediately into action, and the whole day had passed as inactively as if we had been lying off a friendly coast. We lay stretched upon the deck in perfect apathy.

When it became obvious to Owen and Huntley that Gardner was not imminently coming to their assistance, they decided to abandon any attempt at landing. The persisting strong tides and inclement weather contributed to their decision. On the afternoon of the 31st, Gardner received a letter from Owen asking him to send his boats but he refused, in part because of unfavourable winds and in part because he did not think this to be Strachan's intention. The admiral had sent Gardner numerous instructions adding to the general confusion. This sequence culminated in a note of 1 August in which Strachan promised Gardner some pilots but then added the surprising statement, 'Owen is right in not attacking Cadsand; I never approved it, and Lord Chatham will be glad'.

The Cadsand saga effectively ended on 3 August when Huntley's division were ordered to the Roompot and the Veere Gat, a clear sign that the island was no longer an objective. The official memorandum of the operations of the army relegated the episode to a few lines, attributing the failure to land to poor weather and the limited capacity of the landing craft. Owen informed Chatham that the enemy was 'well prepared' and that the landing could not have been made without incurring significant losses. William Dyott agreed: 'It was fortunate we did not attempt to get on shore, as in all probability the 600 men we embarked would have been sacrificed'. Huntley had no clear concept of what was to be done had he landed on Cadsand. When later asked what his principal objective was, he replied 'to do all the mischief possible'.

Strachan perhaps believed that the adverse weather conditions, strong winds from the south-southwest, made the acquisition of Cadsand less important than initially thought. Even with the island in British hands, there was little prospect of ships being able to pass along the West Scheldt past Flushing without some delay. Occupation of the island would hinder French reinforcement of Flushing but this might equally be achieved by a naval blockade of Walcheren. A decisive attack on Cadsand would have divided the British force and left it vulnerable to heavy casualties on the exposed beaches. These considerations allowed Castlereagh to write to Chatham of the 'fortunate failure' of the Cadsand operation. The two commanders on the scene were less phlegmatic, Strachan informing Chatham on 8 August of his regret at their inability to take Cadsand. A major objective of the expedition had not been achieved and the admiral did not have the key to the West Scheldt. The rapid reduction of Flushing was now crucial.[1]

Following the reorganisation of the Walcheren army on the 31st, the British moved south on the late afternoon of 1 August. The French forces intent on opposing this advance were now formally under Osten's command; this was a wise move by Monnet who was no more than an adequate garrison commander. General Graham's right wing pushed down the south-west coast of the island via Zoutland, Dishoek, Vygenter and then Nolle to the west of Flushing. Seaward batteries were at first destroyed with little opposition but at Dishoek and Vygenter a detachment from the 3rd Prussian Battalion offered some resistance and was driven back to Flushing as is recounted by Thomas St Clair whose regiment was on the extreme right of Graham's force.

> The commandant of this post, perceiving our intention of cutting him off from Flushing, immediately commenced a rapid retreat; and Captain Hay, with his light bobs [light infantry], soon entering and pulling down the signal [post], immediately followed them up. A beautiful running fight was now carried on along the sand hills, for three or four hours, but the enemy were too quick to be overtaken by our light infantry who kept fagging after them up to their knees in loose sand.

At Dishoek, the British captured six guns and two mortars but the French garrison again made their escape over the sand hills. Flushing was now in sight and as the troops approached Nolle the town's guns opened fire. St Clair and his men took the Nolle battery and then sheltered behind an embankment. They were still dangerously exposed as French advance troops were in control of the wood to their left. John Douglas, St Clair's regimental comrade, comments that much of the enemy shot and shell passed over their heads but that an exploding shell struck the centre of the column and caused many casualties. The French musketry also did damage; many of the men had bullet marks on their clothes. Graham responded by turning artillery on the wood and then ordering a detachment of light troops to clear it. The day's fighting was shared by the Royals (1st Foot), the 5th and 35th Foot, the 68th Light Infantry and the 95th Rifles. By the evening, with several batteries captured, Graham's men sheltered from the guns of Flushing in ditches and behind dykes. For many of them it was their first taste of battle. John Green of the 68th believed that at least nine tenths of the regiment had not been engaged before. This included Green himself who admitted that, 'the first onset [of fighting] very much terrified me; but gradually, my fears subsided, and I became calm and deliberate'.

On Graham's left, the soldiers of Paget's column moved south to the village of Koudekirke. Here, they met the sixty men of the 3rd Prussian Battalion and the forty Colonial grenadiers posted by Osten. After a brief skirmish and the capture of fifty French prisoners, the remaining defenders fell back to West Souburg where, as related by Paget, stiffer resistance was offered.

> The enemy, having brought forward a field piece which bore upon a material Piquet, Lt Col Johnson with parties of the 68th & 85th Regiments was detached by B. Genl Rottenburg to attack him, and he succeeded in driving him into the town of Flushing, close to the gates of which several prisoners were made. In the course of the day our loss is four officers wounded, & about 90 men killed and wounded; it has primarily fallen upon the Brigade commanded by B. Genl Rottenburg which, as well as all those engaged, behaved with their accustomed gallantry.

Paget believed that the losses of the enemy were 'considerable' and documented the capture of around 200 prisoners. It is probable that after their initial success the British rashly approached too close to Flushing. Lieutenant George Bourne of the 85th remembers 'advancing very near the walls'; his men were obliged to fall back under a destructive hail of grape and canister. After some more skirmishing with the French outposts, the 32nd being brought up to relieve the depleted 85th, Paget made his headquarters on the evening of the 1st at West Souburg.

Although the army memorandum for 1 August states a late afternoon march, it is clear from subsequent timings that Houston's Reserve marched through Middelburg down the Flushing road at the break of day. Contact was maintained with Paget's column on the right and a watch was kept on the fort of Ramakins on the left. At half past eight, Houston's men clashed with Osten's forces at the village of Abeylen midway to East Souburg where the French commander had built a breastwork and cut a deep ditch across the road. William Wheeler describes the difficult British advance against the enemy outposts.

> Before the rear of our Brigade had cleared the city, we received a volley of musketry on our pivot flank (we were marching in column of subdivisions right in front). The word was now given 'Wheel into line,' 'Prime and load'. Before we had time to load, another volley was fired. The contents of this, as of the first, passed over our heads. We could see from whence the fire came but could not see the enemy. To advance upon them was impossible, there being several deep ditches between us. We then broke into open columns of subdivisions and continued our rout in double quick time. We soon came to a windmill, here the road turned suddenly to the left [the fork towards Abeylen and East Souburg], we now saw it was crowded with the enemy in full retreat for Flushing, we followed hard in pursuit about two miles without meeting with anything to retard our progress, when we were suddenly stopped, and the fire from the enemy increased; it was now evident that some impediment was in the way. We could not form into any other order, neither could we render much assistance to the advance as there were deep ditches full of water, each side of the road. A few of us did manage to get across into the field on our left, but was soon obliged to return for we met other ditches, wider and deeper than those besides the road. The enemy at this place [Abeylen] had thrown up a breastwork and had dug a trench.

Osten had sent some *voltigeurs* (French skirmishers) of the 1st Colonial Battalion to support his advanced forces but they were soon pushed back and he was forced to retreat to East Souburg where he met Monnet who was visiting the front line with an aide-de-camp. The French commanders tried to rally their troops but Houston launched a frontal assault and attempted to turn the village; the British now had an unstoppable momentum well described by Wheeler.

> At the entrance of the village, they had planted two 9 pounders, equal to our 12 pounders, these were loaded with grape, in a few seconds more their contents would have been discharged on us, but such was the impetuosity of the charge, they were driven from their ground leaving the guns behind loaded, we punished the enemy severely from this place to the Swann Inn, distance about a quarter of a mile, the road was strewed with their killed and wounded and a great many prisoners were made, from the buttons of the prisoners' clothes it appeared they belonged to the 1st and 2nd Battalions of the Irish Legion and the 1st Colonial Battalion.

The Colonials fell back into the grenadiers of the 3rd Prussian Battalion who joined the increasingly panicky retreat, abandoning the two guns entrusted to them. Osten did his best to hold the situation but, despite the efforts of the general and his two aides-de-camp, a further retreat towards Flushing was inevitable. About forty grenadiers of the Prussian Regiment turned and directed fire at the British before fleeing in the face of overwhelming numbers. Rather oddly, Osten makes no mention of the Irish Battalion which was certainly in the action around East Souburg. We have Wheeler's reference to Irish prisoners, and William Lawless speaks of heavy fighting in which the battalion held their ground for two hours despite being attacked by 'infinitely superior forces'. A company of the battalion's *voltigeurs*, 100-men strong, occupied a farmhouse as an advanced post.

Locals joined the French flight towards Flushing and added to the confusion. Wheeler discovered East Souburg to be almost deserted; all that was left was 'the dead and dying laying about covered with blood, sweat, and dust ... the wounded some in their last agony begging for water, others writhing under pain, calling on someone to shoot them'. On the glacis of Flushing, Osten had seven soldiers at his disposal. As the British column advanced, he ordered Lieutenant Harings of the Dutch Artillery to commence fire with the only available piece of ordnance. The batteries of Flushing, which Osten had warned to prepare for action, now also opened up and the British were brought to an abrupt halt. With Monnet's help, Osten was able to get some of his panicked troops back out of Flushing and he re-established advanced posts about 700 yards (350 toises) from the walls before returning with the remainder of his men into the city. Eyre Coote, now with the Reserve, set up general headquarters in East Souburg.

Fraser's division made the final British push down the east side of the island from Ter Veere through Middelburg towards Ramakins. Little opposition was met during the march. The only obstruction to the progress of the 71st was the men's consumption of a large amount of gin given to them by the villagers of Armuyden. Half of the regiment was rendered incapable and Colonel Dennis Pack was in such a rage that he foamed at the mouth. Order was eventually restored and, by midnight on the 1st, Fraser's force occupied Ruttem with the right towards East Souburg and a battalion of the 77th observing the fort of Ramakins garrisoned by around 130 enemy troops.[2]

Between the time of the landing on the Bree Sand on 30 July and the evening of 1 August the British lost 294 men; forty-six killed, 214 wounded and thirty-four missing, the latter all rank and file. The 3rd Battalion of the 1st Foot, Thomas St Clair's unit, had suffered the most, accounting for almost a third of the casualties. Lieutenant Donald McLean of the regiment was the only officer killed. A few days before landing, he appeared to have a presentiment of his fate, greatly affected as he pointed out to his men that the clean shirts and shaves he recommended might be their last. The French losses during the same period are difficult to calculate as the available returns post-date the siege of Flushing thus including losses in the siege and not accounting for wounded men evacuated to Cadsand. The British had captured the garrison at Ter Veere, around 500 men, and probably another 1,200 prisoners, mostly Dutch. Osten does not give casualty numbers for individual actions, subsuming the figures into the later return, but anecdotal reports support heavy losses, particularly in the fighting north of Flushing on the 1st. Lawless says that the Irish Battalion lost one third of its numbers killed or wounded including two fatalities among the officers.[3]

The failure to take Cadsand and to control the West Scheldt not only meant that there was little prospect of a rapid advance upriver to Antwerp – Grosvenor's and Rosslyn's divisions were sheltering in the Roompot anchorage of the East Scheldt – but also that there was not a proper blockade of Flushing. There was a possible alternative route to the West Scheldt from the East Scheldt via the Veere Gat and The Slough (see map II). This was problematic because the fort of Ramakins remained in French hands and so far only a few gunboats had made the passage in an attempt to link up with Owen's ships at the mouth of the West Scheldt. Strachan had ordered Gardner to remain at anchor off West Capelle and Owen remained distracted by the abortive Cadsand operation so that there was every opportunity for the French to evacuate their Walcheren wounded to Cadsand and, more significantly, to send reinforcements into Flushing.[4]

On 1 August, General Chambarlhac despatched 660 men of the 3rd Battalion of the 65th Regiment from Cadsand across the West Scheldt. The following day, another 983 men of the 8th Provisional Regiment and the 22nd, 45th, 54th, 72nd, and 108th Regiments made the same journey to Flushing. When the boats attempted to re-cross the West Scheldt to Breskens on the 3rd Owen, who was anchored off the Elboog in the estuary of the West Scheldt, sent some boats of his squadron to attack. He ordered the sloop *Raven*, under the command of Captain Hanchett (a 'fire-eater' according to Strachan) to give protection to these smaller vessels. On approaching Flushing, Hanchett saw that the British ships had been blown close to the city's batteries and were under 'a very galling fire'. Deciding to draw this fire upon himself, he ran into the mouth of the Scheldt receiving roundshot from the batteries on Cadsand and grapeshot from Flushing. The other boats retired safely but the *Raven* was extensively damaged and suffered a four-hour ordeal grounded on the Elboog in failing winds. She was refloated the next day and hove into deep water. Nine men were wounded including Hanchett himself who took a heavy blow from part of the main boom.

General Rousseau at Breskens, in describing the incident to the French Minister of War, commented that it 'appeared to have made a large impression on the enemy'. Certainly, the difficulties experienced by the *Raven* seemed to confirm the opinion of the pilots in Lord Gardner's squadron that whilst the French were in possession of Cadsand and Flushing, it was dangerous to enter into the West Scheldt by either the Deurloo or Wielingen Channels. As the British schemed to block the vital communication across the river, the French made two more successful efforts to reinforce Flushing; on the 4th, 320 men of the 48th Regiment crossed in only seventeen minutes in favourable weather and, on the 6th, another 1,160 men of the 8th Provisional Regiment, the 48th Regiment, the 13th and 27th Light Infantry and a Prussian detachment. Rousseau says that the latter reinforcement was made despite fire from British brigs and gunboats on the French craft and on the batteries at Breskens and the incursion of a frigate into the West Scheldt. Unfavourable weather conditions, still unusually bad for the season, made it difficult for the British to keep enough gunboats off Flushing to enforce the blockade until the 7th when sufficient numbers were able to manoeuvre through The Slough to frustrate more French attempts to reach the besieged city. Nevertheless, the beleaguered garrison had been strengthened by 3,123 men in just six days.[5]

Notes

1. General Orders for the Army Aug 2, TNA, WO 28/352; *A Collection of Papers Relating to the Expedition to the Scheldt*, pp. 393, 365; Parliamentary Papers 1810, Vol. XV, pp. cclxvii, cclxxxvi–ix, cci–ii, ccx, ccxc; Journal of the Army, pp. 22–3, TNA, WO 1/190; Bond, G., *The Grand Expedition*, pp. 45–8; Fortescue, J. W., *A History of the British Army*, Vol. VII, pp. 74–5; Christie, C. A., *The Royal Navy and the Walcheren Expedition of 1809*, pp. 194–5; Dyott, W., *Dyott's Diary 1781–1845*, Vol. I, p. 279; *The Walcheren Expedition by a Medical Officer*, pp. 125–6; Berthezène, Lt Gén., *Souvenirs Militaires par le Baron Berthezène*, p. 152; Enthoven, V, *Een Haven Te Ver*, p. 288.
2. Journal of the Army, pp. 11–16; Van Gent, T., *De Engelse Invasie van Walcheren in 1809*, p. 52; Fortescue, Vol. VII, pp. 70–2; Bond, pp. 60–2; Gallaher, J. G., *Napoleon's Irish Legion*, pp. 101–2; Enthoven, p. 288; St Clair, Lt. Col T, *A soldier's recollections of the West Indies and America with a narrative of the expedition to the Island of Walcheren*, Vol. II, pp. 297–324; Green, J., *The Vicissitudes of a Soldier's Life*, pp. 29–30; Douglas, J., *Douglas's Tale of the Peninsula and Waterloo 1808–1815*, pp. 7–8; Osten, Général, *Rapport Circonstancié de ce qui s'est passé dans L'Ile de Walcheren*, pp. 266–8; Bourne, G., *My Military Career*, pp. 38–41; Anglesey, Marquis of, *One Leg*, pp. 106–7; Wheeler, W., *The Letters of Private Wheeler 1809–1828*, pp. 29–32; Barrailier, Capt J., *Recollections of Service at Walcheren*, p. 492.
3. *A Collection of Papers*, p. 79; Bond, p. 106; Osten, p. 285; Gallaher, p. 102.
4. Parliamentary Papers, Vol. XV, p. ccli; Christie, pp. 194, 198; Bond, pp. 52, 82–3.
5. Parliamentary Papers, Vol. XV, pp. xxix–x; Bond, pp. 82–3; Osten, pp. 268–9; *Archives Parlementaires de 1787 a 1860*, Vol. X, pp. 302–3; *A Collection of Papers*, pp. 421–3; Gallaher, pp. 101–2.

CHAPTER 7

Hope on South Beveland

The final part of the three-pronged assault on the Scheldt was the invasion of the island of South Beveland entrusted to Sir John Hope's division made up of the brigades of Generals Disney, Dalhousie and Erskine. Hope's force, the Reserve of the army, had been reinforced by a company of the 95th Rifles, a squadron of light dragoons of the King's German Legion, and some extra mortars and howitzers. It had a total strength of around 8,000 men. The general was to cooperate with Admiral Sir Richard Keats to achieve his objective. The Reserve anchored in the Roompot at 4.30 pm on 29 July. On the following day, that of the landing on Walcheren, Captain Spice of the Royal Engineers and Captain Peal of the navy were sent up the East Scheldt to reconnoitre a suitable landing place on South Beveland. It was found that the river was practicable for ships of the line as far as Zieriksee on the island of Duiveland and for smaller boats up to the South Beveland town of Goes.

Encouraged by the feasibility of disembarkation on the north of the island, Keats started to collect suitable craft to land the troops. Many of the gunboats had been removed from the Reserve to assist the reduction of Ter Veere and the admiral requisitioned the local *schuyts*, flat-bottomed sailboats. From the mast-heads of the ships of the line, sailors watched the French fleet retreating up the West Scheldt towards Antwerp. Although the incident is omitted from official accounts, it seems that four companies of the 28th did go ashore for a short period on 30 July with the objective of destroying an enemy telegraph. Charles Caddell, Solomon Rich and Robert Blakeney of the regiment recall the 'Slashers'' exchanges with a Dutch picquet and the dismantling of the signal post. The next day was very squally. The troops were ordered into the small landing boats at 10am but strong winds sprung up from the south west and the men were ordered to re-embark. Blakeney says that the rapidity of the current was such that the troops had to cling on to the nearest ship. Many boarded the wrong vessel.

The weather remained problematic on 1 August and Keats issued an order

94

that only half the complement of men should be put into the boats. Throughout the morning, the signal to embark was made and reversed several times. At about 10am, the weather moderated and the flats and *schuyts*, about 150 in all, made off in the general direction of Goes. Hope and Keats both boarded the *Sabrina* sloop of war which led the way. The soundings of the treacherous channels had been rushed and a number of the smaller craft went ashore but there was no major accident. The landing was made without opposition between the villages of Kattendyke and Wemeldinge. Hope noted that, 'the shore in general is gently sloped, bottom muddy, & the boats got sufficiently near to prevent the men from being much wet'. The first disembarkation was 3,500 strong, led ashore by the grenadiers of the Guards Regiment and a detachment of the 95th. The absence of any French or Dutch was a relief as the slope of the dyke down to the sea would, in Hope's opinion, have lent itself to stiff resistance as 'an enemy [might] have annoyed us very considerably'. The general instructed his men not to land ammunition immediately but to use the bayonet if any opposition was met. This order was reversed at 2.30pm when most of the remainder of the division had landed.[1]

An advanced column marched on Goes along a road atop a sea dyke. The grenadier battalion of the Guards again led the way with directions to move through Cloetinge and to send out strong patrols towards Goes and Capelle. They were to gain intelligence of the enemy batteries and troop dispositions. It was now oppressively hot and the men stopped at farmhouses to purchase drinks from the locals who were mostly welcoming. Captain Henry Light remembers 'marching along a sandy dyke, receiving friendly salutations from the peasantry and directions to get into the high-road'. Hope's own column, supported by an officer and thirty men of the Rifle Corps, followed the advance party. About halfway to Goes, he was met by the local magistrates who assured him that no opposition would be made. They only requested that no 'outrages' should be committed. Hope agreed and instructed the Deputy Commissary General to consult with the local authorities as to the best way of supplying the people of the town. By 4.30pm, British troops were in the suburbs of Goes and main headquarters were established in the place.

It was by now clear that any enemy forces were in the east of the island near the fort of Batz. The army took up positions for the night: Disney's brigade was deployed across the island east of Goes from Kattendyke through Capelle to Biezelinge, and Erskine's brigade in Goes and in the villages to the south. Charles Steevens and a fellow officer of the 20th were billeted in a private house in Hendrikskinderen and met with 'every civility'. They could hear the sound of gunfire from Walcheren but on South Beveland all was peaceful. Hope wrote to Chatham that the island he had invaded was a country

> as beautiful as a perfectly flat [sic] can be supposed to be, the greatest traces [sic] of happiness & industry is everywhere to be perceived. The villages and farmhouses are neat beyond description & in all their habitations a handy taste is displayed which, though stiff and formal, is extremely pleasant from the cleanliness which pervades through every part of their domestic economy.

He thought Goes to be a 'good looking town'. Here, as elsewhere, the British were made to feel welcome. George Hargrove, an Assistant Surgeon in the Royal Artillery, was pleased that the authorities in the town took great pains to provide proper accommodation for the troops. 'Many expressed their warmest wishes that we should continue in the islands and evinced not a little anxiety at our departure'. Lord Dalhousie wrote to his wife telling her that South Beveland was 'rich beyond description' from one end to the other. He was surprised that there were no beggars or even a lame or a blind man.

There had so far been little contact with the enemy although a few small Dutch patrols were surprised by the speed of the British advance and eighty prisoners were taken by the grenadier battalion of the Guards at Kruyingen. At 3am on the morning of the 2nd, Hope and his staff rode from Goes to Disney's headquarters at Capelle and issued orders for the advance east. There was some urgency as reports had been received that the enemy were planning to cut the sea dyke at Waarde thereby inundating the country around Batz and making the capture of the fort more difficult. The threat of sabotage of the dykes and resultant flooding was to become a recurrent theme of the campaign. Fortunately, on this occasion, the imminent approach of the British forces saved the dyke and the livelihoods of the locals. Disney's brigade advanced upon Waarde. Two miles from this village, the Dutch had constructed a battery on a small eminence designed to cover the anchorage of the French fleet. Again no opposition was met, the twelve-gun battery having been abandoned and spiked. Disney's headquarters were now at Waarde, Dalhousie's at Schore and Erskine's remained at Hendrikskinderen to the west of Goes. Hope anticipated that the reduction of Batz would be more problematic. He had little intelligence as to the exact strength of the Dutch garrison under the command of General Bruce but he understood the fort to be surrounded by a broad wet ditch. If the enemy were determined, it might be necessary to bring up heavier artillery from Walcheren, an arduous task.[2]

The reality, related by Hope to Chatham, was an anti-climax.

Contrary to every expectation, Captain Squire of the engineers, who had been left at Waarde to reconnoitre Batz, arrived at Headquarters late in the night to report that the enemy had evacuated that fort, after having spiked and upset the guns and destroyed as much as they could the carriages.

Bruce had retreated to the fort from Walcheren along the West Scheldt via Waarde; his Dutch force had been depleted by desertion but he still had around 600 men under his command. Despite receiving orders to defend Batz, he judged this not practicable and fled to the east across the Bergen-op-Zoom channel.

Once the British reconnoitring party realised that the fort was abandoned it was occupied by a small detachment of Guards from Disney's brigade at about 7pm. The soldiers were able to watch the enemy fleet under the protection of Fort Lillo and could see the steeples of Antwerp in the distance. Batz was not a strong fortress. Erskine called it 'a very bad work indeed' made mostly out of earth. Engineer Squire, who was to write an account of the campaign, thought it contemptible. Nevertheless, most who entered Batz believed that Bruce could have done more. Squire pointed out the protection offered by a moat eight to ten feet in depth and sixty feet wide and also that the French would have been easily able to supply and reinforce the garrison from the deepwater channel of the West Scheldt. In the event of resistance, some sort of battery would have been necessary for its reduction. Squire concluded that 'if the Dutch General Bruce had acted like a soldier, he might have seriously delayed the success of the operation of the reserve'. Dalhousie agreed that the fort could have held out for a considerable time.

The French command was also unimpressed by the supine surrender of Batz. Lieutenant General Jean-Joseph Tarayre, in command at Bergen-op-Zoom, wrote to General Fauconnet at Antwerp.

> Lieutenant General Bruce was not under my orders but I had advised him of the importance of the fort at Batz which he promised to defend at all costs. I had sent him arms and food and at the moment when he evacuated Batz there were 100 men embarked to reinforce it. I was unable to predict or prevent the cowardice of General Bruce which I hope will not remain unpunished.

Vice Admiral Decrès informed the Emperor of the capitulation. Napoleon was furious at the damage to French prestige, seeing the episode as proof of

Dutch perfidy, and immediately demanded that Bruce be hanged. '*Ce miserable a compromise mon escadre [fleet] et mon terretoire*'. The Dutch general escaped capital punishment but was eventually stripped of his rank by court martial and sentenced to a short period of imprisonment.

The strength of French anger reflected the strategic importance of Batz. On the south eastern extremity of South Beveland, it was a natural depot for any future attack on Antwerp. Even more importantly, its possession gave complete control of the navigation of the adjacent stretch of the West Scheldt and the channel leading to Bergen-op-Zoom. British ships would be able to operate under the protection of its guns to prevent the French flotilla, currently moored around two miles above the fort, harrying the troops on South Beveland.

Having captured the island without suffering a single casualty, Hope rode to Batz on the morning of the 3rd. Two howitzers and three field pieces of Captain Wilmot's brigade of artillery were ordered from Waarde to Batz. Within twenty-four hours, the artillerymen and engineers had unspiked the fort's 24-pounders and three howitzers. Twelve 24-pounders at Waarde were also back in action. The peasantry were encouraged to help in this vital work. George Hargrove noted that the French guns were nearly new and were engraved with the motto 'Confident with the assistance of God'. Disney's brigade was divided between Batz, now with a garrison of 200 men, and the village of Crabbendyke to the north. Early morning cavalry patrols were made along the dykes between the fort and Crabbendyke and Waarde and a night-time picquet established at the small harbour near Batz to monitor any aggressive French naval movements.

On the same day, Admiral Sir Richard Keats landed on the island and updated the naval situation to Strachan. The French flotilla near Fort Lillo did not, he thought, have the appearance of being moored for defence. 'I conclude they are in readiness to move as circumstances may determine them.' He was unable to see any more than ten enemy ships of the line but it was clear that there were more numerous gun brigs and gunboats and that a French bombardment of Batz was a real threat. Despite the capture of the fort, navigation of the Scheldt waterways remained problematic. The narrow channel of the east part of the river between South Beveland and Bergen-op-Zoom was too shallow and ill-charted for the larger ships. It did however allow gunboats and flatboats access to Batz and Keats reported two gunboats arrived and perhaps twenty to thirty more in passage. Other British vessels were preparing to support the land assault on Flushing or were in the Veere Gat and The Slough supervising the movement of transports into the West Scheldt along the eastern coast of Walcheren. Complete mastery of the West Scheldt to within fifteen miles of Antwerp still required the capture of Flushing where the enemy's presence deterred the entry of British ships into that part of the river between Walcheren and Cadsand.[3]

Ter Veere was the main point of disembarkation on Walcheren for the ordnance and entrenching tools needed for the reduction of the forts of Ramakins and Flushing. This task was entrusted to Captain George Cockburn and was a considerable challenge. Richard Henegan a commissary in the Ordnance Department witnessed the scene.

> The beach of Ter Veere was of small dimensions and by the second day it was literally covered mast high with guns, carriages, artillery and engineer stores of every description in one vast heterogeneous mountain; the lighter articles, required in the first instance for batteries, lay at the bottom, the heavier at the top. In short, it would have puzzled any man to have discovered how human hands could have performed such a feat as was here displayed ... .

Small boats plied to and from the beach adding to this colossal mass of equipment. Henegan was in charge of the engineer park at West Souburg and therefore responsible for getting the ordnance to the south of the island. He was hindered by the state of the roads which were narrow, sodden with rain and surrounded by ditches. Enough local wagons, each drawn by two horses, were found to carry the shovels, spades, pickaxes and other siege tools but the guns were quite another matter.

There were many types of artillery in use during the Napoleonic period; each type and size had a specific purpose. Thus there was field, siege, light, garrison and coastal artillery and the individual pieces might be guns, mortars, howitzers or carronades. When used against fortifications the guns fired a solid ball called roundshot while the howitzers and mortars fired explosive shells. The size of the guns was measured by the weight of the projectile; the British used guns varying from 1 pound to 42 pounds although, in practice, they relied mainly on 3-, 6-, 12- and 24-pounders. Anything larger than the 18-pounder gun was regarded as siege artillery. The 24-pounders landed at Ter Veere proved too heavy for the horses which were normally expected to pull the guns and carriages. The local animals were unaccustomed to such a draft and often became stuck for hours. On more than one occasion, the guns overturned into the deep ditch which skirted the road. Large teams of men were employed to haul the guns the eight miles over wet ground. The brigade of seamen under Captain Richardson gave valuable assistance acknowledged in contemporary memoirs; Henegan approvingly refers to the sailors 'making themselves conspicuously useful and contributing not a little to the liveliness of the proceedings'.

On 2 August, Chatham strengthened his force on Walcheren by ordering the landing of Grosvenor's division, around 5,000 strong. This was in part due to the exhaustion of the troops before Flushing who had been on constant alert for three days and nights. By the next day, the new division had marched from East Souburg to take up a position near West Souburg placed on the right between Graham and Paget. Grosvenor was, however, warned that he may have to re-embark at short notice if 'circumstances admitted of the armament proceeding to its ultimate destination'. King's German Legion troops were landed at Ter Veere forty-eight hours later bringing the total number of troops on Walcheren to over 20,000.[4]

The small fort of Ramakins was not expected to offer prolonged resistance. Work commenced on a battery of three 24-pounders and two 10-inch mortars about 700 yards from the fort with a view to breaching the face of a demi-bastion. At daybreak on the 3rd, the British 100-man working party came under fire from the French garrison. A detachment of 95th Rifles were ordered forward under the cover of hedges and ditches to within 250 yards of the walls. Here they were able to pick off the enemy's artillerymen who gained little protection from the parapet. By the forenoon, platforms had been brought up for the guns and the third relief of the working party had almost completed the battery. Realising that he was about to be attacked by several 24-pounders, Ramakins' commandant Captain Wounier surrendered to Fraser at 7pm. The official British despatch described the 127-man garrison as follows.

> The officers and gunners are men who had been invalided and retired from the service. The infantry soldiers are Austrians and Spaniards forced into the French service and deserters from their own formed into a colonial corps.

The terms of capitulation signed by Wounier and Fraser made the garrison prisoners of war; the officers were allowed to keep their swords and the ragbag of soldiers their private belongings. As Strachan was quick to point out to his captains, the fall of the fort allowed the navy to navigate the Veere Gat and its continuation The Slough without fear of molestation, safeguarding a vital link between the East and the West Scheldt. Rosslyn's and Huntley's divisions were to be brought through this channel and assembled off Ramakins.[5]

The British now had to capture Flushing to gain complete control of Walcheren. Chatham was of the opinion that this was a necessary prelude to any further advance of his army. This 'town of smugglers and fishermen' was thought by the British soldiers to resemble Plymouth, although perhaps rather neater and cleaner. Its strategic significance was apparent to all; Commodore Owen described it as the enemy port most dangerous to England. To better understand the assault on Flushing in August 1809 it will be helpful to briefly review the essentials of Napoleonic siege warfare and its obscure nomenclature. Most fortresses of the period conformed to a design that had changed little since the seventeenth century. The besieger was first confronted by the *glacis*, a 'smoothly sloping mound' which led up to the fortress and which could be swept by a hail of cannonballs, grapeshot and musketry. Behind the glacis was the *ditch*. As the name implies this was simply a deep pit. The sides of this pit were *revetted* with sheer masonry walls; the inner of the two walls was the *scarp* and the outer the *counterscarp*. At the top of the counterscarp was the *covered way* where infantry could be posted to fire on, and possibly sally against, the assailants on the glacis. Above the scarps, on the inner face of the ditch, was the *rampart*, which in turn consisted of the *curtain wall* which enclosed the fortress and the *bastions*, protruding triangular or pentagonal works which allowed flanking fire to be brought on the adjacent curtains and the faces and fronts of the neighbouring bastions. The guns in the curtain wall gave flanking fire along the face of the bastions and direct fire over the fort's approaches.

In practice, the exact design of a fortress was determined by the vagaries of the ground and weaknesses might have to be compensated for with additional outworks, and natural strengths such as cliffs and rivers exploited. Most fortresses had stood for many years and their strengths and weaknesses were well known to educated military engineers. Flushing posed particular problems for a besieging force.

> The fortress of Flushing was enclosed by a line of nine bastions; seven of these were unrevetted, being protected by a broad ditch too deep to be forded. The demi-bastions at the extremities were on the rear dyke, and having no ditches, their escarps were revetted. There were only two ravelins [triangular fortifications or detached outworks] in the whole line but the dyke bastions were covered by advanced fleches [simple earthworks in the shape of a shallow V] closed at the gorge with heavy iron chevaux de frise [portable barriers equipped with sword blades etc.]. The whole of the ground outside the line, except certain detached points, was below the sea

level at high water, and could be inundated by sluices constructed in the counterscarp. It was therefore impracticable to form the ordinary approaches or to attack *en regle*.

This attack *en regle*, or in the normal manner, was as formulaic as the fortress's defences. Napier, the great historian of the Peninsular War, noted that:

> There is no operation in war more certain than a modern siege if the rules of the art are strictly followed; and unlike the ancient sieges it is also different in this, that no operation is less open to irregular daring because the course of the engineer can neither be hurried or delayed without danger.

When gun and spade was employed by those tutored in siege work, the time until the fall of the fortress could be accurately predicted.

The most conventional way to force entry was to 'break' the rampart with gunfire. The breach was judged 'practicable' when it was large enough to permit a sufficient number of intrepid men (the first few known as the 'forlorn hope') to clamber over the rubble from the ditch to make the decisive assault. Following proper reconnaissance, the first step in the siege was to 'invest' the fortress, to isolate it from help, and the second to place the batteries optimally to effect the breach. At Flushing this task was to be complicated by the low-lying nature of the land, the battery sites effectively limited to selected areas of high ground. The defenders' guns were unlikely to be idle and the investing troops and batteries had to be well dug in to afford protection. This was where the picks and shovels came in. Wood planking was employed to make emplacements for the guns and the troops were shielded behind *gabions*, wicker baskets filled with earth, and *fascines*, bundles of faggots, and innumerable sandbags.

Cannonballs could be fired over 3,000 yards but to make an effective breach in the wall the guns needed to be much closer, ideally within around 700 yards. The only way to get ammunition up safely was to dig trenches or saps along which wagons could easily pass. These passages could not be straight, as they would be commanded at least in part by the guns of the fort, so the saps were dug in zigzags (parallels). Once the parallels had reached the glacis and the counterscarp had been blown in, and perhaps the guns of the fort silenced, the commander of the town would usually be invited to surrender. In the previous century, provided that the breach was practicable, capitulation at this point was considered honourable as there would be no unnecessary bloodshed. Napoleon had ordered that the first summons of any fortress was to be refused. Such a response would lead to the launching of a mass of men against the breach with the hope (possibly forlorn) of overpowering the defenders.

There was a prevalent opinion that traditional siege operations with their backbreaking and time-consuming toil were misguided and that a fortress could be bombarded into submission. Others, including many professional men, found this repugnant. John Jones, a brigade major on the engineer's staff at Flushing, later wrote a seminal account of British sieges of the Napoleonic era. He believed that 'to bombard a town is merely to shower down upon it shells, carcasses, rockets, hot-shot, and other incendiary missiles'. Surrender only followed the indiscriminate killing of civilians and the random destruction of civic buildings. There was a recent precedent. In 1807 this method of 'inconceivable cruelty' had been used to force the capitulation of Copenhagen and the capture of the Danish fleet. The suffering of the local population led Wordsworth to doubt that Britain was indeed 'a bulwark to the cause of man'.

Although the British engineers at Flushing will have been familiar with the theory of siege warfare, few had much practical experience. Furthermore, their organisation was fragmented and their training ad hoc.

So here was the extraordinary situation of a great power involved in a war two decades long, with three parallel and competitive corps of quasi-engineers, all recruiting artisans of much the same trades from the same source, but without any body of men capable of performing the duties required of real engineers in the field.

Henegan comments that the engineer department was the only one deficient in officers. Many performed their arduous duties with zeal but others were incompetent. Captain Joseph Barrailier recalls a disagreement with a young engineer officer who did not fully appreciate the importance of his men being dug in and under cover. The altercation was overheard and interrupted by Coote who summarily dismissed the engineer; Barrailier was employed as an untutored assistant engineer in the construction of two batteries under the command of Captain William Pasley, one of the most distinguished engineer officers of his time. Lieutenant Colonel Robert D'Arcy was initially in overall charge of the engineers but he was replaced by Colonel William Fyers on 8 August.

The siege work commenced under D'Arcy's supervision at dusk on 3 August when around 6,000 men started work on a battery for six 10-inch mortars (shown as battery F on map IV). This was placed at the highest level

103

which could be found within reasonable distance of the walls, about 1,400 yards from the centre bastion and 1,900 yards from the left flank of the town, against which it was intended to operate. On the 4th, work continued on this battery and 100 seamen and fifty Military Artificers, men usually recruited from regiments of the line to build fortifications, made the fascines and gabions. Over the following forty-eight hours, more engineers' stores were received from Ter Veere and a battery E for ten 24-pounders about 1,000 yards from the central bastion and a battery G on the left of the cantonments on an angle of the eastern dyke were commenced. The object, according to Fyers, was to divert the attention of the enemy in order to favour a real attack on the right.

The two light battalions of the King's German Legion landed from the Veere Gat came on duty in the trenches on the 6th. The weather was dreadful with high winds and rain. Extra blankets were ordered for the men. They sought refuge in hastily constructed huts but these were soon penetrated by the water. The officer of the 81st complained that there was scarcely a change of linen throughout the army and that they were constantly annoyed by the enemy's incessant fire. In order to minimise casualties, selected men were directed to watch the flashes of the town's guns and to cry out 'shot!' as a warning.

> The men who are employed with their shovels digging the earth, upon hearing this, fall flat upon their faces until the shot has passed, which it does with a rushing noise, particularly a shell, and where it falls it makes a terrific excavation, throwing up the mud and sand yards into the air. Luckily it is impossible to fire these missiles with exact precision, or the destruction would be immense, but you must stand your chance of it, fixed in one spot from sunrise to sunset.

Only occasional shots did damage but then the destructive power of the cannonballs caused horrific injuries. One of William Keep's fellow officers was struck by a ball on the left leg and had to be evacuated to Middelburg where the limb was amputated at the thigh. Another man was hit on the head, 'the face fell like a mask on his back, very little discomposed, but a small quantity of blood issuing from his eyes'. The soldier's comrades used their shovels to dig a quick grave.

Many believed that the siege works were not progressing quickly enough. John Squire claimed that the operation 'lacked skill and vigour'. The batteries were too distant from the town's walls, some parallels were dug unnecessarily, and the working parties were poorly organised. Thomas

Graham wrote home on the 6th, 'We have now been a week here without having made scarcely any progress ... Our investment costs us men to no purpose'. Whilst such shortcomings were not likely to be explicitly acknowledged at headquarters, the official memorandum for the army for Saturday, 5 August contains this revealing entry: 'Our works before Flushing go on languidly although our means are ample.'

When the army's senior staff did visit the siege works, they did little to raise morale. Richard Henegan was dismissive.

At certain periods of the day, these officers, splendidly attired, with bran-span new epaulettes, and snow white feathers, attended by aide-de-camp and adjutant, in similar bonne tenue, would show themselves in the centre of the laborious work that was going on so well without them – and then new orders would counteract preceding ones, as if for the sole purpose of displaying superior knowledge, and individual importance.

The procession of visitors from England who wanted to see a siege provided another easy target. One of the tourists brought a large turtle as a present for the army's commander.[6]

Notes

1. Journal of the Army, pp. 11–16, TNA, WO 1/190; NAS, GD364/1/1190, GD45/4/60; Enthoven, V., *Een Haven Te Ver*, pp. 301–3; Parliamentary Papers 1810, Vol. XV, pp. cccxx, 5xxviii; Cadell, C., *Narrative of the Campaigns of the Twenty-Eighth Regiment*, p. 79; NAM, 1992-04-148: 82; Blakeney, R., *A Boy in the Peninsular War*, pp. 129–30; Hargrove, G., *An Account of the Island of Walcheren and South Beveland*, pp. 10–13.
2. NAS, GD364/1/1190, GD 45/14/540; Enthoven, pp. 303–5; NAM, 1968-07-261: 23, 73; Light, Capt H., *The Expedition to Walcheren 1809*, pp. 11–12; Hargrove, p. 42; Steevens, C., *With the Old and Bold 1795 to 1818*, p. 65; Parliamentary Papers, Vol. XV, p. cccxxiii; Fortescue, J. W., *A History of the British Army*, Vol. VII, p. 72.
3. NAS, GD364/1/1190, GD45/14/540; Squire, J., *A Short Narrative of the Late Campaign of the British Army*, pp. 52–3; Enthoven, pp. 305–9; Journal of the Army, pp. 16–19; Cadell, p. 80; *A Collection of Papers Relating to the Expedition to the Scheldt*, pp. 413–5; Bond, G., *The Grand Expedition*, pp. 64–5; Parliamentary Papers, Vol. XV, pp. ccci, ccxliv; Fleischman, T., *L'Expedition Anglaise sur le Continent en 1809*, pp. 35–6; *Archives Parlementaires de 1787 a 1860*, Vol. X, pp. 298–300; *Correspondance de Napoléon Ier*, Vol. 19, pp. 337–8; Hargrove, p. 46.
4. Henegan, Sir R. D., *Seven Years Campaigning in the Peninsula and the Netherlands*, Vol. I, pp. 72–6; Fortescue, Vol. VII, pp. 75–6; Bond, pp. 83–6; Jones,

Sir J. T., *Journal of the Sieges carried on by the Army*, Vol. II, p. 260; Glover, R., *Peninsular Preparation*, pp. 89–90; Wilkinson-Latham, R., *British Artillery on Land and Sea 1790–1820*, pp. 84–5; *The Walcheren Expedition. The Experiences of a British Officer of the 81st Regiment*, p. 50; Parliamentary Papers, Vol. XV, pp. ccccii, 5lv; Enthoven, p. 288; Journal of the Army, pp. 16–24.

5. Fyers, Col W., *Journal of the Siege of Flushing 1809*, p. 150; Enthoven, p. 290; Journal of the Army, pp. 19–23; Fortescue, Vol. VII, p. 76; Osten, Général, *Rapport Circonstancié de ce qui s'est passé dans L'Ile de Walcheren*, p. 269; Parliamentary Papers, Vol. XV, p. xxiv; *A Collection of Papers*, pp. 411–2.

6. Parliamentary Papers, Vol. XV, pp. 6xiv, ccccxcvi, 6xl; Myatt, F., *British Sieges of the Peninsular War*, pp. 12–15; Glover, pp. 94–105; Bond, pp. 84–6; Brett-James, A., *The Walcheren Failure*, pp. 817–8; Whitworth Porter, Maj-Gen., *History of the Corps of Royal Engineers*, Vol. I, pp. 249–50; Jones, Vol. II, pp. 260–2; Fyers, pp. 150–8; Squire, pp. 57–9; Journal of the Army, pp. 26–39; Enthoven, pp. 290–4; *The Walcheren Expedition*, pp. 37–9; Henegan, Vol. I, p. 77; Keep, W., *In the Service of the King*, pp. 58–9, 63; Aspinall-Oglander, C., *Freshly Remembered: The Story of Thomas Graham, Lord Lynedoch*, p. 201; Barrailier, Capt J., *Recollections of Service at Walcheren*, p. 493; Browne, T. H., *The Napoleonic War Journal of Captain Thomas Henry Browne 1807–1816*, p. 46.

CHAPTER 8

Divided Commands

Chatham and Strachan met at Middelburg to discuss the expedition's progress on 1 August and again on the 6th. There was already tension between the two men before the first meeting. In the attack on Ter Veere, Chatham had not consulted Strachan regarding the use of the gunboats. The more they talked, the greater their differences appeared. At the second meeting, Chatham vented his frustration that the army had not been better supported by the navy in the West Scheldt.

> I had also a very long conversation with him [Strachan] on the morning of the 6th, on the Arrangements to be taken for our further Operations when I urged, in the strongest manner, the Necessity of not losing a Moment in bringing up the Cavalry and Ordnance ships, Transports, Store ships, Victuallers, & c. & c. in order that the Armament might proceed without delay to its destination; and I added my hopes that they would receive the Protection of the Ships of War, none of which entered the West Scheldt.

Both commanders agreed that the ultimate destination of the expedition was still Antwerp and that the village of Sandvliet in the upper Scheldt was the natural point of disembarkation. However, Strachan thought that there was a better route for the Army.

> In my interview with Lord Chatham on the 6th, I stated fully the Difficulties I had to encounter from the untoward state of the weather and from the Intricacy of the Channel in passing the vessels through The Slough, as also from the difficulties made by the Pilots who refused to take charge of these vessels, or even to carry the Line-of-Battle ships into the West Scheldt. The strong impression I felt upon this subject induced me to deviate from the Line of Conduct I have always adopted in relation to Military Matters, of not interposing any Opinion; and I ventured to propose to His Lordship to commence the Disembarkation by landing the Cavalry immediately on South

Beveland and marching them to Batz, which might be followed by all
the infantry not occupied in the siege of Flushing ... .

This substantial force could then be ferried across the Scheldt to Sandvliet.

Neither man understood the other's problems. Chatham minimised the
effects of the contrary weather and the treacherous navigation whilst Strachan
did not acknowledge the difficulties inherent in transporting a large force
more than thirty miles along South Beveland's narrow muddy roads before
undertaking a further re-embarkation. Supplying the troops was a constant
challenge; Sontag had made an urgent request to Dutch officials on 4 August
for transport for provisions and this was repeated a week later. The cautious
Chatham was also concerned that Flushing might remain in French hands in
his rear and that the naval force at Batz was of limited size. A disagreement
over the best plan for the expedition was bad enough but there was more.
Firstly, they did not fully appreciate their differences. Chatham later
remembered the admiral accepting his views: 'To all this, and to the several
arrangements explained to him in detail, he fully assented'. Strachan,
however, believed his opinion to have carried weight, an impression which
could only have been strengthened when Huntley's and Rosslyn's divisions
disembarked on South Beveland a few days later. Secondly, despite their
apparent agreement on the subject, the fundamental objectives of the
expedition were now being questioned. Hearing rumours of substantial
French reinforcements, Strachan wrote on the 5th that he believed that an
attack on Antwerp might no longer be 'practicable'. If there was a significant
reinforcement and a French general of the first rank in the city, then they
would be wise not to 'entangle the army and navy in an extensive and
intricate navigation'. He added that he wished that 'this trying business were
well over'.

Sir Home Popham was also becoming discouraged. In a memorandum to
Chatham of the same date, he invoked the possibility of a British 'disaster'
in the face of growing French forces and suggested that the capture of
Antwerp was not essential.

Flushing is the key to the Scheldt ... with that in our possession, the
Enemy is always liable to he destroyed by our Fire ships ... they will
rot at Antwerp.

The disagreements between the commanders were common knowledge
among soldiers and sailors. Ensign Joseph Palmer Wrangle of the Royal
Marine Artillery was planning to start a journal and he eagerly listened to the
gossip. The veterans believed that there was jealousy between the

expedition's leaders and that it was likely to end badly. An officer commented that he was sorry that there was 'some appearance of a different sentiment and even of some asperities'. Chatham was particularly criticised by the men encamped outside Flushing. Thomas St Clair noted that 'It is a curious fact that, during [our] siege and employment in this service, I never once saw our Commander-in-Chief nearer to me than seated on top of the church steeple at Middelburg'. When a Captain Boys came ashore at one of the advance posts near Flushing, he enquired of Colonel Andrew Hay where the senior commander was. 'I don't know. Somewhere in the rear,' replied Hay.

At home, Castlereagh was oblivious of the growing malaise in the high command of his expedition. On the 8th, he wrote to Chatham from Downing Street applauding the rapid acquisition of Walcheren and South Beveland which 'with the exception of the fortress of Flushing, is the best proof of the zeal and energy with which the ulterior objectives of the expedition will be prosecuted.'[1]

The French also had problems. In Flushing, Monnet dithered. He established a *Conseil de Défense* composed of himself, Osten and three other officers but this was quickly disbanded. Orders were announced and then countermanded and the Mayor, Adriaan François Lammens, alleged that Monnet's conversation was 'rambling'. The local population was as much alarmed at the prospect of flooding following the breaching of the dykes as they were by the inevitability of a British attack. In January of the preceding year, many of the city's inhabitants had drowned in a violent storm. Monnet sought to calm them with a grandiloquent proclamation.

> Habitants de Flessingue! I am charged by His Imperial and Royal Majesty to defend our town. I have lived among you for six years, you know the affection I have for you, I have always been satisfied with your conduct ... be calm in the midst of these events of war, I will defend you to the last moment at the head of the brave men I command.

He reminded them that Napoleon was aware of their plight and had promised reinforcements. On the 4th, he wrote to ministers that it would be difficult for him to maintain his defensive position – he needed 8,000–10,000 men to chase the enemy from the island.

The commander did take some decisive steps on the same day that he penned his pessimistic letter to Paris. The garrison and its outposts were divided into two demi-brigades. Osten provides the most detailed description of the arrangement and it is likely that he executed the changes. The right demi-brigade of 1,600 men was made up of two battalions of the Prussian Regiment and a battalion of the 65th Line and was under the command of Major Gauthier. The left, which faced the bulk of the besieging force to the west of Flushing, was composed of a battalion of French deserters, a battalion of the Irish Legion, a battalion of Colonials, some troops of the 8th Provisional Regiment, and a detachment of the 72nd Line. This larger of the two demi-brigades, about 2,000 strong, was under the command of Major Séries, Monnet's aide-de-camp. Osten set up French outposts in a semi-circle around Flushing, up to 700 yards (350 toises) from the walls. At any time, 600 men performed outpost duties and the remainder were held in reserve, mostly inside the town 'cleaning their weapons' and awaiting the call to action. An old hospital a short distance along the Middelburg road served as a depot for the right demi-brigade reserve. These reserves were supplemented by the reinforcements received from Cadsand. The local National Guard camped in the town's squares making patrols through the day and night to keep order.

Monnet worried about the quality of his men and equipment. Although, as the British could testify, the artillery was potentially destructive, it was also outdated and poor. Most was of Dutch manufacture and soon out of service. Several of the ancient gun carriages were broken by the detonation of their own pieces. The artillerymen of the 1st Regiment of Foot Artillery, the Dutch Artillery, and companies of the Veterans and Coast Guards were in short supply and they had to be supported by hastily trained men from the garrison. Few of the *cannoniers* had ever seen action and most were to seek refuge when the British attack commenced.[2]

At his headquarters at Rosendaal, Louis had taken an executive decision. The swelling French forces in the Scheldt – by mid-August there would be around 20,000 troops and up to 17,000 National Guard on the left bank of the river – meant that a proper chain of command was crucial. There remained uncertainty as to how Louis, in command of the Dutch forces, related to Rampon, in charge of the French land forces, and to Missiessy, the master of the French fleet. Louis's fervent wish was for a more senior French officer, preferably a Marshal, to take the matter out of his sweating hands but there was no immediate prospect of this. By 7 August, his anxiety had grown to the point that he felt obliged to take control, announcing himself as commander of the 'Army of the Brabant', all the French and Dutch troops in the Scheldt. Later, in justifying this action to his brother, Louis claimed that the decision was effectively forced upon him, and that he received permission from ministers in Paris.

I was disturbed to see the disunion or rather the confusion arising from several authorities and above all the lack of urgency and the resignation to events. I had a meeting with Generals Rampon and Chambarlhac; and during this, I received a reply from the Arch-Chancellor [Jean Jacques Cambacérès] and the Comte d'Hunebourg [Clarke], who both asked me to take the position of commander in chief.

This left Rampon in command of one of the two corps on the right bank in addition to General Jean-Baptiste Olivier's division on the left bank. The second corps on the right bank, composed of Dutch troops, was under the command of General Jean-Baptiste Dumonceau. Rampon was displeased at this turn of events but accepted the changes pending directions from Napoleon. At Schönbrunn, the Emperor was optimistic regarding events in the Scheldt, informing his Minister of War on the 9th that the British expedition would achieve nothing. He did, however, continue to harangue Louis for his ill-conceived actions and when, a week later, he received Clarke's letter telling him of his brother's uncharacteristic display of initiative, his mood worsened. Both the minister and Louis had overstepped their authority.

What excites my greatest displeasure is that the King [Louis] takes command of my troops without orders from me, in virtue of his title of High Constable of the Empire. He must be profoundly ignorant of our constitution if he thinks the dignity of Constable gives him command of my troops. That is a five hundred year old anachronism. Put a stop to this absurd comedy and send a Marshal ... The King of Holland cannot command our troops; as a matter of fact, he had no right to do it, and, besides, he has not the experience. Where should he have gained it? He never commanded so much as a regiment during the war. How can you believe that any man in France can take command of my troops without my orders? ... I hope you will have received my letter of the 6th; that you will have sent off several Marshals forthwith; and that you will have saved me from the greatest danger I could have run – that of leaving the command in the hands of the Dutch. As for my squadron, the Minister for the Navy [Decrès] must give orders concerning it. All this confusion exceeds my comprehension.[3]

For the first few days of the siege, between 3 and 6 August, there were only minor skirmishes involving the opposing advanced posts outside

Flushing. Picton described these small actions as 'harassing' as they kept the men on the alert for long periods. The general slept in boots and spurs on a bundle of straw. Both the 26th Regiment and the 95th Rifles clashed with French outposts and the British suffered an average of thirty killed and wounded each day. On the 7th, as work continued on the batteries, the French made a more determined sortie against Graham's division on the right of the British line. Osten insists that this was for reconnaissance purposes only; to better understand the disposition of the enemy forces and the most likely site of attack on the town. Certainly, there was no other obvious motive as there were no works in progress at this point and the British forces were more than a mile from the fortress.

Osten organised his men into three columns under the overall command of Major Séries. He emphasised to Séries that the sortie was exploratory and was to be made in the direction of the Nolle battery and the surrounding dunes to the west of Flushing. The left column was led by Major Boeckmann and was composed of 300 men from the French Deserters Battalion. Boeckmann was ordered to seize the breastwork on the dunes in front of the Nolle battery. In the centre, Major Bouis commanded 300 men of the 1st Colonial Battalion and the 48th Regiment. His orders were to take the redoubt to the east of the Nolle battery whilst keeping contact with the left column. On the right, another 300 troops of the 48th Regiment under Séries himself were to advance along the road from Old Flushing to protect the flank of the central column. A Reserve, under Major Pireck, remained in Old Flushing.

The attack commenced at 4 o'clock in the afternoon. Boeckmann's column, instead of attacking the Nolle battery, shuddered to a halt at the first sound of enemy gunfire. Remaining safely out of range, they commenced musketry fire which was not only useless but also dangerous to their own central column advancing to their right. Here, Bouis soon found himself embarrassed by a lack of support and confronted by the Royals posted on the west dyke. St Clair first became aware of the attack when he heard the beating of a solitary French drum.

> I distinguished a column of the enemy formed close under their works, and on the high road in front of us. I immediately sent off one of my men to inform Major Gordon, who commanded our picquets, of this circumstance; but he had scarcely left me, when down came this column in a rush along the road; and, ordering all my men to lie down out of the enemy's sight, they darted past us like a flock of ravens, calling out to each other, 'En avant! En avant!'

Robert Stewart,
Lord Castlereagh.

John Pitt, 2nd
Earl of Chatham.

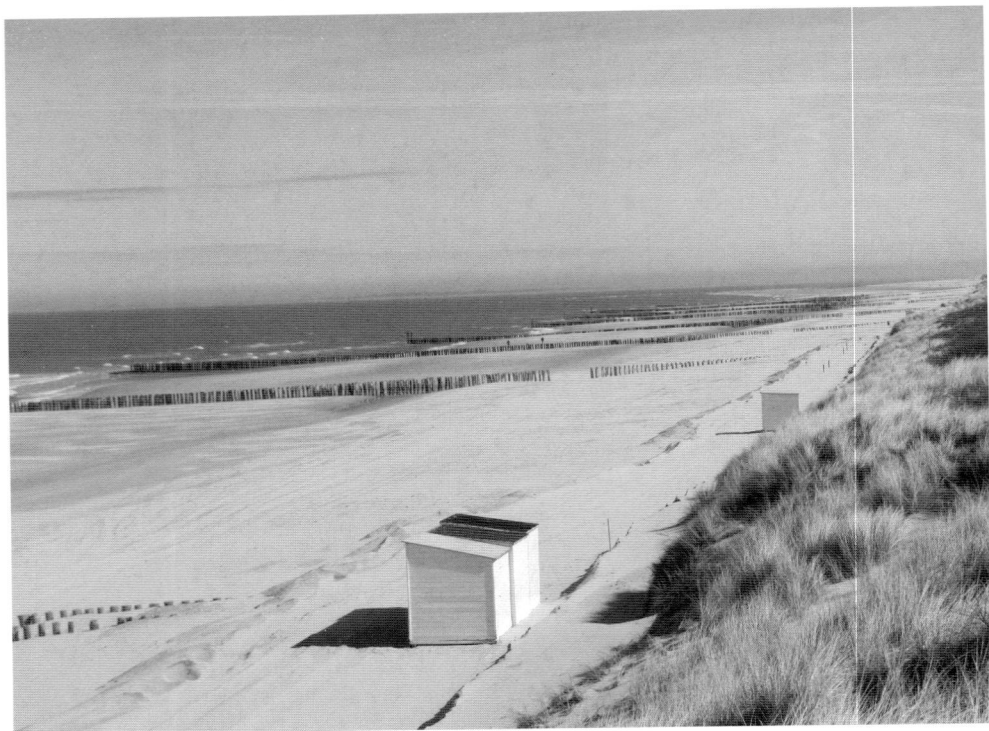

Bree Sand. The British landing site.

Walcheren looking south east from the dyke at Domburg.

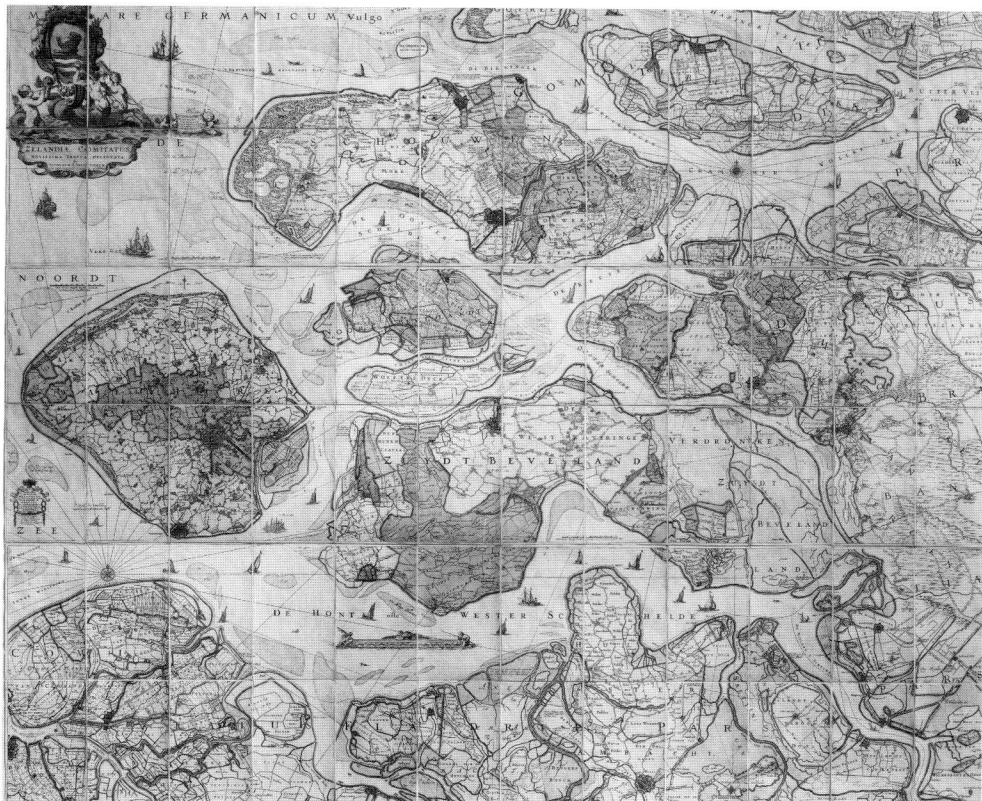

Map of the Scheldt used by a British officer in 1809. (*Zeeuws Archief*)

A local woman.
(*Zeeuws Archief*)

British roundshot from 1809 embedded in the wall of a house at Veere.

British troops in Middelburg. (*Zeeuws Archief*)

The siege of Flushing viewed from the Nolle Battery. (*Zeeuws Archief*)

A mortar fires during the bombardment of Flushing. (*Zeeuws Archief*)

Siege of Flushing. The naval bombardment. (*Zeeuws Archief*)

The centre of Flushing during the bombardment. (*Zeeuws Archief*)

The destruction of Flushing. (*Zeeuws Archief*)

The British fleet in the West Scheldt on August 27. View from Fort Frederick Henry. (*Zeeuws Archief*)

The church at Veere which was used as a British hospital in 1809.

Typical cartoon lambasting Chatham after his return from the 'Glorious Expedition'. The King says, 'Confound such lazy fellows. Is this the way you fight my battles laying in bed till 12 o'clock stuffing turtle and venison with fat Aldermen at Middelburg...'. (*Zeeuws Archief*)

The French advance was checked by picquets of the 35th and 5th Regiments and a charge by the light company of the Royals. Bouis's men showed spirit but they were soon also under fire from Captain Weber Smith's two 6-pounders and with the arrival of two companies of the King's German Legion it was all the major could do to fall back towards Old Flushing. He and many of his men were captured.

Séries's column advanced up the road to Koudekirke with the supporting fire, at least for a short time, of Flushing's guns. His men were engaged by the 5th Regiment and reinforcements from the King's German Legion and were also under fire from a 5½-inch howitzer. As Osten describes, the column was quickly in a perilous situation.

> The attack was lively and, despite the superiority of the enemy who were dug in up to their teeth, this valiant officer [Séries] maintained this position for a long time, in the hope that the left column upon which his attack was dependent would take the Nolle battery; but seeing the unfortunate position of the centre through the fault of the left column, certain moreover that the English were everywhere very superior in number, his movement having allowed him to discover the troops who manned the dykes, he retreated to avoid being cut off and established himself on the small paved road. The firing lasted for three hours and was very lively; but, as night fell, we re-occupied our original posts, such that the day passed without us having lost an inch of ground.

A Scottish soldier of the 71st claimed that many of the French were drunk: 'they could not defend themselves; neither could they run away; we, in fact gave up the pursuit, our hearts would not allow us to kill such helpless wretches a number of whom could not even ask for mercy.' This must have been hearsay as the 71st were not involved in the action. Osten admitted to having lost 340 men, killed, wounded or taken prisoner. He claimed that his enemy had suffered similarly. The British official figures suggest that the besieging army's losses were lighter with five officers wounded and 159 rank and file killed and wounded. It is probable that only thirteen or fourteen men were killed. In his report to Castlereagh, Chatham noted that the French had yielded ground and that his forward posts on the right were now in more advanced positions. Whatever the truth as to the gain or loss of territory, it had been an expensive piece of reconnaissance and not all French officers were impressed. Pierre Berthezène thought the garrison commander to have squandered his ammunition and the blood of his men.[4]

Monnet had another weapon at his disposal. In a letter of 6 August, Napoleon ordered Clarke to remind the commander of Flushing that he should cut the dykes if it became necessary. Two days later, the Emperor reiterated to his minister in Paris that the safety of Flushing depended on the cutting of the dykes and the flooding of the island. 'This operation performed, the enemy will be forced to re-embark and his expedition will have failed'. More agitated directions to Clarke followed on the 9th and the 11th.

> In your letter of the 5th, I cannot see that you have repeated the order
> to General Monnet to cut the dykes and flood the island. You know
> that that is my intention. What alarms me more is seeing that he does
> not speak of using this resource ... .

Napoleon returned to this theme remorselessly in letters written on the 12th and 18th.

Monnet was less convinced that flooding Walcheren was an easy solution. This would lead to the destruction of much of the island and significant loss of life. The civilian population of Flushing would become demoralised and difficult to control. When he met with the town's council, he had conveniently lost Napoleon's orders. It must be granted that it took some courage, or remarkable carelessness, to mislay the Emperor's words. In a later defence of his actions, Monnet insisted that, where possible, he did cut the dykes. Once he understood the strength of the British forces on 1 August, he ordered a cut in the dyke of Ramakins. He intended to make a second breach in the Nolle dyke to the west of the town but this was prevented by the presence of the enemy and the thickness of the dyke. Work was therefore concentrated on gradually enlarging the first cut, thus flooding the land to the east of Flushing. The sluices in the counterscarp of the moat were also opened. These actions had so far not been as devastating as Napoleon had predicted. A combination of Monnet's caution, the elements, and British ingenuity allowed the siege work to continue. The wind was only light and blew from the east and the tides were lower than expected. Chatham ordered the sluices at Middelburg and Ter Veere to be kept permanently open; as Middelburg was three feet lower than Flushing this lowered the water levels around the latter. The general warned the local prefects that they would be held responsible for any 'mischief' by local citizens which worsened the flooding.

So it was that the British soldiers found themselves up to their knees in water rather than their necks, and this was really the case from 9 August onwards. Between the 8th and the 11th, work continued on Batteries A, B (the 'seamen's battery') and E, the mortar Batteries D and F, and the howitzer Battery C. Men also toiled on the redoubts and parallels. Fyer's entry in his journal for Saturday 12 August is a good summary of a typical day's siege work.

> Friday 11th August from 8 o'clock pm to Saturday 12th August, at 8 o'clock pm.
> Field officer for the trenches: Lieutenant-Colonel Pilkington.
> *Left of the Parallel*
> Relief at eight o'clock pm, 600 men.
> Relief at day break, 150 men.
> Relief at one o'clock pm, 400 men.
> This proved a most unfavourable night, being extremely dark, with very heavy rain. The strength of the working-party was employed in uniting the two extremes of the parallel, and raising the Battery B, at which a party of seamen assisted. A small party was employed on the redoubt, and forming the Magazines to the battery E.
> A battery was marked out at C, on the right of E, for two 10 inch Howitzers, intended for enfilading the front of attack, particularly the face of demi-bastion number 3. The platforms of the mortar battery D were completed this morning, and the carpenters began immediately to prepare the materials for the magazine.

Fyers relates similar actions to the right of the parallel. During this period, seventeen wagon loads of tools and materials were received into the Park.

A letter from Captain William Pasley to his fellow engineer John Squire, dated 9 August, suggests that the discord and disillusionment within the department continued through the siege. Pasley pulls no punches.

> I this day landed your horse and send him by your servant. I only landed yesterday morning and saw our works before Flushing ... [he describes the slow progress at some length] ... so D'Arcy was the man but now Fyers has begun since last night. The Corps of engineers is disgraced and damned for ever. The cry of the whole Army & Navy is against us. I found Jones [Captain John Thomas Jones] in a state of despair. Boteler [Captain Richard Boteler] wished that the first shot might take off his head. The French are making counterworks & do them faster than we do ours. We were offered the *whole* Army to act under us. The staff Corps everything at our disposal. Such measures, such power, such circumstances would have put life into a statue, by heavens it would have called a dead

body from the Grave, but what could we do with a parcel of old men or rather old women at our head, with fellows without Souls to direct the operations of Armies. With fellows old in years, poor in spirit, beardless in military experience, destitute of knowledge, not merely block heads but block bodies.

The young engineer officer accuses his seniors of placing the guns by guesswork rather than after proper measurements of distances. Quartermaster General Brownrigg, he says, believed the engineers to be unfit for employment in war.[5]

More British troops disembarked on South Beveland on the 9th. Huntley's division and the infantry of Rosslyn's division were landed from The Slough at a place on the island described as being 'three fourths or four fifths of the distance from the anchorage of Veere to the point on South Beveland opposite to the castle of Ramakins'. It was most likely opposite the village of Armuyden on Walcheren. Certainly the landing site had been very carefully selected and the operation, commencing at daylight and completed by 8am, was uneventful. Once ashore, Rosslyn assumed command of all troops on the island.

As the two new divisions were simply reinforcing Hope's Reserve, there was no immediate enemy threat. There were, according to the General Orders, still a few Dutch troops 'lurking about' on the island but they were of more danger to the local inhabitants than to the British. Despite this, the men suffered. They had been cooped up on ships in the Roompot for ten days. An advance guard of a company of Riflemen and a brigade of guns setting off towards Goes was soon feeling the heat and there were many stragglers. The eight mile march took two hours. William Stewart, the brigade commander, saw the 95th finally enter Wemeldinge at 6pm, 'the heat and late inactivity on shipboard having enervated them and caused many to be speechless on the sides of the road'. The physical demands of marching were increased by the need to traverse the ditches which criss-crossed the landscape. Soldiers improvised as best they could. Ensign Robert Dallas and his comrades in the 9th carried planks which were only partly effective and 'many duckings occurred'. An alternative strategy adopted by the regiment is revealed by James Hale. 'We were ordered out most days, in order to practise jumping these ditches, that if the enemy should make an attack on the island, we should not be unacquainted with jumping'. Steevens of the 20th used a pole to leap the ditches until he injured his back.

Upon reaching their final destinations on the island, the men were very well accommodated in houses and barns. A number of memoirists remember a subsequent period of pleasant rest and recovery. The 43rd were billeted in Goes and the village of Cloetinge. Ensign John Cooke shared the handsome house of the local burgomaster.

> We were surrounded by abundance, our days occupied in the sports of the field, and our evenings passed at each other's quarters in idle and pleasant conversation. Pay was issued almost to the day it was due. Provisions of all descriptions were offered for sale at a very low rate; tea, sugar, and coffee were not half the price of the same in England. Wines, brandy, hollands [gin] and liqueurs might be purchased for a mere trifle, and fat fowls or ducks for tuppence the pair.

This account is at odds with Hope's expression of 'extreme anxiety' regarding the supplying of his troops at this time. The general was also displeased by the indolence of his men. In reporting to Chatham, he made little effort to conceal his frustration.

> Our operations since entering the island of South Beveland have been so idle & so uninteresting as to scarcely afford one incident worthy of recording. The troops who landed in Walcheren have had everything to do, & we have been tame spectators of their activity from the tops of all the steeples in the island, from which, the surrounding country can be seen for a great extension in every direction.[6]

In response to a request from Admiral Keats, Hope sent a small detachment of men from the Reserve to Schouwen and North Beveland to round up sailors who were 'straggling' from their ships. Enemy aggression against the main British force on South Beveland was unlikely but there had been attacks on the fort of Batz. The first of these, on 5 August, involved twenty-five French brigs from the anchorages at Forts Lillo and Liefkenshoek. A heavy cannonade commenced at midday and continued for two hours. Inside the fort, the Royal Artillery under the command of Captain Wilmot returned fire with the 24-pounders. The French attack was ineffectual. Assistant Surgeon Hargrove noted that almost all their shot fell short or passed harmlessly overhead. A second attack was also witnessed by the doctor.

> On the 8th August they came down again; this morning, they prolonged their visit to three hours and a half, firing 24 pound shot

and grape, the latter scarcely reached the shore, we had fourteen 32
pounders [actually 24-pounders] and two howitzers opposed to them,
and must have disabled a number of them; one of their vessels in
particular they could scarcely get on, and toward this we directed all
our fire; during the evening a Portuguese deserter came ashore and
informed us that the vessels and their crews had been severely cut up,
numbers killed and wounded; the only sufferers we heard of on our
side were two poor harmless sheep that were shot through while
grazing on a hill beyond the fort; some of the houses in the fort
suffered considerably but as the soldiers were all ordered to line the
breastworks while the firing continued, and as the inhabitants retired
into the country, no accident happened.

A third and final assault by the enemy flotilla was made on the 11th. Six
gunboats under Dutch colours sailed from above Lillo attempting to reach
the town of Bergen-op-Zoom but became grounded on the banks of the
narrow channel. The fort opened fire and the gunboats were soon on fire and
abandoned. Their precipitate retreat to Lillo was encouraged by the arrival
of two British naval forces.[7]

Sir Home Popham approached in command of a flotilla of around forty-
five gunboats in addition to some sloops and gun brigs. He had received
fire from enemy batteries at Flushing and the opposite shore during his
passage of the West Scheldt but had sustained no serious damage. Sir
Richard Keats arrived with thirty flatboats via the East Scheldt. Both naval
commanders took up anchorage at Batz. To the west, Strachan had not made
the advance up the Scheldt originally planned, a point of contention
between him and Chatham. His hopes of forcing the passage between
Flushing and Cadsand with the frigates and ships of the line in early August
were frustrated by a combination of adverse winds and a lack of pilots.
Further reasons for keeping his ships in the estuary were the need to
facilitate the blockade – 'I was under the necessity of detaining our flotilla
to prevent supplies being thrown in to the garrison of Flushing' – and to
cooperate with the army in the attack on the fortress. It was the admiral's
opinion, expressed in a letter of 8 August to Gardner, that ships of the line
would be needed to bombard Flushing into submission. He wrote to
Chatham offering the use of his ships' armament should the fire of the land
batteries alone prove inadequate.

On 11 August, the weather relented. A favourable westerly breeze enabled
Captain William Stuart of the *Lavinia* to lead ten frigates under the guns of
Flushing and Breskens. General Picton ordered land Battery G to open on

Flushing in an attempted diversion but this fire was countermanded when observed at headquarters. Inside the town, Osten commenced a vigorous attack on the British frigates. He was hindered by the lack of artillerymen, his few *cannoniers* being assisted by auxiliaries of the National Guard. Fire was exchanged between the ships and French batteries on both banks and many *cannoniers* were killed and wounded. Marine Robert Fernyhough describes the action from the deck of the frigate *Statira*.

> Our squadron of ten frigates was led in gallant style by Lord William Stuart in the *Lavinia* and engaged with the batteries nearly two hours. The cannonading was tremendous, about 600 pieces of ordnance firing at the same time, which, adding to the bursting of the shells over us, was a magnificent, yet an awful sight. I assure you my sketch [attached to the letter to his family] is very inferior to the appearance of the engagement, although it shows you our correct position during the action. To a spectator, the sight must have been imposing. The frigates could only be distinguished at intervals, emerging from the smoke. I had the command of six thirty-two-pounders, on the quarter-deck with the royal marines; and we fired, I believe, forty rounds out of each gun during the two hours; they became so heated that two or three of my guns dismounted and wounded several of the men; we were in consequence obliged to reduce the quantity of powder.

Fernyhough and his comrades were soon 'as black as sweeps'. The marine lost the skin off his fingers from the friction of working the gun ropes. British losses were light. A shell struck the *L'Aigle* and fell through the deck before exploding and killing one man and wounding four others. In total, there were two killed and nine wounded. Strachan had originally intended to accompany the frigates up the West Scheldt once they had cleared Flushing but, in the event, he remained in the estuary with the ships of the line.[8]

By Saturday 12 August, the land batteries outside Flushing were nearing completion. At noon, everything was reported ready except the seamen's battery (B) which would be finished during the night. Despite the discharge from the sluices at Middelburg and parties of 2–300 men working incessantly to keep the drainage ditches clear, raise their banks and damn the water off from the trenches, the flooding now passed over the crest of the parallel at low spots and threatened the communication between the batteries. In some places, the water was so deep that poles had to be driven into the ground to mark the roads. In Middelburg, Sontag asked the Dutch officials to provide maps and lists of locals with knowledge of the dykes and flooding. The soldiers were becoming anxious, one writing home on the 11th, 'the water begins to flow very fast. If Flushing does not fall within less than ten days we must re-embark or we shall all be drowned'. Chatham announced that the bombardment would commence on 13 August.[9]

Notes

1. Bond, G., *The Grand Expedition*, pp. 81, 90–3; Fortescue, J. W., *A History of the British Army*, Vol. VII, p. 82; Parliamentary Papers 1810, Vol. XV, p. 1125; *A Collection of Papers Relating to the Expedition to the Scheldt*, pp. 758, 783; ZA, De Archieven Der Gewestelijke Besturen van Zeeland 1799–1810: 647; *The Walcheren Expedition. The Experiences of a British Officer of the 81st Regiment*, p. 90; Wrangle, J. P., *A Journal of the Walcheren Expedition 1809*, pp. 184–5; St Clair, Lt Col T., *A soldier's recollections of the West Indies and America with a narrative of the expedition to the Island of Walcheren*, Vol. II, pp. 325–6; Brett-James, A., *The Walcheren Failure*, p. 818; Castlereagh, Viscount, *Memoirs and Correspondence of Viscount Castlereagh*, Vol. VI, p. 301.
2. Fleischman, T., *L'Expedition Anglaise sur le Continent en 1809*, pp. 41–2; *Archives Parlementaires de 1787 a 1860*, Vol. X, p. 304; Osten, Général, *Rapport Circonstancié de ce qui s'est passé dans L'Ile de Walcheren*, pp. 270–2; Enthoven V., *Een Haven Te Ver*, pp. 299–300.
3. Rocquain, F., *Napoléon Ier et le Roi Louis*, p. 207; Loyd, Lady M., *New Letters of Napoleon I*, pp. 148–9; Lecestre, L., *Lettres Inédits de Napoléon Ier*, Vol. I, pp. 343–7; Fleischman, pp. 30–1; Bond, pp. 74–6.
4. Journal of the Army, pp. 30–1, TNA, WO 1/190; Havard, R., *Wellington's Welsh General*, p. 101; Jones, Sir J. T., *Journal of the Sieges carried on by the Army*, Vol. II, pp. 262–3; Enthoven, pp. 290–2; Osten, pp. 272–5; St Clair, Vol. II, pp. 326–9; Douglas, J., *Douglas's Tale of the Peninsula and Waterloo 1808– 1815*, p. 8; Bond, pp. 88, 94–5; *A Collection of Papers*, pp. 86–7; *A Soldier of the Seventy-First*, p. 43; Berthezène, Général, *Souvenirs Militaires*, p. 154.
5. *Correspondance de Napoléon Ier*, Vol. XIX, pp. 311, 317, 322, 334, 342; Lecestre, Vol. I, p. 349; Jones, Vol. II, pp. 263–7; ZA, De Archieven Der Gewestelijke Besturen van Zeeland 1799–1810: 647; Enthoven, pp. 297–9; Fyers, Col W., *Journal of the Siege of Flushing 1809*, pp. 153–6; *The Walcheren Expedition*, p. 66; Bourne, G., *My Military Career*, p. 42; Pasley, C. W., *Captain Pasley at Walcheren August 1809*, pp. 17–19.
6. Journal of the Army, pp. 39–41; Parliamentary Papers, Vol. XV, pp xxx, cccxxxix, 5lxxviii, Enthoven, pp. 300, 306; NAM, 1968-07-261:56; Verner, W., *History and Campaigns of the Rifle Brigade*, Vol. II, p. 33; Dallas, R. W., *A Subaltern of the 9th in the Peninsula and at Waterloo*, p. 63; Hale, J., *The Journal of James Hale*, p. 48; Cooke, Lt J., *A True Soldier Gentleman*, p. 58; Steevens, C., *With the Old and Bold 1795 to 1818*, pp. 65–6; NAS, GD364/1/1190.

7. Squire, J., *A Short Narrative of the Late Campaign of the British Army*, pp. 68–71; Bond, pp. 89, 95–6; Fortescue, Vol. VII, pp. 80–1; Enthoven, pp. 305–6; Hargrove, G., *An Account of the Islands of Walcheren and South Beveland*, pp. 47–9.

8. NAS, GD364/1/1190; Bond, pp. 95–7; Christie, C. A., *The Royal Navy and the Walcheren Expedition of 1809*, p. 194; Jones, Vol. II, p. 267; *A Collection of Papers*, pp. 423–7, 786–7; Brenton, E. P., *The Naval History of Great Britain*, Vol. II, p. 296; Osten, pp. 277–8; Fernyhough, R., *Military Memoirs of Four Brothers*, pp. 139–40.

9. Jones, Vol. II, p. 267; Fyers, pp. 156–7; Bond, pp. 99–100; *The Walcheren Expedition*, pp. 49–50; ZA, De Archieven Der Gewestelijke Besturen van Zeeland 1799–1810:647; Bourne, p. 42.

CHAPTER 9

Bombardment

The army's commander was becoming concerned. He had new intelligence of growing French forces between Bergen-op-Zoom and Antwerp. A captured French naval officer reported that Bonaparte had ordered Monnet to cut the sea dykes and inundate the whole island. All could see that the water was slowly rising. On the 11th, Chatham updated Castlereagh.

> The several batteries will, I hope, be ready to open on the Place either tomorrow or the following day, and I shall look with great Anxiety as to the Result, as the speedy Reduction of Flushing, particularly under present Appearances, is of the last Importance; as till then, so very large a Portion of the Force under my command is unavoidably detained before it.

Although bombardment was considered by many of his officers to be both an unprincipled and uncertain method of reducing the town, there was no alternative.[1]

At 1pm on Sunday 13 August, seven of the eight British land batteries, a total of fifty guns (twenty-six 24-pounders, fourteen 10-inch mortars, six 8-inch mortars, two 10-inch howitzers, two 8-inch howitzers) opened fire. The arrangements for the ammunition were two days' consumption from the magazines at a rate of 200 rounds per gun and 100 per howitzer, and one day's consumption at the same rates of firing in depot at East Souburg. At the same moment, two divisions of gun and mortar-boats on the south-east and south-west of the town under the command of Cockburn and Owen also commenced fire, as did some batteries of rockets on the left of the trenches. This intense barrage continued until dark. The garrison returned fire, mainly against the Nolle battery (A), and disabled one gun and damaged another. A mortar-boat was also struck and was forced to limp back to Zoutland Bay before sinking. Strachan was still unable to bring up his ships of the line due to the weakness of the wind and they remained moored off Dishoek.

Relieved that their labours in the trenches were finished, the British troops watched the bombardment with keen interest. William Keep was among them.

> Our task was over, and the soldiers of the artillery took possession, leaving us little more to do than to observe the effect their fire produced upon the town, and singular and terrific it was! Especially at night when the shells, sent an immense height into the air, appeared like falling stars, producing on their descent into the town a distinct reverberation, and the Congreve Rockets with their trains of fire crossing each other, illuminated the heavens, the whole of which was reflected in the waters around us, then rapidly increasing in the ground we occupied, so that to keep our feet dry we climbed the trees, watching with anxiety the result of our operations.

Keep admitted that the scene eventually became 'appalling to witness'. A soldier of the 71st was stunned and bewildered by the noise of the 'bursting of bombs, of falling chimneys which added to the incessant roar of the artillery'. John Green was near a mortar battery which was throwing shells as fast as possible. He saw houses and churches on fire and could occasionally hear the screams of the inhabitants, a fact confirmed by the officer of the 81st Regiment: 'when there was an interval in the noise, it was filled with the shrieks of the women from the city. Even the dogs howled, and several owls and bats flew frightened round the light'. Monnet and his staff were spotted in the tower of the Town Hall using the telegraph but they were soon forced to make a hasty retreat and the device was destroyed.

The fire of the land batteries fell mostly on the left demi-brigade. When the British guns opened, the 1st Colonial Battalion suffered casualties and, with the exception of an officer and a handful of men, immediately fled. Chef de Bataillon Séries had to shut the gates to prevent them re-entering the town. He then placed himself at the head of the Carabinier Company of the Irish Legion and reoccupied the ground abandoned by the Colonials before also reclaiming the posts of the Deserters Battalion which had been quickly abandoned.[2]

At sunset, General Thomas Graham ordered an assault on the French post on the west dyke. The attacking force was made up of the Royals, the second battalion of the 14th Regiment and a light company of the King's German Legion. Covering fire was to be provided by the Nolle battery (A). St Clair says that the necessary preparations had been made earlier in the day.

> At six in the evening, the rockets commenced playing against the town. This was the signal for our advance, and the illumination from

these monstrous fireworks was so great that every step before us was
as clearly visible as in daylight. The light company [led by Captain
Hay] rushed forward, and [Captain] Rowan's and my company after
them. The enemy, who had observed us strengthening our advanced
post, had not been idle in making preparations to oppose us, but all
was in vain: they could not resist the rush made upon them by three
youthful captains, full of vigour and a thirst for glory.

The French troops forced back in to Old Flushing by the Royals' attack were
a battalion of French deserters commanded by Captain Boeckmann. Their
hasty retreat left the remaining French forces to the right exposed and the
Colonial and Irish battalions also fell back into the town's suburbs in the face
of the advancing 14th Regiment and German troops. Osten insists that
Séries's demi-brigade kept up a firefight lasting three hours and that little, if
any, ground was ceded. He estimated that his losses at around 100 men killed
or wounded. Some fell into enemy hands; John Douglas of the Royals saw
six French prisoners being marched to the rear by a soldier's wife who had
an entrenching shovel on her shoulder. The British lost only one man killed
and six wounded although there were the usual narrow escapes. In Douglas's
regiment, Lieutenant Mackenzie would have been fatally wounded but for a
few guineas in his purse turning the ball away. Colonel Fyers, observing
events through his spyglass, was only spared because the musket ball which
struck him in the chest passed first through a few inches of sand at the crest
of a parapet.

As night fell on the 13th, the British reinforced the newly won ground at
the west dyke. A communication trench was dug to join with the redoubt at
the southern end of the parallel. Osten warned the commanders of the right
and left demi-brigades to remain vigilant in view of the possibility of night
attacks. He gave explicit instructions as to the advanced line they were to
hold around Flushing.

I ordered them to hold firm as long as possible in this new position
and, if they were forced to beat the retreat, to fall back with pride and
in good order, forbidding them under any circumstances to return
back into the town before having set fire to all the houses along their
route. The commander of the right also received an order to spike the
guns of the moulin à poudre battery.

At 2am on the 14th, Osten visited Old Flushing which was now in flames
and gave more orders for the placement of the 48th and 65th, Deserters and
Prussian battalions. At some points the advanced posts of the two armies

were no more than a few yards apart. St Clair was separated from the enemy by only a paling. He struck up a conversation with two sentries on the French battery whom he found to be 'intelligent and sensible fellows'.[3]

Later in the morning, the seamen's battery (B) consisting of six 24-pounders joined the assault. Smoke blowing across from Old Flushing had allowed the British to complete their final battery unmolested. Mortars were directed over the west of the town but the guns were more particularly used to enfilade the rampart of the western sea line causing extensive damage to the French traversing platforms, carriages and guns. Such was the rate of fire from both guns and mortars that ammunition intended for the siege of Antwerp had to be used. On South Beveland, Dalhousie recorded in his diary that the constant cannonade at Flushing sounded like distant thunder.[4]

The silencing of a number of enemy guns and the strengthening wind allowed Strachan to weigh anchor from Dishoek and enter the West Scheldt from the Deurloo Channel. At 10am, seven line of battle ships approached Flushing receiving fire from the town. On a signal from the Nolle battery, the squadron poured forth its broadsides. The scene was observed by the army's senior officers including Robert Brownrigg.

> Each ship was laid alongside the town, for above an hour & half at a distance from 1,400 to 1,800 yards which with the land batteries pounded in the most tremendous fire into the place that is possible for the imagination to conceive; the whole was speed by [sic] in flames and, at the expiration of an hour, scarcely a shot was returned from the walls. At 2 the enemy guns were completely silenced. I was during this awful period with Lord Chatham on the sand hill immediately above the Vygenter battery and never before witnessed so fine and magnificent a sight – horrible it is true – as far as the poor inhabitants of the place were concerned. Sir Admiral Strachan led in the squadron most gallantly in the St Domingo, seconded by the Venerable – Lord Gardner followed – and the other ships in close line of battle. The two armoured ships [St Domingo and Blake] unfortunately got aground, the St Domingo with the stern to the town but, surprising to say, her loss, and that of the other ships of the line have been very trifling.

The best naval account of Strachan's attack on Flushing is that of Major Marmaduke Wybourn of the Royal Marines who was on the *Blake*.

> It was found that the Army could not succeed in storming the Town of Flushing, which is inaccessible on the Land side, & Sir R.

Strachan formed the desperate resolution of attacking by Sea (he is the bravest fellow in the world). We had lain just out of reach of shot since the 11th & yesterday the signal was given to prepare for battle at Sea; we and the other Flagship got within Pistol shot of the Walls – the havoc we made was shocking, when to our consternation we both struck the Ground, all the other ships passed by further off, seeing the danger; for three hours & a half we were thus left to ourselves, the batteries cutting us to pieces and no alternative but to wait the Tide rising. We all thought there could be no possibility of escaping. We on the poop, which is the roof of the Captain's Cabin, were in such a line with the Guns, that it is amazing any of us escaped; almost the first shot killed my best Sergeant, a fine fellow, it took off both thighs, left Arm & right hand, the poor fellow called out to me, but I could not bear to look at him. Fortunately he died in half an hour, under amputation, 5 more men wounded by the same shot & you may judge what were our expectations; when this took place five minutes after we began I confess I never was more alarmed. The Blake is much damaged. Providence alone spared our lives. It is thought bad enough to pass by Batteries, fear seldom occurs in equal battles, but when a ship is under stone walls, & in a position not to get one Gun to bear on the Enemy, it is the worst of forlorn hope ... By the blessing of God, we lost but 13 men killed and wounded ... We have learnt since, that so destructive was our fire before we got aground that the French could not stand at their guns.

The French response was also compromised by their shortage of artillerymen; there was only one company of the 1er Régiment Francaise and a weakened Dutch company. Within an hour, half of these men were missing. Osten made repeated visits to the batteries where he found that some men had perished at their posts but that many 'non accoutumés à la guerre' had run for cover.[5]

By 4pm, the French guns were silent. The left demi-bastion was almost in ruins and the outwork at its front was abandoned. All parts of the town were in flames. Monnet and his staff were forced to flee the Hotel de Ville and the powder magazine was only saved with difficulty. Many of the firemen had been killed or wounded and the water pumps were mostly out of action. Osten observed that some had had their pipes deliberately punctured by 'malveillants' (literally 'malicious people'). The local population, already discontented, were now desperate. A number of delegates were sent to Monnet to beg him to surrender.

Outside the walls, the assailants watched the burning buildings. Safe from the fire, they were still under threat from the rising water level. The French remained intent on cutting through the east dyke to let in the sea; if achieved, this could throw four or five feet of water over all the batteries except those on the top of the dykes. Chatham, realising that Flushing's guns were quiet, ordered a cease-fire. Eyre Coote summoned the town to surrender with its garrison prisoners of war; the letter was taken into Flushing by Lieutenant Colonel Walsh who carried a flag of truce. An answer was requested within the hour. Monnet replied that he would communicate his decision once he had consulted with 'la conseil pour la défense de la ville'. Four hours elapsed and it was obvious that the garrison were busy remounting guns and repairing embrasures. Monnet was informed that, unless the town surrendered, hostilities would recommence at 9pm. When this second ultimatum was ignored, the British batteries duly opened fire again. At 11pm, the French commander sent a letter with a flag of truce requesting a forty-eight hour cease-fire. Coote replied that only immediate surrender was acceptable and the bombardment continued.[6]

Whilst these messages were being exchanged, a further attack was made on the French outposts at 11pm. The battery of three 24-pounders (G) on the left of the British line was so far from Flushing that it was not only unable to reach the town but also to silence a troublesome French battery of two guns on the east dyke about 500 yards from the walls. Occupation of this dyke would allow the British battery to be sited at a proper distance. The enemy's advanced battery was to be carried by assault and, if it was not possible to retain the ground, the guns were to be spiked. Captain Pasley played a pivotal role in the planning of the attack and he describes the outcome in his usual opinionated style.

At 11 this was approbated by him [General Fraser] & also by Sir Eyre Coote, but the execution of it was put off till the next night the 14th. Sir Eyre Coote however wanting to improve upon my plan, ordered us to keep possession of the French battery if possible, he was also anxious that I should fill up the cut that the Enemy made to let in the sea-water. I could have told him that both these things were impracticable till we had entrenched properly & made batteries to support us on the ground, which I was contented with taking the first night, but a Commander-in-Chief must have his way. Colonel Pack of the 71st was appointed to command the party for the attack, whom I, of course, was to accompany in order to put the ground we gained in a state of defence, if tenable, or if not tenable to give, as Engineer, an official opinion. We took the Battery in a moment, driving in their sentries & pickets like sheep, some of whom I believe were drowned, running into deep water in their fright. There was a very strong party in the battery, part of whom ran away with little resistance, the rest, about 40, were taken prisoners and sent off. In the attack on the Battery I was wounded by a Bayonet which passed through my thigh but gave little pain & did not prevent my walking.

By the light of the shells & the fires in Flushing I saw that this battery was completely covered by the Town. I therefore repositioned it untenable [sic] to Colonel Pack. In the meantime a large party of French formed in line just under the Battery where we were & kept up a heavy fire upon us. At that time all our men were all dispersed by twos and threes owing to the darkness & confusion, & I do not believe there was one third of the numbers of the enemy. Colonel Pack was collecting his soldiers to charge them. At this time I was shot through the body & completely knocked over. When I recovered myself a little I found I could walk & thought it best to go off before I got stiff. After I was nearly exhausted I met some soldiers coming to carry off our wounded who took me to a hospital.

Pasley had a lucky escape. The bayonet wound passed near a large artery and the musket ball grazed his spine. After their initial setback, the French had responded by sending up two companies of the right demi-brigade who fired on the British assault force. Osten asserts that Pasley's men were driven back to their original positions. Certainly, the British were forced to retreat. Both sides claimed to have spiked the guns. The French admitted to losing around fifty men killed, wounded or made prisoner, whilst the British suffered two officers killed and three wounded and thirty-six rank and file killed or wounded from a force of 150 men. Pasley drew his own conclusions. 'The occasion of our great loss was employing too few men in the enterprise.'[7]

At 2.30 on the morning of the 15th, Monnet offered to surrender, requesting only that the garrison be treated as French troops. Coote agreed, asking in turn that the French make no more attempts to flood the land in front of Flushing. The bombardment stopped although the navy's guns were not silenced until 3am when Strachan learnt of the capitulation. Why had Monnet chosen to surrender at this particular moment? In essence, he believed that honour had been served – 'a besieged city never surrenders on the first day of bombardment' – and that further resistance would be both futile and self-destructive. He later wrote an eloquent memorandum to describe the situation in Flushing and to justify his decision.

The rubble from the houses was obstructing the streets, preventing movement and almost paralysing all the services. The people were irritated that I had ill received and then sent back the enemy's negotiators and the various deputations of the town who had come to ask me to put an end to the horrors of the siege. Consternation and the greatest disorder reigned in the place; armed cowards were pillaging and patrols ordered to fire into the air had not been able to stop the brigandage which was growing everywhere. The exhaustion and demoralisation of the troops joined to the cowardice of the foreign corps, of whom a good part had passed over to the enemy, all presented as desperate a scene as one can imagine.

The conflagration was so general that within six hours the town would have been consumed and the powder magazine, protected with difficulty, would have blown up; there was no shelter for the preservation of any of the provisions of war, no hospitals to receive the sick, no building where the troops might take much needed rest. After all these considerations, the council [of war] could not help feeling ... that this resistance could only produce even greater misfortunes without preventing the surrender of the place, that which induced it to finally listen to the repeated summonses of the enemy to capitulate.

Among those pressing Monnet to surrender was the mayor, Lammens. There is no evidence that the governor consulted his fellow military officers; Osten makes no reference to his own involvement in negotiations and simply states that Monnet notified him of the decision. The general informed the commanders of the two demi-brigades. Osten was unhappy with the performance of some of his officers and men, particularly the Battalion of Deserters and its commander, Major Boeckmann, who had fled at the earliest opportunity. A number of officers were arrested but no action was taken. On the other hand, Osten believed that the 65th and 48th Battalions of the Line and detachments of the 72nd Regiment and the 8th Provisional Regiment composed of conscripts but led by good officers, had all conducted themselves well. Officers receiving special mention included Lawless of the Irish Legion.

British officers expressed surprise at the suddenness of the fall of Flushing. Henegan understood the suffering in the town but he thought that the defenders were still capable of holding out as no practicable breach had been made. Picton agreed that more obstinate resistance might have been expected: 'We were all much pleased to find that our conclusions, or rather apprehensions, were erroneous; and I believe none more so than our commanders who are not calculated to struggle with much unexpected difficulty.'[8]

Chatham immediately wrote to Castlereagh informing him of the surrender. He praised the conduct of the troops and gave due acknowledgement to the 'constant and cordial cooperation' of the navy. At 1pm on the 15th, Adjutant General Colonel Robert Long and Captain George Cockburn were sent into the town with powers to arrange the articles of capitulation. They returned to Middelburg at midnight with conditions which were ratified by Chatham and Strachan. There was a feeling among senior British officers that these proceedings were unnecessarily drawn out; Brownrigg refers to 'accidental causes of delay' and Gomm thought that the negotiators had been 'too long about it'.

For the French, the terms were signed by Captain Leveque of the Engineers and Captain Montonnet of the Artillery and ratified by Monnet. It was agreed that the garrison would be allowed to march out of the place with the appropriate honours of war. They were to lay down their arms on the glacis and would then to be sent to England as prisoners. Those not fit enough to be removed were to remain under the care of French physicians and surgeons. The local population was given reassurances that their property would be respected and that 'no inhabitant would be molested on account of any opinion or conduct he may hitherto have held'. French citizens who had lived in Flushing for at least five years might be permitted to remain on condition of swearing an oath of allegiance to the British.

Detachments of the Royals and the 71st Regiment took command of the gates of Flushing. Further delays now occurred. The 16th was given over to the preparations for the embarkation of the garrison. The French evacuation was originally planned for noon on the 17th but Monnet represented that there would not be sufficient daylight to march his men to Ter Haak, the point of embarkation. It was the morning of the 18th when the garrison finally left the town in front of a British army forming a line from the gates to the place appointed for the piling of arms. Monnet and Chatham stood side by side during the formalities which were witnessed by William Keep.

> We formed an avenue of great extent for them to march out with all the honours of War. Our Regiment [77th] formed one side of the square at the extremity of it, where they were to lay down their arms, the 36th, 79th Highlanders and 82nd, the other faces, and here we awaited their arrival with all the ceremony of a Grand Review, and indeed they had all the honour of this to themselves for such a set of

miserable Banditti looking fellows were never seen. Their uniform and accoutrements of the most motley kind, the officers with top boots drawn over rusty pantaloons that livery stable grooms might have been ashamed of, and making a truly shabby appearance. I believe the few decent French among them disowned the rest and said they were Poles and Jews ... It was almost farcical to see these men received by their captors with the ceremonies performed, and I believe our Generals and Staff Officers (of which there was a great number splendidly attired) felt somewhat ashamed of the ostentation displayed when they discovered for whom it was done, for it was found that Flushing is looked upon as a condemned hole and the receptacle for deserters and all the refuse of the French Army.

An article of capitulation for the surrender of Middelburg had stated that other places surrendering without opposition would be offered the same advantageous terms. On 15 August, the deputies of the towns of Zieriksee and Brouwershaven and the whole of the islands of Schouwen and Duiveland surrendered to the Earl of Rosslyn and Admiral Keats. Chatham passed this news on to Castlereagh commenting that this would allow his army to draw ample supplies of cattle, spirits and biscuit from the captured territories.

A letter from Keats to Strachan, dated 15 August, updates the naval situation. Keats himself commanded eighteen sloops and gun brigs and four divisions of gunboats in the Saeftingen shoals, a location chosen by Home Popham as it effectively cut communication between the east and west parts of the Scheldt. Six frigates were anchored off Waarde awaiting an opportunity to come up and most of the flat boats from the East Scheldt had been ordered to Batz. Some of the sloops and gun brigs were running low on provisions and water. With respect to the enemy, it was believed that the main flotilla, formed of thirteen men of war and an unknown number of ships of the line, had retired behind the protection of Fort Lillo, anchored off and below Antwerp perhaps as far down as Fort St Philippe. There were forty-four French gun vessels in the East Scheldt between Tholen and Bergen-op-Zoom. Keats thought, however, that it was unlikely that the enemy would make any immediate attack. Equally, he believed that his own ships could achieve little without the active cooperation of the army.[9]

At Flushing, the 3rd Battalion of the Royals and the 14th Regiment were ordered to break into open column and lead the entry into the town. St Clair caught glimpses of pretty female faces through the few windows which had not been closed up to keep out the shot. If this reminded him of his march through Chelmsford two months earlier, there was little else similar. Flushing was, according to Thomas Graham, 'a complete ruin'. This was a slight exaggeration as some of the works on the land front remained in perfect state. On the other hand, the left bastion and the sea defences were much damaged and most of the houses had been hit. Around 250 dwellings were uninhabitable and fifty completely destroyed. A dozen warehouses and two churches, the Oostkerk and the Franschekerk, had been wrecked. The Town Hall with all its finery was gutted, only the outer wall remaining. In parts of the town, the locals had succeeded in fighting the fire only to succumb to flooding from a breached dyke. Captain Neil Douglas of the Cameron Highlanders was appalled by what he saw: 'Some entire streets were destroyed and the Houses having fallen inwards and being blackened with the Smoak looked like a place that had long been in ruins.' William Dyott agreed; it was 'utterly impossible' to describe the horror and dismay etched in the countenances of the wretched individuals left on the streets to lament the loss of their family and friends. People of all ranks dug in the smoking rubble searching for survivors. The total civilian losses were uncertain, perhaps 330 killed and 500 wounded. Almost all British memoirists strike the same note of awestruck horror, one officer observing that 'no one would become a soldier who saw war really as it is'. William Gomm remained phlegmatic, commenting that, whilst the destruction of Flushing was a necessary human violation, it was less upsetting than the burning of Copenhagen as 'it is not the Government seat of a nation, nor can it supposed to have contained anything of value, in a literary point of view, that can have suffered'.

The British soldiers made their billets as best they could. William Keep judged it 'a most diabolical place'. Whilst exploring what was left of the city, George Hargrove entered the sumptuous East India House which had been appropriated for the sick and wounded French troops. The young doctor was taken aback.

> I beheld a crowd of poor wretched Frenchmen, their Wives and Children indiscriminately mixed together, the latter too the victims of raging war, dying and dead, many breathing the last sigh amidst those noisome vapours uniformly attendant on rooms crowded with wounded soldiers, which perhaps the hurry and confusion of the moment could not have averted.

In another room, he found a heap of French uniforms torn to pieces and covered in blood mixed up with broken bayonets, swords and caps.[10]

The number of French casualties can only be estimated as the returns are inconsistent. Osten states 2,950 men killed, hospitalised, made prisoner or deserted from the time of the British disembarkation up to the fall of Flushing. British figures suggest that this is close to the truth. A return of prisoners and deserters taken between 30 July and 15 August totals 1,800; probably these were mostly Dutch with the majority captured around Flushing and the remainder at Ter Veere and Ramakins. An indeterminate number of French sick and wounded were transferred from Flushing to Cadsand before the blockade. Chatham believed this evacuation to exceed 1,000 men. The strength of the French garrison in Flushing at the time of the capitulation (5,800) was approximately 2,000 less that when it had been maximally reinforced prior to the siege. Thus we can say that the French probably lost around 3,000 men in the two weeks following the British landing, of which approximately 2,000 were casualties at Flushing. When Chatham alludes to total French losses of around 9,000 in a letter to Castlereagh of 18 August he presumably means the whole of the French garrison.

Close to 5,500 prisoners of war were embarked on twelve British ships for the voyage to England. William Richardson noted them to be a mixture of French, Dutch, Germans and Russians but there were certainly other nationalities. The sailors were irritated by the bluster of the French. A veteran officer, who had been on board since his capture at Ramakins, had insisted that Flushing would never be taken. He now boasted that Antwerp was invulnerable. Whereas the French were generally treated with respect, the attitude to the mercenaries was mixed. Brownrigg declared in a letter to Gordon, 'The Germans and Spaniards you may immediately take into our service but don't know what you will do with the Irish who are no doubt all rebels, and if they had their desserts should be hanged'.

The surrender terms agreed by Monnet made no special provision for the Irish Legion and it was understandable that these men were desperate to escape capture by the British. At least a few succeeded. Lieutenant Terence O'Reilly and Chef de Bataillon William Lawless, who had been seriously wounded in the last days of the siege, first concealed themselves in the house of a sympathetic French doctor. After an unsuccessful attempt to cross the West Scheldt in a small boat they remained in hiding for more than six weeks in a farmhouse outside Flushing and then back in the city. The men eventually made a successful escape in an open boat transporting vegetables. Lawless took with him the eagle from a flag that Napoleon had presented to the regiment in 1804. On returning to Paris, he was received by the Emperor and awarded the Legion of Honour. Those Irish officers who did fall into British hands feared mistreatment and many changed their names and took refuge in French units. A number were incarcerated in England and some escaped.[11]

The official returns allow a more precise statement of British losses. Between 2 and 6 August, a period which included some of the early skirmishing around Flushing, there were twenty-six killed, 127 wounded and four missing. The significant skirmish of 7 August resulted in fourteen killed, 141 wounded and five men unaccounted for. The equivalent figures for the third period, for 8 to 15 August, up to the fall of Flushing, were thirty-one, 105 and one. The frigate action of 11 August and the siege cost the navy nineteen killed and 103 wounded. If we add the casualties sustained during the landing on Bree Sand and up to 1 August, this gives a total of army and navy losses of 136 killed, 690 wounded and forty-four missing. The small number of casualties suffered during the siege reflects the subjugation of Flushing by bombardment rather than by breaching of the walls and a formal assault. Wellington's storming of the fortresses of Badajoz, Ciudad Rodrigo and Burgos in the Peninsula three years later was to cost him 8,000 men.[12]

Notes

1. Enthoven V., *Een Haven Te Ver*, pp. 293−4; *A Collection of Papers Relating to the Expedition to the Scheldt*, pp. 92−3; Parliamentary Papers 1810, Vol. XV, p. xxxii; Squire, J., *A Short Narrative of the Late Campaign of the British Army*, pp. 55−7.
2. Journal of the Army, pp. 56−60, TNA, WO 1/190; Jones, Sir J. T., *Journal of the Sieges carried on by the Army*, Vol. II, pp. 268−9; *A Collection of Papers*, p. 433; Enthoven, p. 294; Keep, W., *In the Service of the King*, p. 49; Green, J., *The Vicissitudes of a Soldier's Life*, p. 36; *A Soldier of the Seventy-First*, p. 43; *The Walcheren Expedition. The Experiences of a British Officer of the 81st Regiment*, p. 87; Osten, Général, *Rapport Circonstancié de ce qui s'est passé dans L'Ile de Walcheren*, p. 279; Gallaher, J. G., *Napoleon's Irish Legion*, p. 104.
3. Jones, Vol. II, p. 270; Enthoven, p. 294; Bond, G., *The Grand Expedition*, p. 101; St Clair, Lt Col, *A soldier's recollections of the West Indies and America with a narrative of the expedition to the Island of Walcheren*, Vol. II, pp. 335−41; Douglas, J., *Douglas's Tale of the Peninsula and Waterloo 1808−1815*, p. 9; Osten, pp. 279−81; Gallaher, p. 104.
4. Journal of the Army, pp. 56−65; Jones, Vol. II, pp. 270−1; Osten, p. 281; NAS, GD45/4/60.
5. *A Collection of Papers*, pp. 433−4; Fullom, S. W., *The Life of General Sir Howard Douglas*, pp. 106−7; Brenton, E. P., *The Naval History of Great Britain*, Vol. II, p. 300; Enthoven, pp. 294−5; Wybourn, Major T. M., *Sea Soldier*, pp. 140−2; Osten, pp. 282−3.
6. Jones, Vol. II, pp. 271−2; Bond, pp. 103−4; Fyers, Col W., *Journal of the Siege of Flushing 1809*, p. 157; Osten, p. 283; Enthoven, pp. 294−5.
7. Journal of the Army, p. 64; Squire, pp. 64−5; Enthoven, p. 294; Pasley, C. W.,

Captain Pasley at Walcheren August 1809, pp. 19−20; *Vicissitudes of a Scottish Soldier*, pp. 93−4; *A Soldier of the Seventy-First*, p. 44; Osten, pp. 283−4.

8. Osten, pp. 284−5; Bond, pp. 104−5; Enthoven, pp. 295, 300; Henegan, Sir R. D., *Seven Years Campaigning in the Peninsula and the Netherlands*, Vol. I, p. 79; Havard, R., *Wellington's Welsh General*, p. 105.

9. Journal of the Army, pp. 65−7; *A Collection of Papers*, pp. 94−105, 111−5, 450; *Archives Parlementaires de 1787 a 1860*, Vol. X, pp. 309−10; Enthoven, p. 295; Bond, p. 105; Jones, Vol. II, p. 273; Dyott, W., *Dyott's Diary 1781−1845*, Vol. I, pp. 282−3; Keep, p. 55; Gomm, WM, *Letters and Journal of Sir William M. Gomm*, p. 136.

10. St Clair, Vol. II, pp. 347−9; Brett-James, A., *The Walcheren Failure*, pp. 60−1; Jones, Vol. II, pp. 273−4; Dyott, Vol. I, p. 282; Keep, pp. 56−7; Hargrove, G., *An Account of the Islands of Walcheren and South Beveland*, pp. 25−7; *The Walcheren Expedition*, p. 94; Squire, p. 66; Gomm, p. 134.

11. Fortescue, J. W., *A History of the British Army*, Vol. VII, p. 80; Osten, p. 285; *A Collection of Papers*, pp. 97, 107−9, 112, 116−7; Jones, Vol. II, p. 273; Bond, pp. 106−7; Richardson, W., *A Mariner of England*, p. 270; Enthoven, p. 296; Gallaher, pp. 105−7.

12. *A Collection of Papers*, pp. 79, 85, 91, 106; Bond, p. 106. Fortescue, Vol. VII, p. 80.

CHAPTER 10

A French Marshal

S ome of the French prisoners of war brought back to England were eventually released through diplomatic channels. Monsieur Le Chanteur, *Commissaire Imperial de le Marine* at Flushing, was held at Bishops Waltham. Nine years earlier, Le Chanteur had helped a captured British officer, Colonel Thomas Scott, brother of Sir Walter Scott, to return home after his ship had fallen into French hands. Now, with the roles reversed, Le Chanteur wrote to Major General Scott. He obtained his passport back to France in February 1810.

The arrival of Osten and Monnet on British soil provoked a mixed response from the home press. The former was described by the *Edinburgh Annual Register* as being 'much beloved at Walcheren'. The Flemish general, the columnist continued, had 'on every occasion shown himself the friend of any English sailors who have been cast away on the island'. It was noted that it was Osten who had led the sorties out of the garrison. Monnet, in contrast, was a man of 'vulgar manners and appearance' and was greatly disliked. *The Times* agreed that Flushing's ex-commander was a coarse character with a common face but *The Star* was more generous in its assessment of his conduct. 'Who should have thought that this town should have resisted for 14 days against an army of 20,000 men.' Those on the scene, British and French, also had mixed views of Monnet's performance. The officer of the 81st judged him a coward, never endangering himself during the siege, but, on the other hand, the defence of the town was brave and he 'might certainly have surrendered it at any moment ... No one speaks well of the fallen'. Jean Jacques Pelet was critical of his fellow officer's actions. Monnet, he said, had adopted a poor strategy, attempting to dispute the approaches to Flushing against an army which had all the advantages. Both British and French were united in applauding Osten's bravery.

News of the fall of Flushing reached Paris on 19 August. General Rousseau telegraphed Clarke informing him of the capitulation. The Emperor was in turn informed by his Minister of War. He initially received the news at Schönbrunn on August 24 but, judging from the tone of his correspondence, it was several days before he believed the vital port to be lost. He was, in the words of Savary, 'astonished' at this turn of events. Only a few days earlier, he had written to Fouché assuring him that Flushing,

> is impregnable because it is necessary to cross the ditch which is full of water and, in the final resort, one can cut the dykes and flood the whole island. If Flushing was to be taken in less than six months, it would be necessary to arrest and put on trial all the generals, colonels and senior officers who were responsible for its defence.

Now that he knew the worst, the Emperor concluded that Flushing's fall was the result of 'cowardice amounting to treason'. It could, he informed Clarke, have been defended whilst there was still a piece of bread to eat. His ire was especially directed at Monnet. 'If Flushing is taken, I can only attribute it to the commandant losing his head.' In a rush of letters in late August his attacks become more personal and vindictive. The 'vile coward' had disobeyed his orders to cut the sea defences. He had given up the place to 'a few bombs'. Monnet was out of the Emperor's grasp in England but at the end of 1809 he was tried in Paris in his absence by a council of senior officers. They found little fault with his military conduct during the siege but he was judged to have mismanaged the capitulation by delegating the negotiations to junior officers. There were also financial irregularities. These misdemeanours allowed the council to find him guilty of the more serious charges of cowardice and treason and to sentence him to death. The conclusions were published in *Le Moniteur*, Napoleon's organ of propaganda. Monnet avoided execution and returned to France in 1814 when he had his old rank returned to him by Louis XVIII. Osten was held on parole at Lichfield but escaped to Holland in February 1810 with the help of his daughter and a smuggler called Waddell who acted as an 'escape agent'.

Napoleon's frequent letters to Clarke contained more than condemnation of Monnet. Throughout August, he continued to try to influence events in the Scheldt from afar giving remarkably detailed instructions pertaining to troop dispositions in the region. Decrès, the *Ministre de la Marine* at Paris, also came under fire. A letter of 10 August is typical of the Emperor's correspondence at this time.

> I have received your letter of August 4. You do not tell me where my fleet is. If it is at Antwerp I have nothing to fear; if it is not there I have the greatest fear for it. Your writing is not clear. You do not inform me why my reassembled fleet has not entered Antwerp. The enemy's plan is very well developed ... .

On the same day, he accuses Clarke of fatal hesitation. 'No doubt you expect the English to come and capture you in your bed.' He does admit that it is difficult for him to keep up.

> Events change at every instant; it is impossible for me to give orders which only arrive fifteen days later. The ministers have the same power as me since they can hold meetings and take decisions.

It is unlikely that his ministers believed this; on the following day, Napoleon continued his tirade against Cambacérès, accusing him and his peers of 'shocking inactivity'. Public opinion would have to be managed. Cambacérès was instructed to print a daily bulletin as 'imagination always exceeds reality'.[1]

The Emperor's repeated accusations of complacency and lassitude were, to a degree, unfair. Whilst the British besieged Flushing there had been substantial reinforcement of the wider French defensive position in the Scheldt. The significant number of National Guardsmen in this army has been alluded to. This was mostly the initiative of one man. French ministers were nervous of raising such a large body of men outside the regular army, partly because there were uncomfortable similarities with the *levée en masse* of the Revolutionary years and partly because they believed the Emperor might disapprove. Joseph Fouché, Minister of Police and in temporary control of the Ministry of the Interior, grasped the nettle. In his memoirs, he claims that

> I perceived the danger. Invested, during the Emperor's absence, with a great part of his power by the union of two ministries, I instilled energy into the council of which I was the life and caused it to pass several strong measures.

This immodest assessment of his role is supported by Count Réal, a Prefect of Police, who witnessed a meeting of Fouché, Cambacérès and the other ministers held to discuss their response to the British threat to Antwerp. Fouché advised an immediate levée of the National Guard.

> What would the Emperor and the Army say if France, whom they are fighting at a distance [in Austria] to defend, should allow her soil to be insulted with impunity whilst waiting for them to return to her help?

Cambacérès retorted that he had no wish to have his head chopped off and that they must wait for instructions from Napoleon. 'For my part,' replied Fouché, 'I shall do my duty even when waiting for orders.'

On the same day, the Minister of Police issued a magnificent appeal to the valour of the French nation and mobilised the National Guard. Prefects were instructed to demand suitable men from the mayors of towns throughout the Empire. These dignitaries in turn appealed to the patriotism of their citizens through the posting of public notices. In the Nièvre, the people were told that,

> An English expedition threatens our frontiers from Boulogne to the Scheldt and one can see the vessels of our eternal enemy floating on the ocean from all points on the coast.

This audacious raising of the National Guard had been opposed by all other members of the council with the exception of Decrès. The discontent with Fouché was not limited to Paris; General Pelet believed the Minister of Police to have unnecessarily spread alarm and to have been motivated by self-interest. Crucially for Fouché, the Emperor approved his actions. In the letter to Clarke of 10 August, he specifically excludes Fouché from his charges of inaction. A week later, he writes to the Minister of Police giving directions for the organisation, command and arming of the National Guard units. Whilst publicly supporting Fouché's levée, Napoleon was bound to be suspicious of a man who effortlessly took control in his absence. Fouché had not helped his cause by declaring in a circular to the mayors of Paris that the mobilisation proved to Europe that 'if the genius of Napoleon gives brilliance to France, his presence is not necessary to repulse his enemies'. The Emperor found a reason to remove him from office in 1810.

This growing force needed proper command. We have seen that Louis was a reluctant leader of the Army of the Brabant. Despite the strengthening of his hand, he remained melancholic and pessimistic. His brother constantly berated him for his perceived shortcomings. He had not invested adequately in his army. 'The finances of a King are not those of a prior of a convent.' Louis's insecurity was evident in his correspondence to Clarke. In a letter of 12 August, he acknowledges the reinforcements but complains of their quality and the shortage of officers. 'They cannot reliably defend Antwerp ... My ships and my docks are perhaps being burnt. East Friesland is perhaps at this moment occupied by the Duke of Brunswick.'[2]

There was a need for a senior officer of the Empire to bring cohesion and calm to the Scheldt operations. Louis had already requested a Marshal and, on 10 August, Napoleon obliged by approving the appointment of Marshal Jean-Baptiste Bernadotte, Prince of Ponte-Corvo, to the overall command. Clarke communicated directly with Bernadotte two days later.

The Emperor, informed of the descent of the English on Holland, has judged it appropriate to entrust you to the command of the 24e division militaire and of that part of the 25e division militaire on the right bank of the Meuse. The general of division Senator Rampon and the generals and troops assembled on the Scheldt between the island of Cadsand and L'Ecluse up to the left of the Meuse pass under your command. The general of division Sainte-Suzanne will keep command of the coast between the island of Cadsand and the Somme. The Marshal Duc de Valmy [Kellerman] will continue to command the neighbouring departments of the Rhine on the right bank of the Meuse. As a result of a direct order of the Emperor, an important corps of reserve will be assembled at Weser under his command. The Marshal Duc de Conégliano [Moncey] has been ordered to return to Lille to command another corps of reserve of which you will subsequently know the composition. The Emperor gives on this occasion, Prince, a new proof of his confidence of your devotion to himself and to the defence of the State. His Majesty has thus anticipated, before knowing of it, the offer you have made of your services.

A biographer has described Bernadotte as the most puzzling of all the fourteen generals who were created Marshals of the Empire by Napoleon in the spring of 1804. A tall and handsome man, he was capable of great bravery on the field. Conversely, none of Napoleon's other generals had his knack of narrowly missing major battles. His corps was at Ulm and Austerlitz but he angered the Emperor and was threatened with court martial when he failed to make contact at Auerstädt in 1806. In the summer of 1809, he was again under a cloud. At the battle of Wagram in early July he had issued an *ordre du jour* giving disproportionate credit to the Saxon troops under his command. Bernadotte was probably motivated by a desire to fire up his men but when it was reported in the German press that 'Saxon troops had won the battle of Wagram' there was a storm of French indignation and Napoleon was irritated enough to bring the matter to Clarke's attention.

If you have any occasion to see the Prince of Ponte-Corvo please convey to him my displeasure at the ridiculous order of the day which he has published in all the newspapers. It is all the more out of place because he himself was complaining about the Saxons the whole day. The order of the day contains other inaccuracies ... .

The Emperor went on to describe Bernadotte as a man enamoured with money and averse to the dangers and fatigues of war.

140

The choice of Bernadotte for command in the Scheldt is an example of Napoleon's pragmatism. The Prince of Ponte-Corvo was French, experienced and available. The Emperor was keen to ensure that all Dutch troops were unequivocally under French control and Bernadotte's seniority would confirm this. Furthermore, Fouché had played a part in Bernadotte's appointment. In his memoirs, the Minister of Police describes his attempts to persuade the general to take the post: 'if he refused to fulfil the commission conferred upon him by the Minister of War he would appear to assume the air of a discontented person ... that in case of need we ought to serve the Emperor in spite of himself.' Napoleon probably judged that it was better to have these scheming men on side than publicly out of favour. Having agreed to proceed to Antwerp, Bernadotte made a strident declaration of loyalty. 'If I am offered only a company of veterans for the defence of the Empire I shall not hesitate to accept such a command!' Rather as for the raising of the National Guard, Clarke and his fellow ministers were taken aback at the appointment of a man who had recently incurred Napoleon's censure. A solution to the Scheldt command problem had been found but the Emperor's wariness of a plot was well understood by Fouché: 'he [Napoleon] never pardoned either Bernadotte or myself for this eminent service and our intimacy became more than ever an object of suspicion with him.'[3]

On 15 August, the day of the surrender of Flushing, Bernadotte was in the outskirts of Antwerp conferring with the King of Holland. It was also the celebration of the Emperor's birthday and the two men inspected the troops entrusted with the defence of the Scheldt. According to de Rocca, the Dutch Guard was brilliantly dressed but the French, in stark contrast, were a 'feeble and poorly disciplined mass'. Captain François Dumonceau, son of the general, agreed with him. They were the 'residue of the depots' mixed together pell-mell into provisional battalions and squadrons. De Rocca was impressed by the new commander's demeanour.

> Marshal Bernadotte moved through the ranks, informing himself of the detailed needs of each corps; he placed himself at times at the head of pelotons and squadrons to show the young officers what they had to do. In showing respect to all, he gave them the confidence they lacked.

The Marshal also reprimanded and cajoled and stressed the need for improvement. He showed a young soldier how to use his rifle. The cavalry of both armies slipped in the mud, several horsemen falling into the ditches. On the next day, King Louis left for Amsterdam with half of the 4,000 Dutch

Guards to organise the National Guard and to make arrangements for the defence of the other parts of the coast of Holland. Bernadotte remained in Antwerp where his organisational prowess was soon apparent. The local Commissary General of Police informed Paris that the Prince of Ponte-Corvo had found that there was much to do.

> Not one piece of the country was prepared. This morning he found an important fort guarded by three conscripts. The troops had no organisation. Everything was in dreadful chaos. S. A. [Bernadotte] lost no time; four days later after his arrival everything is almost in order.

De Rocca believed that Bernadotte had resolved many of the command rivalries and galvanised the French forces. The Marshal was not slow to take credit for his actions, writing to the Emperor on the 18th to inform him that he had already done all that was humanly possible to bolster the defences of the region.

> The English might do us some harm but I hope that on the frontiers of the Empire they will not succeed in soiling the laurels with which Your Majesty has decorated your armies.

The army under Bernadotte's command was substantial. Sixty thousand National Guardsmen were under orders for service in the Scheldt by mid-August. These men were divided between Antwerp, Cadsand, Boulogne, Ghent, Brussels, Lille, Ostend, and St Omer. On the front line between Cadsand and Bergen-op-Zoom Bernadotte had 19,000 infantry in addition to the 16,000 National Guards under the command of Generals Rampon and Soulès. The infantry numbers included 900 artillerymen and there were 2,300 cavalry. The total strength of the Army of the North, excluding reserves and the Dutch at Bergen-op-Zoom was just under 40,000 men.

There had been other important command appointments. Marshal Bon-Adrien Jannot de Moncey, Duc de Conegliano, was given the 16th Military Division (*L'Armée de la Tête de Flandre*) which was made up of forces north of the Somme River including Cadsand but excluding the camp of Boulogne and Bernadotte's men on both banks of the Scheldt. The Emperor trusted Moncey and probably thought him a suitable person to keep an eye on Bernadotte. General Claude-Sylvestre Colaud was appointed Governor of Antwerp and General Jean-François Dejean, Inspector General of Engineers, was also ordered to the city.[4]

The construction of new defences and the repair of the existing fortifications was a French priority. Antwerp was still in a poor state at the beginning of August. General Saint-Laurent found that many of the guns were unserviceable, the carriages broken, and the gunpowder kept in the open. Louis did his best to help and on the 9th he was able to report the strengthening of existing forts and the erection of new fortifications. Rampon confirmed that new works at Lillo and Liefkenshoek had resulted in both being in a 'respectable state'. Pelet wrote a week later that 'great works' had already been completed and that he thought the city to be safer from attack. Despite this progress the general is critical of Bernadotte and in truth there was still much to do. The Marshal demanded the further reinforcement of Lillo (400 men and fifty guns) and Liefkenshoek (250 men and fifty guns), the rebuilding of a number of old forts (La Croix, St Marie, St Philippe, Frederick Henry, La Perle, Isabelle) and ordered the flooding of larger areas below Antwerp.

The French flotilla remained stationed above the defensive boom stretched across the Scheldt where it was protected by several of the forts. Further up river a number of ships were chained together to provide another block to navigation. In the approaches to Antwerp, there were three ships of the line also supported by forts and riverfront batteries. Napoleon had definite views as to the optimal garrison and defensive strategy for the city which he believed to be the ultimate British target. On 13 August, he gave Clarke detailed instructions regarding the senior command and manpower. 'Thus organised,' he explained, 'Antwerp is inpregnable.'[5]

Now in control of Flushing, another fortress the Emperor had considered invulnerable to British attack, Chatham ordered the bulk of his army to South Beveland. An attack on Antwerp remained the key objective. Whilst the 6,000 men of Fraser's division were left to guard Walcheren, Grosvenor's division was embarked at Ramakins on the 19th and then Graham's over the next two days. This took longer than expected due to a shortage of transports. Rottenburg's brigade crossed to South Beveland on the ferry from Armuyden and then marched across the island to Batz. Adverse winds continued to hinder British naval movements and cavalry and ordnance transports destined for South Beveland were delayed in The Slough.[6]

Chatham wrote to Castlereagh on 19 August telling him that Grosvenor's and Graham's troops would soon be rendezvousing at Batz and joining the forces of Rosslyn, Hope and Huntley. A General Order of the same date stipulated that as military operations on Walcheren were now terminated the army would no longer be designated as wings but would be composed of an advanced guard of the light troops and cavalry under Rosslyn, the Reserve under Hope, and the four current divisions under their respective officers. The army's commander intended to leave Middelburg for South Beveland the next day. In fact, Chatham did not depart until the 21st making the fourteen-mile journey to Goes. On the morning of the 22nd, he had a conference with Sir John Hope at the village of Schore, midway between Goes and Batz, before returning to the former place in the evening. Hope had explored the feasibility of crossing the Bergen-op-Zoom channel but had found that this was possible for only a very small corps. The following day, the headquarters of the army passed through Schore and Waarde reaching the village of Crabbendyke about thirteen miles along the road from Goes. It was not until noon on the 24th that Chatham and his staff were established at Batz. This was eight and a half days after the fall of Flushing and this ponderous progress convinced many that the general's indolent habits had returned. Rumours spread that he rarely rose from bed until the early afternoon, that he enjoyed the company of his pet turtle, and that he was afforded 'the luxury of a London kitchen' while his men had to subsist on meat and biscuit. Captain Frederick William Trench, serving in the Quartermaster General's Corps, believed the commander's apathy to be 'extraordinary' and presumed that he must be awaiting vital orders from England. In his journal, he noted that Chatham could not be persuaded to reconnoitre the country, the general always taking the shortest route.

In fairness to Chatham, at least some of the initial delay at Middelburg was caused by his lengthy correspondence with Castlereagh regarding the provisioning of his army. Britain was trying to fight a war on more than one front and resources were limited both in Spain and in the Scheldt. At the outset of the expedition, the Commissary General had received strict orders from the Treasury not to pay the local inhabitants more than the market price for their goods. It was expected that expenses might be deferred by the use of bills from London. This proved impractical and the commissaries were reluctant to impoverish the local population. 'We have not only drained them of their cattle but have often taken their cows, which were of greater value to them for the support of their families than can be made good by the highest price paid for beef.' Horses, wagons, and drivers were also taken into British service despite it being the harvest time. Chatham supported an appeal for extra money but this was brusquely rejected by the Treasury, a decision which was explained by Castlereagh in a private letter to Chatham of 17 August.

> When I inform you that we do not possess the power of sending you
> from hence [England] a single foreign coin of any sort, and that, in the
> last extremity, rather than disband the army, that British armies must

be sent, you will not be surprised that you should receive peremptory orders to enforce the system agreed before you left London. If any comparative indulgence can be shown, perhaps it may be advisable to manage the feelings of Walcheren people most, if we are to keep the island, not by applying a different system, but by making South Beveland contribute most to the wants of the army. I need not suggest what the impression in England would be if guineas were going out to pay our army abroad; besides, it could not be done without an Order in Council and other proceedings which would embarrass.

On South Beveland, Lord Rosslyn reported that the shortage of money was a cause of 'great inconvenience'. An officer complained that his men were unable to keep themselves warm and dry.

There is a miserable deficiency of everything that is necessary to this purpose. We have no flannels or blankets; even our shoes are so execrable as not to exclude the wet; the leather is like so much brown paper and tears off the sole after it has got one or two wettings.

Chatham defended his commissary from attack and refused to enforce contributions from the local population. This was not, he argued, a situation where the extreme rights of war applied. Walcheren had surrendered upon terms which included respect for property. London eventually relented but the promised extra 40,000 Dutch dollars did not reach Chatham until September.[7]

The British Army was starting to suffer from a more sinister affliction. Chatham's force was at first extremely healthy; there was no sign of excessive sickness until after the fall of Flushing. On 19 August a fever broke out among the men. Rifleman Harris and his comrades were whiling away the time in a South Beveland village when, in his words, 'an awful visitation came upon us'. Inspector of Hospitals John Webb wrote to the Surgeon General in London on the 20th stating that each regiment had an average of six to eight men affected by the fever. Around 150 men would not be fit enough to make the transfer to Walcheren and would have to be admitted to hospital. There were about 600 French sick in the hospitals of Flushing and Ter Veere. The Inspector asked that additional medical officers be sent to join his staff. This was probably a routine request but, within a week, the sickness had spread rapidly and Webb again asked for extra doctors. As yet, the great majority of men had only mild disease but Webb warned that if the army remained inactive in such a 'swampy' country then the situation was likely to deteriorate.

William Dyott noted in his journal that 'great sickness prevailed in the army'. The weather continued rainy and unsettled matching the mood of the troops. Even before the onset of illness, it appears that many were becoming dispirited. Senior officers were sceptical as to the chances of a successful attack on Antwerp. On Sunday 20 August, Thomas Graham and Thomas Picton wrote home remarkably similar letters. Graham, debilitated by an eye ailment, announced the intention to proceed up the Scheldt. 'I doubt much our doing more; there has been so much time, and they have such means ... .' Picton, now Governor of Flushing, also advocated caution.

> In my opinion, we shall not attempt anything further; although we make great demonstrations, as if we were determined to proceed immediately. According to the accounts we have here, a very respectable [French] force has been collected at Antwerp; and all the country through which we must unavoidably pass has been completely flooded. Under such circumstances, I trust we are too wise to commit the safety of the fleet and army; and that we shall prudently content ourselves with the laurels which we have already gathered.

On South Beveland, William Maynard Gomm believed all was in the balance; it was a 'toss up' which way the army went next. Dalhousie recalled that before the expedition's departure, he and Erskine had expected a short campaign. 'Lord Chatham was like the piper who was longer in tuning his pipe than playing it.' Now, he informed his wife that the tune was likely to carry on for some time.

Whilst Chatham made his way to Batz, Strachan came up the river to Waarde with five ships of the line. A meeting between the two men had originally been planned at this South Beveland village for the 23rd but the admiral had discovered that the enemy were constructing works higher up the river at Sandvliet and Lillo and he judged it more important to explore this activity than to meet Chatham. All British naval movements were closely observed by the French on the left bank of the Scheldt. On 17 August, British frigates had exchanged fire with the garrison at Terneuse with little damage to either side. Strachan and his senior officers thought that little could be achieved by the navy acting alone. On the 22nd, Strachan had informed William Wellesley Pole at the Admiralty that the enemy were in considerable force on both sides of the river.

> It is said 15,000 men are collected in the neighbourhood of Sandvliet; the beach near that place appears favourable for landing the troops. I

have directed Sir Richard Keats to undertake the arrangement. To Captain Cockburn I have given command of the flotilla and to Sir Home Popham that of the fire vessel department. It is the opinion of Sir Richard Keats and myself, and I believe every sea-officer, that, without the cooperation of the army, we cannot effect the ultimate objective of the expedition.

Keats had earlier communicated with the Earl of Rosslyn offering him naval support to achieve their ultimate objective, something he felt the need to spell out, 'namely, the destruction of the enemy's ships of war near Antwerp'. The general replied that he had received no instructions whatsoever as to subsequent operations and that he was awaiting the arrival of Lord Chatham at Batz.[8]

As the British pondered their next move, the French consolidated and reorganised their forces. On 20 August, Clarke specified that Bernadotte would continue to command the Army of the North but that his jurisdiction on the left bank was to be reduced to the area between Hulst and Tête de Flandre. Moncey was to receive some troops from Bernadotte and was designated commander of the Corps of Observation on Cadsand responsible for the area between Hulst and Ostend. Bernadotte sulked at this diminution of his immediate forces but more reinforcements poured in from the surrounding military depots and, by the 26th, Clarke was able to declare that there were 100,000 troops in the Scheldt to combat the English invasion. The Army of the North totalled 33,000 men, the Corps of Observation on Cadsand just over 40,000 and the remainder were made up of the 12,000 National Guardsmen of the Army of the Reserve at Lille commanded by Bessières, and around 14,000 men in the camp at Boulogne and other depots. There were also some 6,000 Dutch troops at Bergen-op-Zoom commanded by Marshal Jean-Baptiste Dumonceau.

Bernadotte was determined that as many of these men as possible should be concentrated around Antwerp to protect the fleet and the docks. On the 22nd, he had almost 30,000 troops in the vicinity of the city, about half being troops of the line. How many of these men were ready to face an immediate British attack was less clear; the Marshal believed only around 12,000. The quality of the troops entrusted with the defence of this outpost of Empire remained a cause for concern. Napoleon warned Clarke that the French should only fight a battle if it was necessary to save Antwerp or only 'if it was four against one and in a good position protected by redoubts and batteries'. When the Emperor sent General d'Hastrel from Paris to Antwerp to act as Bernadotte's *chef d'état major*, he warned him that he would find most of the senior officers to be useless. Clarke had resorted to recruiting men who had previously been rejected or discharged from military service.

D'Hastrel received a cool reception from Bernadotte who believed him to be Napoleon's spy, a suspicion the marshal later admitted when the two men became friends. The Emperor's determination to influence events in the Scheldt was always destined to be frustrated by his commitments in Austria and the limitations of contemporary communications. The sending of orders via the Minister of War in Paris served to increase the delays and make Napoleon's opinions retrospective. It took about six days for Clarke's letters to reach the Imperial Headquarters at Schönbrunn. On 24 August, Napoleon complained to his aide-de-camp that he had received no news from Antwerp since the 16th.[9]

The Emperor had informed d'Hastrel that 'The fleet must defend Antwerp and Antwerp must defend the fleet'. Earlier in the month, Missiessy had kept his options open but he now moved his ships to safety above the city; this had the secondary benefit of releasing 6,000 sailors for garrison duty in the Scheldt fortress. If Napoleon could not manage the detail, he could at least give encouragement. On the 27th, he replied to Bernadotte's letter of nine days earlier.

> The fleet, the garrison, the army and yourself must not be separated from Antwerp ... I am confident of your bravery, skill and experience. If our enemies try something against Antwerp they will be repulsed.

The Emperor judged that a little flattery was necessary. His correspondence of this period is suffused with optimism. He assures Clarke that the English expedition will achieve nothing; the French can only lose by imprudently attacking them.

> If I was commanding the English forces, I would judge it not possible to besiege Antwerp with less than 60,000 men, and even then I should fear being beaten and thrown into the sea. This English operation lacks any sense. Every day we have thousands of men more and every day they have thousands less. Every day we believe more in our success and every day they fear more a reverse and see a catastrophe approaching.

A few days later, he returns to the same theme: 'all that is needed to defeat the English is patience and the passage of time.'

Others were starting to share the Emperor's positivity. Engineer Dejean considered that the greatest danger to Antwerp had passed by the 23rd. Had not the enemy already been assembled at Batz for several days without attacking? Surely they had missed their chance. The most senior French commanders, Bernadotte and Moncey, were more circumspect. There remained the need to concentrate around Antwerp those forces thinly spread along the banks of the Scheldt. In trying to defend all areas, the French could be fatally weakened. Bernadotte thought the situation to be improving but still critical. Many French veterans expected more fighting. De Rocca and his comrades watched every movement around Batz. 'We learnt that the English General in Chief had just arrived there and we believed that he was going to attack us incessantly with all his forces.'[10]

Notes

1. Thierry, E., *Notice sur M Le Chanteur Principal de la Marine*, pp. 19–20; *Edinburgh Annual Register for 1809*, Vol. II, p. 256; Fleischman, T., *L'Expedition Anglaise sur le Continent en 1809*, pp. 43–5; *Archives Parlementaires de 1787 a 1860*, Vol. X, pp. 308–9; *The Walcheren Expedition. The Experiences of a British Officer of the 81st Regiment*, pp. 79, 84–5, 128–9; Pelet, Général, *Mémoires sur la Guerre de 1809*, Vol. IV, p. 326; Savary, M., *Memoirs of the Duke of Rovigo*, Vol. II, p. 139; Lecestre, L., *Lettres Inédites de Napoléon Ier*, Vol. I, p. 352; Fischer, A., *Napoléon et Anvers*, p. 164; Wauwermans, Général, *Napoléon et Carnot*, pp. 93–4; Abell, F., *Prisoners of War in Britain 1756 to 1815*, p. 382; *Correspondance de Napoléon Ier*, Vol. 19, pp. 330–3, 392–9, 401–11, 441–5.
2. Bond, G., *The Grand Expedition*, pp. 77–80; Fleischman, pp. 49–52, 55–6, 70; Fouché, J., *The Memoirs of Joseph Fouché*, pp. 236–9; Hayward, A. L., *Indiscretions of a Prefect of Police*, pp. 196–8; Pelet, Vol. IV, pp. 322–3; *Correspondance de Napoléon Ier*, Vol. 19, pp. 322–54; Rocquain, F., *Napoléon Ier et Le Roi Louis*, pp. 209–11.
3. *Archives Parlementaires*, Vol. X, p. 305; *Correspondance de Napoléon Ier*, Vol. 19, pp. 328–30, 288–9; Palmer, A., *Bernadotte*, pp. ix–x; Barton, D. P., *The Amazing Career of Bernadotte 1763–1844*, pp. 222–4; Fleischman, pp. 53–6; Pelet, Vol. IV, p. 331; Fouché, pp. 237–9.
4. Fleischman, pp. 56, 68–9; Bond, pp. 79, 109–11; De Rocca, Mr, *Campagne de Walcheren et D'Anvers en 1809*, pp. 102–6; Dumonceau, F., *Mémoires du Général Comte François Dumonceau 1790–1811*, p. 258; Fischer, p. 168; Wauwermans, pp. 89–90.
5. Bond, pp. 72, 76, 111–4; *Archives Parlementaires*, Vol. X, p. 304; Pelet, Vol. IV, pp. 333–4; Wauwermans, p. 84; Fleischman, p. 61; *Correspondance de Napoléon Ier*, Vol. 19, p. 339.
6. General Orders for the Army 19 Aug, TNA, WO 28/352; Parliamentary Papers 1810, Vol. XV, p. xl; *A Collection of Papers Relating to the Expedition to the Scheldt*, p. 118; Enthoven, V., *Een Haven Te Ver*, p. 295; Journal of the Army, pp. 69–74, TNA, WO 1/190.

7. Journal of the Army, pp. 67–74; Squire, J., *A Short Narrative of the Late Campaign of the British Army*, pp. 75–6; Fortescue, J. W., *A History of the British Army*, Vol. VII, pp. 81–5; NAM, 1974-01-137, 1968-07-261: 65; Bond, pp. 112–3; Glover, R., *Peninsular Preparation*, pp. 15–16; Castlereagh, Viscount, *Memoirs and Correspondence of Viscount Castlereagh*, Vol. VI, pp. 304–6; Parliamentary Papers, Vol. XV, p. 5lxxix; *The Walcheren Expedition*, p. 109.
8. Parliamentary Papers, Vol. XV, pp. cccclxxx, ccclxxxviii; Journal of the Army, p. 74; McGuffie, T. H., *The Walcheren Expedition and the Walcheren Fever*, pp. 194–5; Hargrove, G., *An Account of the Islands of Walcheren and South Beveland*, p. 53; *A Collection of Papers*, pp. 587–90; Harris, B., *Recollections of Rifleman Harris*, pp. 173–4; Dyott, W., *Dyott's Diary 1781–1845*, Vol. I, p. 284; Robinson, H. B., *Memoirs of Lieutenant General Sir Thomas Picton*, Vol. I, pp. 243–6; Aspinall-Oglander, C., *Freshly Remembered. The Story of Thomas Graham Lord Lynedoch*, p. 20; Gomm, W. M., *Letters and Journal of Sir William M. Gomm*, p. 136; NAS, GD45/14/540; Brenton, E. P., *The Naval History of Great Britain*, Vol. II, pp. 301–3; Fortescue, Vol. VII, pp. 81–2.
9. Bond, pp. 114–9; Fleischman, pp. 61–2, 67–8; D'Hastrel, Général Baron, *Mémoires (1766–1825)*, pp. 138–9; *Correspondance de Napoléon Ier*, Vol. 19, pp. 382, 394.
10. Fleischman, p. 69; Wauwermans, p. 73; *Correspondance de Napoléon Ier*, Vol. 19, pp. 359, 382; Bond, pp. 111, 115–7; De Rocca, pp. 109–10, 113–4.

CHAPTER 11

Retreat

On 24 and 25 August, British gunboats ventured up the Scheldt and exchanged fire with the French forts of Frederick Henry and Doel. In Keats's words, the intent was to 'annoy and obstruct' the progress of the enemy's works. Many of those aboard the British ships near Antwerp believed that this aggression was pointless. William Wheeler's regiment was on the transport *Anne*.

> We are at present anchored before the city. The whole of the French fleet are strongly moored in the harbour, where they are as snug as their hearts can well desire, protected by formidable batteries and two large chains drawn across the mouth of the harbour, to make themselves doubly secure. The city is protected on the land side by an immense army, and troops are daily arriving to reinforce those already in camp. It is evident we are a day behind. Some heavy cannonading takes place every time the tide serves, between our light vessels and gunboats and their batteries outside the eminence of the harbour. This does not appear to be of any service and must be attended with loss of life and a useless expenditure of ammunition.

Home Popham and Brownrigg explored the right bank of the Scheldt above Batz. The beach at Sandvliet was not well suited for a landing but there was a possible landing site at a creek a little to the north. This was all in accordance with the longstanding plan but when Chatham and Strachan met with the army's lieutenant generals on 26 August the mood was pessimistic. There were now 'so many difficulties' that Chatham decided to call another meeting with his senior staff on the next day to make a definite decision as to what to do next. The discussion was to focus on a paper drawn up by Brownrigg in which he methodically detailed the progress of the expedition, the strengths of the opposing armies, and possible plans for an attack on Antwerp. He opened by describing the failure to land on Cadsand and the slow reduction of Flushing: 'With these uncontrollable obstacles to contend with, the prospect soon vanished of being able by a rapid and simultaneous effort, to carry the object of the Expedition to its ultimate extent, and which could alone ensure the complete success of the enterprise.' The obstacles referred to by Brownrigg included the weather, the enemy's resort to flooding, and the nature of the ground around Flushing. He then turned to the respective sizes of the two forces.

> The strength of the enemy, by concurring intelligence, appears to be nearly as follows: In Bergen-op-Zoom, 6,000; Breda, 2,000; cantoned between Bergen-op-Zoom and Antwerp, 15,000; In Antwerp, 11,000; On the left bank of the Scheldt, 3,000; In Tholen, 500; Total 37,500.

> Our total number, including artillery, cavalry and infantry, amounts to about 30,000 effectives; of this, 6,000 are left in Walcheren, and 2,000 must necessarily be left in South Beveland, giving a disposable force of only 22,000 men for the siege of Antwerp, and other operations connected with it.

Brownrigg believed that there were two possible ways of approaching Antwerp. The first would be a combined army and navy operation involving the reduction of the forts of Lillo and Liefkenshoek and the investment of the city from both banks of the river. This had the disadvantage of dividing the army; with 8,000 men needed for the guarding of depots, stores and provisions and for escorts and 4,000 for the attack against Liefkenshoek and the occupation of the left bank of the Scheldt, this would leave only 10,000 for the actual siege. The Quartermaster General concluded that although this plan of operations was the best in principle, there were insufficient troops to carry it through. There was a real risk of a relatively small British force being forced to raise the siege and then being defeated in an action with the loss of the ordnance and cavalry. The detached corps on the left bank would be unable to lend any support.

The second plan gave up significant naval cooperation and the occupation of the left bank. Instead, the whole available army would land on the right bank and advance directly on Antwerp. But again there were problems. The failure to control both banks of the river deprived the land force of naval support, there would be the fortress of Bergen-op-Zoom to deal with, and the lines of communication would be vulnerable. As Antwerp would be incompletely invested, it would be possible for the French to reinforce it from the left bank. Brownrigg estimated that the final attack on the city could not be commenced in less than three weeks from the time of landing. This was 'during the most sickly season of the year in a country strictly hostile and incapable of furnishing any supplies whatsoever'. He continued:

Thus the safest and best way of attacking Antwerp far exceeds our means; while the alternative is liable to all the disadvantages of a want of naval cooperation, and an incomplete investment of the place.

He ended with a discussion of the possibility of damaging Antwerp's arsenal and shipping without recourse to a formal siege. A bombardment of the city could be undertaken from the left bank after reduction of the forts of Liefkenshoek and Tête de Flandre. However, this area was flooded and it was unlikely that significant harm would be caused to the sluices and docks that rendered the city such a powerful naval arsenal. The marching of a force with ordnance along the right bank to target the enemy fleet, most of which remained four miles above Antwerp, was judged 'rash and inadvisable'. In the final paragraph, Brownrigg concluded that the ultimate objective of the expedition could not be attempted with any rational hope of success.[1]

The lieutenant generals met at Batz on the 27th as planned. They considered the Quartermaster General's memorandum and also discussed the strength of Antwerp. The defences of the city were understood to be repaired with the major fortifications now in good order, the ditch deepened, guns mounted on the bastions, and batteries constructed on the quays. The forts of Lillo and Liefkenshoek would have to be captured prior to the formal siege of Antwerp leading to a further delay of three to four weeks. During this time, the generals believed, 'the means the enemy will have of augmenting his forces are incalculable'. In contrast, the British force was afflicted by disease and was diminishing. There was only one possible outcome.

The matter, therefore, for consideration, is whether under all the circumstances so stated, it is advisable to undertake operations so serious and extensive? We are under the opinion that, under all the circumstances that have been laid before us, the undertaking of the siege of Antwerp is impracticable.

Strachan responded to this conclusion by asking if it were possible for the army and navy to cooperate in assaulting Lillo and Liefkenshoek. The generals could see 'no possible advantage' arising from such an attack or from any other minor operations. This vital document, signalling the start of the end of the expedition, was signed by Coote, Rosslyn, Huntley, Grosvenor, Hope, Paget and Brownrigg.

Chatham apparently readily accepted this decision by committee, immediately informing Strachan that he also believed attacking the two forts to be futile. An explanatory letter was sent to Castlereagh two days after the meeting. Because of the growing strength of the enemy, the unexpectedly strong state of Antwerp, and increasing sickness in his own army, the Commander in Chief believed it his duty to abandon his original objective.

> It is my intention to withdraw gradually from the advanced position in the island [South Beveland], and sending into Walcheren such an additional force as may be necessary to secure that important possession, to embark the remainder of the troops and to hold them in readiness to await His Majesty's further commands, which I shall most anxiously expect.

Brownrigg wrote to Hope that he believed that the futility of an attack on Antwerp would also be strongly felt at home. 'I trust that Lord Chatham will stand fully justified ... .' Castlereagh made the usual conference with the King and confirmed that Chatham should leave a garrison on Walcheren and return with the rest of his army to England. Chatham was instructed to cooperate fully with Strachan and the navy in taking any measures the admiral thought appropriate to obstruct the navigation of the Scheldt and also to consider the possible destruction of the enemy works at Terneuse.[2]

Whereas the army's senior generals and the Secretary of State for War were resigned to a retreat, Strachan seems to have been less convinced. Certainly, his enthusiasm for an attack on the forts and his correspondence with Chatham and the Admiralty suggest a man in two minds. In a private letter to Chatham, the admiral complains of a lack of provisions for both the navy and the army. He insists that the general report this to the government at once: 'I am sure your Lordship will be of my way of thinking that not a moment should be lost in communicating home.' Strachan then acknowledges that because of this supply problem, the increasing levels of sickness and the growing power of the enemy, there is little to be gained from further operations. Fortescue describes this letter as 'wild' and ascribes it to Strachan's irascible nature and to the fact that he was unwell at the time. 'Altogether, the letter was not such as one gentleman should have written to another.' Parts of the letter are a little intemperate but, judged by modern standards, Fortescue's criticism appears excessive.

A second letter was despatched to the Secretary of the Admiralty in which

Strachan showed no understanding of the army's difficulties and inferred criticism of Chatham. He stressed the 'unqualified' naval support he had offered. The admiral was later forced to admit that he regretted the tone of this letter which he did not think would be published.

It was only a statement of facts; but I might have put it together in such a manner as not to be offensive, for in the way it was worded it appeared like casting a reflection upon Lord Chatham and the principal officers of the army.

Strachan was not tactful and his attempts to distance himself from a decision with which he agreed were clumsy. He later admitted that when he wrote his letter to the Admiralty,

It was with an impression that the country would be very much dissatisfied that more was not done, and I thought it was due to myself and to the Navy, to state to that branch of the government that I was under [the Admiralty] that we were desirous to go on, or that we had taken all the measures necessary to go on.

Strachan's careless correspondence attracted predictable criticism from the army's generals who voiced concerns regarding his character. Brownrigg wrote privately to Hope on 9 September.

The admiral is a man who is least calculated of all others in his profession to have had the direction of the current service. His opinions are as variable as the winds, and without intending harm, for he is good natured in the extreme, he confuses all things and gets into difficulties beyond number – he is now execrating himself for having sent the letter ... He is far from being a strong-minded man and is full of apprehension.

Brownrigg insisted that Chatham still received Strachan with 'cordiality' but the friction between senior officers was not conducive to a good relationship between the services. There were naval mutterings of 'a tribe of generals whose names are scarcely known out of St James's'.[3]

The news of discord in the British high command reached Bernadotte, communicated to him at Antwerp on 30 August by pilots who had served in British ships. The Marshal remained vigilant and had received fresh orders from Napoleon. He was to remain at Antwerp to prevent a British landing on the right bank of the river between the city and Bergen-op-Zoom. While the 'Army of Antwerp' remained entrenched, Moncey's Army of Tête de Flandre was placed so as to be able to reinforce Bernadotte from the left. In support were Marshal Kellerman's forces at Wesel, well situated to attack the British from the rear, and the Army of the Rhine under Marshal Bessières at Lille. The French understood that time was their greatest asset. In de Rocca's words, 'The slowness of our enemies gave us the time and opportunity to reinforce our army and to instruct the recruits that arrived every day.'[4]

British preparations to evacuate South Beveland and the smaller garrisons on Schouwen, North Beveland and Wolversdyle were underway by 28 August. All guns were removed from South Beveland with the exception of those at Batz still needed to cover the evacuation. As the cavalry transports were now unlikely to be required, they were returned to England. While artillery was being dismantled on South Beveland, new guns were established on Walcheren along The Slough and Veere Gat and on St Joostland Island. These were well situated to cover the passage of troops between South Beveland and Walcheren in small boats and across a floating bridge built by the Royal Staff Corps linking St Joostland and Armuyden. It had been estimated that around 19,000 troops were required for the defence of Walcheren. The proposed force under Graham's command was as follows: 1 troop 9th Light Dragoons eighty men; Rottenburg's Brigade 2,000; Alten's Brigade 1,500; Hay's Brigade 2,500; Ackland's Brigade 2,000; Dyott's Brigade 2,353; Brown's Brigade 1,900; Picton's Brigade 2,350. The remaining numbers were made up of detachments of cavalry, artillery and engineers.

Frederick Trench declared that he was 'mostly glad' at the outcome of the generals' meeting; under such a leader he believed little more could be achieved. The troops were weary of the sickness and boredom on South Beveland and surrounding islands and they were relieved at the order to withdraw. Charles Steevens of the 20th expected the French to occupy their old quarters on Wolversdyle, 'and quite welcome they were to them, for we were very glad to quit such an unhealthy country'. His sentiments are in contrast to contemporary memoirs of the Peninsula where every British retreat was related with dismay. Marine Wrangle also expressed the prevailing mood.

> At 12 am [29 August], several transports coming down the river and upon one coming within hail we spoak her and enquired where bound when to our great surprise she answered 'For England'. The expedition is given up. This was delightful information indeed. It sets all hearts rejoicing and we begin to anticipate the pleasing order to weigh.

Chatham moved from Batz to Goes on the 29th and then returned to Middelburg a few days later leaving the final evacuation of South Beveland to Hope. Unsurprisingly, the commander in chief failed to agree with Strachan regarding the correct order of things. The admiral was anxious that the troops remain on South Beveland for another ten days or a fortnight to allow him to execute his brief to destroy the navigation of the Scheldt. Chatham declined, arguing that there were no enemy troops on the island and that Strachan should have the wherewithal to prevent the French from landing artillery. Home Popham tried to play the peacemaker, apologising to Chatham for anything improper in Strachan's correspondence and stressing that his naval superior was only trying to comply with the Admiralty's orders. He was sure that the admiral would also apologise for any offence caused. In the event, Strachan succumbed to pressure and agreed to provide his full support to the immediate evacuation of South Beveland. There was, however, no disguising the rift between the two men. In a letter to the Admiralty of 31 August, Strachan comments with obvious irritation, 'I have to inform you I have not yet heard from Lord Chatham'.[5]

The expedition commander's reluctance to maintain a force on South Beveland was in large part because of the spiralling levels of sickness. On 28 August, the Journal of the Army reported that disease was affecting an 'alarming proportion' of the men. Chatham informed Castlereagh. He believed the total number of sick to be close to 3,000 but this was an underestimate. The Journal of the Army added that the levels of disease 'had now unfortunately far exceeded what could have been speculated upon even by those who best knew the effects of this unhealthy climate'.

The army's doctors were not spared and Webb wrote to Coote warning that their sufferings from disease and over-work were such that it was becoming difficult to provide a proper medical service.

> Under these circumstances of great and evident difficulty, and with the certainty of our wants increasing rapidly, and our means of meeting them diminishing by the sickness of medical officers, I beg to submit to your consideration the absolute necessity of sending expressly to England for medical aid, and of applying that a fast sailing vessel should be appointed to bring out the assistance that is so urgently required.

Those doctors who remained well, George Hargrove among them, held hourly meetings to discuss the relentless tide of disease. A normal rate of sickness for the army in England was around forty cases per thousand men.

In the British force in the Scheldt in the third week of August this figure was sixty-two and by the end of September it had risen to 500. An epidemic of a disease referred to as 'Walcheren Fever' was not only affecting operational decisions but threatening to destroy the army.[6]

Notes

1. Parliamentary Papers 1810, Vol. XV, pp. cccxiv–cccxviii; Journal of the Army, pp. 77–9, TNA, WO 1/190; Enthoven, V., *Een Haven Te Ver*, pp. 309–12; *A Collection of Papers Relating to the Expedition to the Scheldt*, p. 462; Bond, G., *The Grand Expedition*, pp. 117–22; Wheeler, W., *The Letters of Private Wheeler 1809–1828*, pp. 36–7.
2. Journal of the Army, p. 79; Parliamentary Papers, Vol. XV, pp. cccxviii–cccxx, cccxcix, xli–ii, vii; *A Collection of Papers*, pp. 119–20; Castlereagh, Viscount, *Memoirs and Correspondence of Viscount Castlereagh*, Vol. VI, pp. 319–20; NAS, GD364/1/1190.
3. Parliamentary Papers, Vol. XV, pp. 5xlvi, cccc, clii–iii; *A Collection of Papers*, pp. 462–7; NAS, GD364/1/1191; Fortescue, J. W., *A History of the British Army*, Vol. VII, pp. 86–7; *The Walcheren Expedition. The Experiences of a British Officer of the 81st Regiment*, pp. 90, 107; Wrangle, JP, *A Journal of the Walcheren Expedition 1809*, pp. 184–5; McGuffie, TH, *The Walcheren Expedition and the Walcheren Fever*, p. 202.
4. Bond, pp. 118–9; De Rocca, Mr, *Campagne de Walcheren et D'Anvers en 1809*, pp. 112–4.
5. Journal of the Army, pp. 79–87; Fortescue, Vol. VII, pp. 87–8; Squire, J., *A Short Narrative of the Late Campaign of the British Army*, p. 77; Bond, pp. 122–5; Parliamentary papers, Vol. XV, pp. xlii–iii; Enthoven, p. 326; NAM, 1968-07-261: 88; Steevens, C., *With the Old and the Bold 1795–1818*, pp. 66–7; Wrangle, p. 188; *A Collection of Papers*, pp. 467–8.
6. Journal of the Army, p. 80; Marshall, H., *Contribution to Statistics of the Sickness and Mortality which occurred among the troops employed in the expedition to the Scheldt in the year 1809*, pp. 308–15; Castlereagh, Vol. VI, p. 314; *A Collection of Papers*, pp. 133–4; Parliamentary Papers, Vol. XV, p. xlv; Hargrove, G., *An Account of the Islands of Walcheren and South Beveland*, pp. 57–8.

CHAPTER 12

Fever

Soldiers who had recorded their favourable first impressions of Walcheren were now seeing the island in a different light. William Keep was pining for home, informing his mother of the 'wretchedness' of his surroundings. 'What a contrast it formed to the happy spot from which your letter was directed.' He pictured her seated at a cheerful window 'with the balsams and the balmy breezes you was literally inhaling, compared to the vapours that hang over this unfortunate island and doom its Invaders to destruction'.

This sinister aspect of the Scheldt was more quickly perceived by the doctors of the expedition. Perhaps the best description is that penned by the most senior medical man, John Webb.

> Independent of the existing records of unhealthiness of Zealand, every object around us depicts it in the most forcible manner; the bottom of every canal that has communicated with the sea is thickly covered with an ooze, which when the tide is out emits a most offensive and noisome effluvia; every ditch is filled with water which is loaded with animal and vegetable substances in a state of putrefaction; and the whole island [Walcheren] is so flat, and so near the level of the sea, that a large proportion of it is little better than a swamp, and there is scarcely a place where water of a tolerable good quality can be procured.

Webb noted that despite the best efforts of the locals who were scrupulously clean, most appeared pale and listless and that during the sickly season, from about the middle of August to the first frosts, nearly a third were attacked by fever.

If the local population was so affected what was the likely fate of an army? Dutch troops were the best acclimatised but those forces on Walcheren suffered severely. One regiment had arrived on the island three years earlier 800 strong and by the time of the British invasion it had been reduced to eighty-five men. Troops ordered to the Walcheren garrison from Amsterdam took leave of their friends with the same feeling of foreboding as if they were going to the West Indies. A British army sent to the region in 1747 had been largely destroyed by a fever well described by the eminent army doctor, John Pringle.

> In Zealand, the sickness was great among the four battalions which had continued there since the beginning of the campaign. Those men, partly in camp and partly in cantonments, lay in South Beveland and in the island of Walcheren, two districts of that province, and both in the field and in quarters were so very sickly that at the height of the epidemic some of those corps had but 100 men fit for duty: this was only about the seventh part of a complete battalion.

When the army entered winter quarters, there were still four sick men for every man fit for duty. This account was included in Pringle's *Observations on the Diseases of the Army* which remained an important text in the early nineteenth century. Senior army doctors such as Pepys and Keate were familiar with it and neither man was surprised at the outbreak of disease affecting the new expedition. Pepys had actually discussed the subject with Pringle and later declared that the epidemic of disease on Walcheren was entirely predictable. Seasoned military men were also aware of the proverbial sickliness of the region. Good officers were worried about the health of their soldiers. Thomas Picton had expressed concern before the disembarkation from England. He was not alone but Major General Harry Calvert was later to admit that 'The healthiness or unhealthiness of the island of Walcheren certainly had no influence upon [my] opinion one way or the other, it was merely a military question'.

If it was permissible for army men to address purely military matters, it was unclear that the government could legitimately take such a blinkered view. Soldiers on Walcheren presumed that senior politicians were unaware of the risk to which they had been exposed. William Keep wrote home from Flushing on 11 September.

> Had the ministers been informed of the unhealthiness of this place, different means would doubtless have been adopted. It seems extraordinary that they were not, as it is proverbially the place of transport for the Military Delinquents of France, and they sent us here at the very time of the year in which the fever prevails.

Political commentators at home decried this lack of foresight. The expedition was 'the fruit of statistical ignorance in everyone – everywhere from the

Prime Minister to the commander in chief, and from him to the surgeon's mate'. This ignorance could have been immediately dispelled by 'every Middelburghian or any Dutchman'. The government appeared to have had little dialogue with the doctors of the Medical Board. The Physician General had not been consulted regarding the diseases of Holland before the sailing of the expedition, indeed not before 10 September. It is probable that this failure of consultation was not entirely due to ministers' lack of medical knowledge. Castlereagh was cognoscente of the sickliness of the Scheldt. Two years earlier, he had written to Lord Hawkesbury informing him that Walcheren was 'excessively unwholesome' late in the year. According to his latest intelligence, a malignant fever was 'raging' at this time. The precedents were clear for all who wished to see them. Fortescue's assertion that 'no one could have foreseen such an appalling plague' is overly generous.[1]

What was the virulent disease which was first called 'Zealand fever' or 'Flushing sickness' but which came to be known as 'Walcheren fever'? It is difficult to penetrate archaic medical terminology but we can reach some conclusions by reading the descriptions of the disease left by the soldiers who suffered the symptoms and the doctors who treated it. We have a number of accounts of the fever left by men who were lucky to survive. Fortunately, not all believed, as one Scottish soldier, that 'describing the torments of the ague cannot be interesting'. William Keep soon developed the malady.

> The disease comes on with a cold shivering, so great that the patient feels no benefit from the clothes piled upon him in bed, but continues to shiver still, as if enclosed in ice, the teeth chattering and cheeks blanched. This lasts some time and is followed by the opposite extremes of heat, so that the pulse rises to 100 in a small space. The face is then flushed and eyes dilated, but with little thirst. It subsides and then is succeeded by another paroxysm, and so on until the patient's strength is quite reduced and he sinks into the arms of death.

John Dobbs of the 52nd notes that each fit started with a feeling of depression and uneasiness at the same time in the late afternoon. He was attacked every third day. Rifleman Benjamin Harris describes being 'struck with a deadly faintness, shaking all over like an aspen'. His teeth chattered in his head such that he could not hold on to his rifle. Headache was a common symptom and was sometimes severe as related by Captain Henry Light.

> Nothing could describe the agonising pain that fixed itself in my head. I can only compare it to the pressure of a burning iron on the most vital parts, with a sensation as if the burning instrument was

worked round and round in quick succession. My surprise has often
been that I preserved my senses.

Those affected experienced profound debility. Light was confined to his bed
and was too weak to shout for assistance. Private James Todd, of the 71st,
complained that the 'country disorder' took him completely off his feet. The
disease was no respecter of rank. General Thomas Graham was invalided
home: 'I am more helpless than can be imagined'. During an attack, the
peripheries of the body became cold and the nails turned blue or white.
Another common sign was enlargement of the spleen. Benjamin Harris had
to endure a large swelling on the left side of his abdomen and he carried 'an
extra paunch' for many years.[2]

These soldiers' stories give vital clues as to the likely nature of the
affliction but it is necessary to consult contemporary medical writings to gain
a more objective understanding of Walcheren fever. I will follow George
Hargrove who gave a description of the disorder in his sketch of the
expedition.

I shall briefly relate the principal outlines and chief characteristics of
the disease, without engaging in prolix detail, which would both be
unnecessary and irksome to those readers who do not belong to the
medical faculty.

Hargrove gives the best account of the fever, not least because he had the
opportunity to observe it from the outset. Most other medical texts are by
doctors who only encountered the disease in soldiers returned to England.
His description of an acute attack contains much in common with the soldiers'
narratives.

The cases that came under my observation in the first instance were
marked by a surprising degree of debility and lowness of spirits, by
the suddenness of the attack and by an almost instantaneous increase
of the different symptoms. The first case that I was called to of our
regiment was a sentinel on guard at the park of artillery at the village
of Waarde who fell down while at his post of duty and was nearly
deprived of the power of utterance; when I came to the guard room,
I found this poor man writhing in agony, who told me he felt as if his
brain was burning and his bowels twisting round, and in order to
procure a momentary suspension from his sufferings, he was obliged
to bend himself nearly double, he said he was so weak he was certain
he could not survive it long; on examination I found his skin hot and

162

covered with a clammy moisture, his tongue white, his pulse full and quick, his breathing quick and accompanied with a vast deal of anxiety and frequent sighing ... .

When he later attended the hospitals on Walcheren, the doctor noticed some change in the patients. The original 'intermittent and remittent fevers' were now often replaced by a 'low malignant and contagious disease, such as occurs in confined and crowded gaols'. The sufferers were listless and despondent, inclined to constipation, and covered by 'petechiae', small skin haemorrhages. Those who survived the acute attack often developed enlargement of the liver and spleen and a tendency to 'obstinate dysenteric complaints'. This was a chronic relapsing disorder. Hargrove gives several examples of men who first became ill on Walcheren who remained sick for months or even years. Gunners Robert Larkin and Charles Goodie, fit young men, were victims of Walcheren fever and both were still requiring treatment in the spring of 1812. Others became unwell only after their return home. Of 130 members of a light infantry company of the Scots Guards which left England, only forty men marched back into London and all except two subsequently developed a fever.

George Pearson Dawson, a surgeon at the hospital at Ipswich, treated many very sick men returned from the Scheldt. Some developed the disease in England and Dawson's description of an acute attack of fever is very similar to Hargrove's. However, he observed that;

> in many cases, symptoms varied, and would make their appearance under such various circumstances and at such irregular periods as to render description difficult ... A soldier seemingly in good health was admitted into the hospital for a bowel complaint, which was removed in a few hours, next morning he was seized with a severe fit of Ague, and the succeeding day was attacked with fever and delirium.

Dawson admitted that he was perplexed by the symptoms. He emphasises the terrible appearance of the men under his care: 'they seemed as if they had been resuscitated from the grave'. These living skeletons crawled around the hospital. Some expired in agony with convulsions. 'To see soldiers who had fought their country's battles die in this way was horrible.' Others ended their lives more peacefully, dying from 'sheer debility'.

John Bunnell Davis was a temporary physician at Ipswich. In his account, he stresses the presence of both intermittent and continued fevers and the frequency of bowel complaints. Many of his patients died of diarrhoea and dysentery. Davis's particular contribution is his analysis of over forty postmortems. Soldiers dying from the disease had large livers and spleens and ulcerated and inflamed intestines. There was often an excess of fluid (oedema) in the abdomen, lungs and brain.

Military and medical men agreed that not all were equally predisposed to Walcheren fever. Most obviously, there was a difference between the local residents of the Scheldt and foreign soldiers. The French doctor Jean-Baptiste Trésal served at Middelburg and observed the disease at close quarters. Whereas the natives developed a continuous weakening fever, strangers were prone to intermittent fevers which plagued them even after their return home. Not all soldiers were equally affected. British soldiers in the Scheldt believed that they were more likely to contract the disease than their French adversaries or other nationalities.

> Of all the foreigners in the English army, none of them suffer in any proportion to the English. The rot seems amongst us alone; and every ditch, every field, and every street are full of our dying and dead ... We catch colds and fever as if we were so many women ... The French do not suffer one tenth part in the wear and tear of a campaign, whereas a few days' rain or a soaking mist will invalid a whole British army.

Not all British soldiers were equally vulnerable. Thomas St Clair recalls that, during their stay on South Beveland, the men were housed in a large church and the officers were billeted on local families. 'Many of our finest soldiers fell violently ill of that fatal malady. The officers were not such sufferers ... .' Sickness levels were greatest among the rank and file, considerably lower among the drummers and sergeants, and lowest in the commissioned officers. Interestingly, it was noted that British troops who were natives of more mountainous areas were more often affected that those from flatter and wetter districts. There was also a significant difference in the prevalence of disease in the army and navy. As predicted by the people of Middelburg, the sailors fared better than the soldiers, especially when the ships were at least two cable lengths from the shore. There was some sickness on board and the crews at Middelburg suffered more than those off Flushing. A Captain Marryat, then a midshipman on the *Imperieuse* frigate, was invalided home having declared that Walcheren was 'no longer a place for a gentleman'.[3]

Most of the doctors who studied Walcheren fever decided that the multiplicity of symptoms and signs could not be explained by a single disease. There is little doubt that malaria was present. Often referred to by the soldiers as 'ague' and by the doctors as 'intermittent fever', this mosquito-transmitted infection causes a debilitating relapsing fever associated with enlargement of the spleen. Unlike today, malaria was common in both Holland and England in the early nineteenth century. The relative resistance of the British troops from low-lying districts probably indicates that they had developed a degree of immunity to the disease. Many historians have understandably attributed Walcheren fever to malaria alone but there are problems with this hypothesis. The high mortality rate in such a short period is not compatible with the types of malaria known to have been prevalent in the Netherlands at this time. Only the most virulent form, '*falciparum malaria*', could have caused such decimation and this was restricted to the Tropics.

Typhus is a disease which thrives in conditions of overcrowding and deprivation. It has been said that the history of typhus is the history of human misery. Epidemics have long been associated with war. It is caused by *rickettsia*, microorganisms somewhere between bacteria and viruses, and in its epidemic form is transferred from person to person by the human body louse. Characteristic symptoms and signs of typhus include malaise, rigors (shaking fits caused by fever), headache and the appearance of skin petechiae. Fatal cases develop drowsiness and coma, death occurring between five and fourteen days. The disease was seen in the troops returning from Corunna and we can be confident that it was present on Walcheren. When John Webb describes the fever assuming a more serious form, degenerating into 'that species of low fever which often prevails in gaols and other ill-ventilated places in England', he is almost certainly referring to typhus.

Although there is no overwhelming evidence, it is also probable that some of the troops contracted typhoid, another cause of 'continued fever'. This infectious disease is passed from person to person by contaminated water and food. Hargrove refers to the 'unwholesome' drinking water on Walcheren. The troops were ordered to guard fresh water sources but there were few springs in the countryside and the soldiers quenched their thirst with stagnant ditch water. The locals were reluctant to drink the Middelburg water preferring supplies imported from Germany. Complaints of listlessness, furred tongue, and severe headache observed in Walcheren fever sufferers may all have been symptoms of typhoid. The disorder might also have been the cause of the intestinal ulcers seen at autopsy.

To these three infectious diseases, we can add dysentery. This miserable disorder is caused by a variety of bacteria and is characterised by the passage of bloody diarrhoea. In severe cases, there is increasing weakness and dehydration. Dysentery particularly affected men already debilitated by other maladies. It blighted the Corunna campaign and was the cause of more deaths during the Peninsular War than any other single disease. Several doctors describing the disorder in the Scheldt refer directly to dysentery and relate the typical onset of bowel symptoms in sick soldiers.

The available sources suggest that Walcheren fever was not a newly discovered killer disease but a lethal combination of old diseases – malaria, typhus, typhoid and dysentery – acting together in a group of men weakened by previous campaigning and a life of drunkenness and poverty in the lower reaches of society.

The enormity of the epidemic both stunned and demoralised the troops. William Keep informed his father that 'nothing in the East or West Indies can equal the sickness that has prevailed here'. Rifleman Harris was to remember Walcheren as the place where he met the 'worst enemy of all'. The officer of the 81st reported that his healthiest men were no better than 'walking corpses'. 'Everyone wants to be at home, and everyone without disguise begins to express this wish.' In order to preserve some semblance of morale, men who died 'almost by the minute' were buried at night. Military bands no longer played at the funerals. Captain Henry Light saw corpses dumped unceremoniously into pits thirty-feet deep. At Middelburg, the funerals were so frequent that

> a single lantern preceded and brought up the rear of the party, a first, second, then a third, and like the magic glass of Macbeth's witches, half bewildered our senses when the number followed so closely one after the other.

Despite the authorities' best efforts to throw a veil over these depressing scenes, men became panic-stricken. An officer believed that their reaction was part of the malaise: 'Whenever this happens in an army, or indeed in any multitude, the most harmless disease becomes contagious and fatal.'[4]

The desperation of both doctors and soldiers was exacerbated by their failure to understand the causes of the disease or diseases which had struck down the army. The Napoleonic Wars predated by a full century the emergence of the science of microbiology with its insights into the disease-causing organisms found in water and on insects and rodents. Most army doctors held views that were little different from those of the physicians who treated the Black Death in the Middle Ages. They believed that diseases were caused by 'miasma' or 'miasmata', invisible poisons in the air exuded from rotting animal and vegetable material, the soil and standing water. George Hargrove commented that the low-lying Scheldt was full of stagnant marshes 'and the summer and autumnal months are so intensely hot, as to account at once for the miasmata continually evaporating from the surface'. The experienced physician, Gilbert Blane, also thought Walcheren fever to be the result of 'poison from exhalations from the soils' but he admitted that the nature of this poison was entirely unknown. A few army doctors were starting to favour the 'contagion theory' in which disease was somehow passed from person to person. There was, however, little support for this in the medical accounts of Walcheren, most authors emphasising that the fever was not contagious. This was despite the common observation that the disease spread rapidly in overcrowded or poorly ventilated conditions such as prevailed in Flushing.

Beyond these broad theories of disease causation, there were plenty of more specific aetiologies invoked. Assistant Surgeon Robert Rennie believed the unprecedented level of sickness among the troops to be attributable to:

> 1st, the nature of their food; 2ndly, the quality of their liquor; 3rdly, their carelessness and irregularity – especially their indulgence in unripe fruits and tank-water; 4thly, the dampness of their lodging, which was too frequently, though necessarily, in houses or churches, or barns neither dry or well ventilated.

The soldiers were suspicious of the stench arising from the half-extinguished fires in Flushing, the flooding of their lines, and the exhalations from the corpses of the enemy.

On occasion, medical men came close to the truth. There are numerous references to the drinking of stagnant water and it was also noticed that soldiers who were exposed to the night air were more prone to the illness.

> On referring to the return of the sick that came under his charge to England, Mr Jones informed me that he observed one company of the right wing bore no proportion to the others, having only one man ill; and on enquiring into the cause of their exemption from disease, it was found that when the troops entered their cantonments strict orders had been given to prevent their smoking in any of the barns for the fear of accidents from fire. In consequence of this order, it was customary for the men in the evening, after they had thrown off their accoutrements, and many of them part of their dress, to take their pipes and sit under the trees, or rest themselves in other open and exposed situations, where they enjoyed the conversation of their comrades, in some instances probably to a late hour; while the men belonging to the company alluded to, being quartered in a rather

better description of house, were in the habit of smoking their pipes in a large kitchen with the servants of the Dutch family.

George Hargrove noted that those who stood guard in the late evening and early in the morning suffered the most. He thought this because of the 'heavy mists or dews' which were present at these times. The real cause of at least one of the prevalent diseases was seen everywhere by all but not recognised. William Keep complained that his mosquito bites were annoying but they were not as bad as in some of his men whose faces were so swollen that they could hardly see or put their caps on at parade. At night, Keep bound his hands and face in silk handkerchiefs. Others rubbed brandy or oil into their skin to deter the insects. Hargrove agreed that the bites were unpleasant but he thought the mosquitoes little more than a nuisance: 'the buzzing noise they make is more alarming than any harm they inflict.'[5]

Hampered by this lack of understanding of the epidemic which was enveloping them, doctors' and soldiers' efforts to stop its spread were haphazard. Physicians visiting the stricken expedition were quick to give guidance.

The troops should not be oppressed with duty or enjoy less than four nights in bed; on the evening of the nights on which they mount guard, an extra allowance of spirits to each man would be extremely beneficial; and when relieved next morning, a comfortable warm breakfast of strong coffee should be in readiness. The barracks ought to be of the best description, well guarded from cold and damp ... On no account should the ground floors be used as sleeping apartments. The more lofty the buildings the better; for the tenants of the upper stories not only enjoy the best health but when taken ill, have the disease in the mildest form; an instance of which came under our observation when we visited Fort Ramakins.

The author, an Inspector of Hospitals, writes at length also stressing the importance of good quality clothing and shoes and a nutritional diet. This was sensible advice although some details are less convincing: 'the broth [is to be] well spiced with pepper'.

Official advice, issued via the General Orders, included directives not to eat fresh fruit or to drink warm buttermilk, not to lie in the full sun or on damp ground, not to fish in the stagnant ditches, and to boil or to add vinegar to drinking water. Other recommendations were equally well intended but were too late to save the expedition. These included the gradual habituation of soldiers to the climate by reinforcing the garrison outside the sickly season and housing troops in vessels offshore. Physician Adam Neale believed that only radical steps could prevent a future disaster on Walcheren.

> Having felled the trees and removed the hedgerows, the next means to be accomplished is the removal of the shallow watery surfaces exposed to evaporation. This may be accomplished by the expeditious employment of pumps acted upon by powerful steam engines ... .

Soldiers held their own views as to how to stay clear of the fever. Most of these prophylactic regimens involved tobacco and alcohol. Major General Erskine counselled his battalions to drink four glasses of brandy each day – on rising, at breakfast, after dinner and in the evening. Officers congregated in their favourite taverns on the Flushing quay smoking Havana cigars and sipping their medicinal gin and water. Thomas St Clair attributed his escape from 'the horrid ague' to smoking the best local tobacco in a meerschaum pipe.

The attempts to treat Walcheren fever will not be related in detail but a few words on early-nineteenth-century medicine will give some understanding of what the sick soldiers endured. Much of the medical treatment of fever was misguided and harmful. It was designed to remove the impurities that were believed to be present in the blood. The typical 'antiphlogistic' regimen involved the administration of drugs such as laxatives and emetics combined with other treatments including bleeding, blistering and drenching with cold water. Alcohol and tobacco were regarded as panaceas. The following medical account is typical.

> The general plan of treatment at first was to open the body by means of five or six grains of the submuriate of mercury, with an equal quantity of c. ext of colocynth, followed by the senna infusion, and sulphate of magnesia after which the submuriate and antimonial fluid were given every three to four hours in small doses, and continued, either with or without mercurial friction upon the side, according to the state of the patient and the period of the disorder, or until the mouth became slightly affected. The warm bath, fomentations, and blisters to the side were also employed.

The hapless patient, already debilitated by disease, was assailed with a mixture of toxic drugs such as mercury and 'drastic purges'.

In obstinate cases, further measures might include more mercury, the removal of blood with a lancet or cupping glass, and the ingestion of Peruvian bark. The latter drug was widely used on Walcheren and was probably of benefit in malaria. Hargrove describes it as a routine choice for treatment: 'The Peruvian bark, it will be easily imagined, was a favourite medicine and the immense quantities that were hourly required induced us to make up dozens of bottles daily in the form of a strong infusion.' Quinine, extracted from Peruvian bark, remains an important drug in the management of malaria. Its efficacy in the Napoleonic era depended on the exact type of bark used and the dosage.

Many soldiers experimented with their own 'cures'. Some tried a homemade mixture of gunpowder and brandy and others purchased their favoured medicines. According to Harry Ross-Lewin of the 32nd, there was disagreement between the local Walcheren doctors and the British Army medical staff as to the best way to manage the disease.

> The Dutch Physicians were quite adverse to our system of treating the sick and very fairly proposed to take charge of one hundred of the soldiers in hospital and to allow any of our medical men to select an equal number, in order to see which could affect a majority of cures out of their respective list of cases. This offer was rejected; but why remains to be answered.[6]

In early September, the scale of the epidemic and the number of deaths continued to increase. John Webb, soon to fall ill himself, reported that the rapidity with which the disease had spread was 'almost unexampled in the history of any military operations'. At the beginning of the month there were upwards of 5,000 men sick on South Beveland. By the 3rd there were 8,200 and by the 7th just under 11,000, some of whom sailed back to England in transports. A return for 10 September for Walcheren shows that of the 18,870 rank and file and non commissioned officers on the island, almost 7,000 were sick and over 200 had died within the previous week. These official figures may have underestimated the ravages of the fever. On 3 September, the second battalion of the 23rd had 244 men on the sick list and a week later there was not a single man fit for duty. The entire regiment was eventually moved from Middelburg to Flushing in carts.[7]

It was against this melancholy backdrop that the evacuation of South Beveland was completed. All the artillery except some pieces at Goes had been embarked by 2 September. The removal of the sick from the island posed more problems. In the East Scheldt, Keats was reluctant to send his men of war and larger transports beyond the anchorage at Zierikzee because of contrary winds and possible fire from the Dutch batteries on Tholen. Smaller boats were landed at Wemeldinge to carry the men to the larger vessels downriver whilst officers were embarked from the dyke on North Beveland. Getting the men on board was not easy. Benjamin Harris describes the pathetic scenes: 'those who were a trifle better than others crawled to the boats; many supported each other; and many were carried helpless as infants.'

Some sick were ferried across The Slough on the ferry at St Joostland Island. This apparently straightforward escape carried its own hazards. Captain John Ford of the 79th had to rescue invalids abandoned on the beach on South Beveland at low water: 'The tide was flowing fast and these helpless men would all be drowned.' The chaos continued on the other side of the water. The sick of Dillon's brigade were removed from the boats only to be made to wait for wagons to convey them to Middelburg. Those who could walk suffered, in the words of George Bourne, 'a dreadful rainy march'. At Borselen, on the south-west coast of South Beveland, Montresor's brigade with 600 sick were refused accommodation on the men of war which Strachan was determined to keep in active service to cover the retreat. Rear Admiral Otway contrived to find enough transports to get them off the island. He was distressed by what he saw: 'God send us better prospects.' He would soon also fall ill.

By mid-afternoon on 4 September, Hope had supervised the embarkation of the remaining guns and stores and the destruction of magazines. The rearguard descended the Scheldt and within forty-eight hours all British soldiers were on Walcheren or on board ships anchored off Flushing or in the Roompot. The navy remained in control of the Veere Gat and The Slough passage and the West and East Scheldt as far as South Beveland.[8]

With the army in retreat and the navy employed only to protect Walcheren and transport the sick, the role of the expedition's medical services attracted increasing attention both on the scene and at home. The weakness of this medical force has been decribed. The medical staff was not in proportion to the size of the army and some regiments were without surgeons or assistant surgeons. Both Inspector of Hospitals John Webb and Adjutant General Robert Long had put in writing before the expedition's departure their anxiety that the resources of the medical department were inadequate. There were also criticisms of the quality of some parts of the department; men with 'inferior professional qualifications' were allowed to accompany the expedition as dispensers of medicines. On 25 August, only a few days after the first appearance of the disease, the medical staff was reduced to six physicians, eighteen surgeons, three apothecaries and purveyors, and twenty-eight hospital mates. There were, of course, also the regimental doctors of whom there were forty-six surgeons and seventy-five assistant surgeons at this time. Webb was becoming frantic, writing to the Surgeon General Thomas Keate on the 27th to bring the shortage of doctors to his attention. He tried to enlist the help of local Dutch doctors but the language difficulty and their perceived shortcomings meant that they were of limited help.

There is urgency in Castlereagh's letters in early September. He was beginning to understand that his expedition was threatened by a medical catastrophe. On the 2nd, he asks the Army's Commander in Chief David Dundas to ensure that additional medical assistance is sent to Walcheren 'without delay'. He also requests that the Medical Board be consulted as to the likely nature of the prevalent disease and the need for medicines. By the following week, he is demanding immediate steps to provide transports and hospital ships and suggesting a meeting between the Surgeon General and Military Secretary to discuss possible strategies to prevent the spread of the fever. Of the Medical Board members, Surgeon General Keate was the most proactive. He had earlier sent repeated letters to the Agent of Transports requesting hospital ships for the expedition, had fretted at the slow embarkation of medical officers at Deal, and had proposed the employment of London hospital surgeons and their best pupils to manage the sick returning to England. He now tried to raise the sorely needed extra doctors. On 5 September, he was able to inform Webb that two physicians, four staff surgeons, and around twenty other medical officers (probably hospital mates) were making their way to Deal. Keate advised the inspector that he may have to ignore the usual distinctions between the medical specialities. 'In emergencies of duty you do well to avail yourself of the services of every medical officer, whether physician or surgeon, in the way most beneficial to the sick and wounded troops.'

The soldiers were aware of the desperate shortage of medics to care for them. Benjamin Harris saw naval doctors come ashore to assist the regimental surgeons.

[They] had more on their hands than they could manage. Dr Ridgway of the Rifles [Assistant Surgeon Thomas Hughes Ridgway] and his assistant having nearly five hundred patients prostrate at the same moment. In short, except myself and three or four others, the whole concern was completely floored.[9]

The crisis extended to hospital accommodation. At Middelburg there were some suitable buildings including the former French hospital and the spacious warehouses of the Dutch East India Company. These hospitals were crowded but were reported to be well run. Sick officers in Middelburg were instructed

172

to present themselves to the staff surgeon on duty. There was also an airy hospital in a large church at Ter Veere able to accommodate 400 patients and additional general hospitals at Armuyden, Zoutland and Ramakins. The greatest problems were at Flushing where the bombardment had removed the roofs from many of the buildings and the ground floors were mostly flooded and uninhabitable. Workmen were sent from England to repair the damage but they soon fell ill and progress was slow. Sick soldiers were quartered in cold damp churches without beds with only a greatcoat for a blanket and a haversack for a pillow.

Thomas Picton, ill with fever, informed the resident commissioner of the navy on 31 August that there were 800 sick men of different regiments in the town, '600 of whom are lying upon the boards without beds or palliases'. With rare exceptions – for instance, the well-sited and organised Royal Artillery hospital at Flushing – the medical services were overwhelmed. Rudimentary standards of treatment became difficult to maintain. Parades were held at which jugs of bark were passed along the line but these were abandoned when the men were unable to stand. The sick were so widely scattered that the doctors stopped making rounds and instead sat in a 'sort of watch-box' dispensing their medicines. Every morning at Ter Veere, several hundred men crawled out of the general hospital towards the town square where there were hogsheads containing a nauseating mixture of port wine and bark. The dead filled the fields and local labour was employed to dig more graves.[10]

When William Dyott's aide-de-camp, Thurston Dale, was seized by the fever, Dyott decided that his best chance of cure was a quick passage home. The expedition's leaders shared this view and the first sick troops were transported back to England as early as the beginning of September. Castlereagh's directive that Chatham should return with the army excepting the force to garrison Walcheren reached the General on the 10th. He had already anticipated the order, advising Strachan that the crowded state of the ships and the increasing sickness necessitated a prompt return to home shores. 'The smallest delay in [the sick] sailing might be productive, in the opinion of the medical men, of the most fatal consequence.' On 7 September, those troops bound for England sailed away. Some arrangements had been made for the sudden influx of invalids; Leith's and Houston's brigades alone landed nearly 1,100 sick and this pattern was repeated in other battalions. Many were landed at Harwich where the worst cases were admitted to a general hospital, the less ill transported by boat to Ipswich, and the convalescents by wagon to Colchester. Transport ships bringing the sick home were immediately cleared and returned to Walcheren to repatriate more of the rapidly dwindling army.[11]

In a letter of this period, the Surgeon General commends Inspector Webb for his prudent management of the sick and wounded French prisoners. This reminds us that Britain's enemies were not immune to Walcheren fever. There was a history of French suffering in the region. The future Marshal Macdonald commanded on Walcheren in 1794. Five out of every six of his men were struck down by fever and the general was so violently attacked that he had to return to France to recover. When he visited the Scheldt the following year his illness relapsed. In 1809, Captain James Hope was informed by the locals in Middelburg that the French suffered just as much as the British. Thomas Picton believed that the French garrison in Flushing had lost 1,000 men during the previous year and that it was commonplace for two thirds of their force to be in hospital. Others reported that Monnet had lost half his garrison, around 1,500 men, after an unusually wet autumn. The 1809 returns for the French military hospitals at Middelburg and Ter Veere show 724 deaths in just over ten months.

French forces in the Scheldt continued to lose considerable numbers to disease even after their displacement from Walcheren. Many of the National Guards raised by Fouché were soon occupying the hospitals of Antwerp, Malines (Mechelen) and Brussels. On 7 September, Bernadotte reported 'frightening' levels of sickness. The daily admission of 250 men into the hospitals was damaging morale and encouraging desertion. Louis reminded his brother that his army was greatly depleted. By the end of the month, there were 13,000 French soldiers in hospital in the vicinity of Antwerp and the Dutch forces were at half-strength. William Keep voiced the common view of soldiers of both armies.

> How many brave fellows have resigned their breath in this destitute island? The French may very well call it The Tomb, for to such of that nation as have been sent here the grave was prepared.[12]

French officers tried to protect their charges from fever by adding Dutch gin and vinegar to their wine rations. Monnet advised that the garrison on Walcheren should be static in order to allow habituation to the air. He quoted the case of a French Regiment which suffered during its second year on the island only half the sickness and mortality it had endured during the first, and which was affected hardly at all in the third year.

Napoleon preferred to send troops to unhealthy areas at the last possible moment to limit their exposure. The Emperor had predicted that the British would perish in the Scheldt. There are numerous references to the dangers of the region in his correspondence of August and September, 1809. On 9 August, to Clarke: 'Fever and flooding will deal with the English ... They will lose two months in front of Flushing; the fever and flooding will do the rest'. A week later, he reassures Fouché:

> Before six months, of 15,000 English on the island of Walcheren there will remain only 1,500, the rest will be in the hospitals ... They will not defend the island of Walcheren ... If it is necessary for them to have 20,000 men to guard it, they will lose 10,000 from fever and we will be able to retake it when we want.

On the 18th, he reminds the Minister of War in Paris that Walcheren is defended by 'fever and bad air'. For every extra month Britain remained in the Scheldt, he calculated that a third or even half of her army would fall sick. Napoleon was capable of sacrificing enormous numbers of men in ill-prepared schemes of dubious military merit. He did, however, have more understanding of disease than his enemies.[13]

Notes

1. Parliamentary Papers 1810, Vol. XV, pp. xi, cxxx, cvii, clvii; Keep, W., *In the Service of the King*, pp. 57, 61; Marshall, H., *Contribution to the Statistics of the Sickness and Mortality which occurred among the troops employed on the expedition to the Scheldt in the year 1809*, pp. 315, 326; Pringle, J., *Observations on the Diseases of the Army*, pp. 57–8; Dawson, G. P., *Observations of the Walcheren Diseases*, p. 2; Havard, R., *Wellington's Welsh General*, p. 97; Castlereagh, Viscount, *Memoirs and Correspondence of Viscount Castlereagh*, Vol. VI, pp. 189, 338; Fortescue, J. W., *A History of the British Army*, Vol. VII, p. 92.
2. *Vicissitudes of a Scottish Soldier*, pp. 99–100; Keep, pp. 59–60; Harris, B., *Recollections of Rifleman Harris*, pp. 75–6; Light, Capt H., *The Expedition to Walcheren 1809*, pp. 38–9; *Soldier of the Seventy-First*, pp. 44–5; Dobbs, Capt J., *Recollections of an Old 52nd Man*, pp. 16–7; Aspinall-Oglander, C., *Freshly Remembered. The Story of Thomas Graham Lord Lynedoch*, p. 202.
3. Hargrove, G., *An Account of the Islands of Walcheren and South Beveland*, pp. 54, 77–9, 94, 99–100; Dawson, pp. 8, 20–4, 48–9; Davis, J. B., *A Scientific and Popular Account of the Fever of Walcheren*, p. 180; Castlereagh, Vol. VI, pp. 338–46; Blane, G., *Facts and Observations respecting Intermittent Fevers*, pp. 2–3, 8–9; Borland, J., Lempriere, W., Blane, G., *Report on the prevailing malady among His Majesty's Forces serving in the Island of Walcheren*, pp. 183–4; Feibel, R. M., *What Happened at Walcheren: The Primary Medical Sources*, pp. 64–7; Parliamentary Papers, Vol. XV, p. xii; *The Walcheren Expedition. The Experiences of a British Officer of the 81st Regiment*, pp. 125, 133–4; St Clair, Lt Col T., *A*

soldier's recollections of the West Indies and America with a narrative of the expedition to the Island of Walcheren, Vol. II, pp. 360−1; Marshall, pp. 314−20; Brett-James, A., *The Walcheren Failure*, p. 63; Lloyd, C., Coulter, J. L. S., *Medicine and the Navy 1200−1900*, Vol. III, p. 175.

4. Howard, M. R., *Walcheren 1809: A Medical Catastrophe*; Howard, M., *Wellington's Doctors*, pp. 155−93; Howard, M. R., *Medical Aspects of Sir John Moore's Corunna Campaign 1808−1809*; Feibel, pp. 64−7; Kempthorne, G. A., *The Walcheren Expedition and the Reform of the Medical Board 1809*, p. 135; Cantlie, N., *A History of the Army Medical Department*, Vol. I, pp. 403−4; General Orders for the Army 11 Aug, TNA, WO 28/352; Keep, pp. 64−5; Harris, p. 187; *The Walcheren Expedition*, pp. 109, 124, 136; Light, pp. 24−5; McGuffie, T. H., *The Walcheren Expedition and the Walcheren Fever*, p. 196.

5. Howard, *Wellington's Doctors*, pp. 182−3; Hargrove, pp. 63, 81, 70; Blane, pp. 16−19; *The Walcheren Expedition*, p. 135; Castlereagh, Vol. VI, pp. 339−42; Dawson, pp. 8, 13; Borland, p. 184; Marshall, p. 308; Fellowes, J., *Observations on the Remitting and Intermittent Fever*, p. 343; Keep, p. 51; NAS, GD45/14/540.

6. Borland, pp. 185−7; Blane, pp. 6−7; Enthoven, V., *Een Haven Te Ver*, pp. 330−1; Castlereagh, Vol. VI, pp. 40−6; Hargrove, pp. 83−95; General Orders for the Army 31 Aug; Brett-James, p. 62; McGuffie, p. 196; St Clair, Vol. II, p. 299; Howard, *Wellington's Doctors*, pp. 162−6; Dawson, p. 9; Fellowes, p. 363; *Vicissitudes*, pp. 105−6; Gunn, J., *The Memoirs of Private James Gunn*, pp. 104−5; Ross-Lewin, H., *With the Thirty-Second in the Peninsula and other Campaigns*, pp. 136−7.

7. Parliamentary Papers, Vol. XV, p. xii; Blane, p. 12; Marshall, p. 309; Journal of the Army, pp. 87−8, TNA, WO 1/190; Graves, D. E., *Dragon Rampant*, p. 105; McGuffie, p. 197.

8. Journal of the Army, pp. 87−9; Bond, G., *The Grand Expedition*, pp. 126−7; Fortescue, Vol. VII, pp. 87−8; Harris, pp. 174−5; Ford, Capt J., *Flushing*, p. 111; Bourne, G., *My Military Career*, pp. 59−60; Brett-James, p. 64.

9. *A Collection of Papers Relating to the Expedition to the Scheldt*, pp. 583−90; TNA, WO 17/249; Cantlie, Vol. I, pp. 396−9; McGuffie, pp. 194−5; Parliamentary Papers, Vol. XV, p. cccclxxv; Harris, p. 174.

10. Cantlie, Vol. I, p. 399; Brett-James, pp. 63−4; Dyott, W., *Dyott's Diary 1781−1845*, Vol. I, p. 286; Blane, p. 3; General Orders for the Army Sept 5; Marshall, p. 307; Parliamentary Papers, Vol. XV, p. cccclxxiii; McGuffie, pp. 196−7.

11. Parliamentary Papers, Vol. XV, p. ccclxxv; *A Collection of Papers*, pp. 122−3, 598; Dyott, Vol. I, p. 286; Castlereagh, Vol. VI, p. 321; McGuffie, p. 197; Fortescue, Vol. VII, p. 88; Marshall, p. 309; Kempthorne, p. 136.

12. Parliamentary Papers, Vol. XV, p. ccclxxvi; Macdonald, Marshal, *Recollections of Marshal Macdonald*, pp. 47−8; McGuffie, p. 195; Havard, R., *Wellington's Welsh General*, p. 106; NAS, GD364/1/1191; ZA, Het Archief van de Econoom van de France Militaire Hospitalen in Middelburg en Veere 1799−1814, 4−5, Registre des Morts 1808−1809; Fleischman, T., *L'Expedition Anglaise sur le Continent en 1809*, pp. 62−3; Pawly, R., *Le Walcheren des Français*, pp. 26−8; Keep, p. 65.

13. Blane, pp. 9−10; Pawly, p. 26; Fleischman, p. 63; *Correspondance de Napoléon Ier*, Vol. 19, pp. 322−3, 360, 40; Howard, M., *Napoleon's Doctors*, p. 67.

CHAPTER 13

An Unexpected Calamity

The Emperor received the news of the British retreat from the telegraph at Strasbourg on 7 September. He wrote to the Comte de Champagny that he believed the expedition to be effectively at an end. De Rocca and his comrades were shocked at this sudden turn in events.

> The enemy, to our great astonishment, still attempted nothing. We saw the number of their ships diminish every day. At first we thought they were making for Holland to attack the towns of Willemstadt and Helvoet-Sluys; then we believed that the Island of Cadsand was threatened by an immediate attack and we prepared to send help unable to convince ourselves that the English had abandoned their plan of bombarding Antwerp.

Perhaps the British were trying to confuse the French, tempting them to disperse their forces. However, by 30 August, there were no more than sixty ships in front of Batz and four days later there was hardly a vessel in sight. It seemed that the enemy was now content to retain Walcheren. From Cadsand, on 9 September, General Rousseau informed the Minister of War of the passage of a large British fleet of ships of the line, frigates and transports down the West Scheldt. Only a few days earlier he had expected to be attacked but now he was confident that the enemy was in retreat: 'I am in no doubt that this is the end of the English Expedition.'

In Antwerp, the police reported the city to be as quiet as in peace-time. Maritime Prefect Malouet echoed the sense of relief: 'The enemy has gone away. I don't know where.' Most of the population applauded the British retreat, no doubt relieved that that their city had been spared the miseries inflicted on Flushing. Many French officers believed that they had been saved only by the enemy's incompetence. Pelet was among them.

> If the English had advanced rapidly, either through South Beveland on Lillo and Antwerp or with their fleet pursuing ours, they would have found the forces and defences of the Scheldt unprepared. There

is every reason to think that at this moment they could have destroyed our fleet and burnt our shipyards.[1]

When the expected attack failed to materialise, Bernadotte was at first suspicious that the British were temporising, adopting a new strategy of threatening his forces at several points. He had warned General Moncey at Ghent of the enemy movements downriver. However, these fears were short-lived and, on 1 September, the Marshal issued a triumphant Order of the Day to his army.

Soldats

It is ten days since a formidable expedition reached Batz; the enemy made no secret of his plans ... Six hundred ships and 40,000 men threatened Antwerp, its fleet, its shipyards, all the works conceived by the genius of the Great Napoleon. Uncertain of defeating you with normal arms, the enemy combined against you a thousand tools of destruction. You are saved! When I counted 15,000 of you, I placed you at the point of honour. The enemy has vainly attacked Vieux-Doel and Frédéric-Henri ... Frustrated in his hopes, he leaves today and believes he will find easier pickings on other shores ... Soldats! You have fought little, but the gains you have made are incalculable; the shores of the Scheldt will attest for centuries that gigantic force can fail in the face of energy, devotion and valour.

Louis was also asserting himself, writing to Napoleon from Haarlem on September 6 vigorously defending his own actions and criticising the Emperor's behaviour: 'in treating me as if I was a traitor, you dishonour your family, the kings of your dynasty and your name.' A couple of days later, the King was corresponding with his brother again, confirming the British retreat to Walcheren but now in a more characteristic vein.

I have written several times to your Majesty without any response since his letter of August 5. I have written always through Monsieur Lavalette [Postmaster General]. I sent a courier, Sire, because I have great need of reassuring and encouraging news from Your Majesty. He can have no idea of my difficulties and worries in such a moment.

Louis complained that his army was sick and fretted over rumours of Napoleon's ill health before expressing his concern that the English might attack other parts of Holland. The Emperor's response to this tirade of gratuitous self-justification, criticism and supplication was brutal.

AN UNEXPECTED CALAMITY

I received your letter of the 8th at Brunn. You tell me of a great action that the Dutch have made to retake Batz; this is ridiculous. The English have evacuated Batz, as they will evacuate Flushing, because of disease.

Louis's management of his realm and his defence of the Scheldt was lambasted and he was warned to shut up. 'I repeat that my wish is that you should not speak of me directly or indirectly in your harangues.'[2]

The reoccupation of South Beveland commenced on 4 September after a French flotilla found Batz to be abandoned. It was a matter of honour for the Dutch that they should recapture the fort before the French. The only way this could be achieved quickly was to ford the treacherous Bergen-op-Zoom channel. This operation was entrusted to General Cort Heyligers who was to attempt the transit to South Beveland with carabinier and voltigeur companies of the *3ᵉ Régiment de chasseurs à pied*. Marshal Dumonceau, in overall command of the Dutch forces, arrived at 3pm to supervise the crossing which is best described in the journal of Captain of Carabiniers Schuurman.

> Without a guide and with the river's unknown channels and depths, the danger of the enterprise was obvious. After dragging the water and the mud for several hours, a navigable place [Kreekerak] was found. This place and the fort of Batz were very difficult to see with the naked eye. When they started to cross the Kreekerak a violent storm erupted. The rain made the shore invisible to our troops and the rising tide was such that the men had water up to the chest! The weakest were helped by their comrades. Some men, holding their *giberne* and rifle over their heads, were sent in skirmishing order to position themselves more quickly.

A Lieutenant Wolf van Westerveld finally found the way across. Submerged in water above his shoulders, he cried out, 'Ici! Ici!' Schuurman continues:

> fortunately, we had reached the other side of the channel. Because the tide was rising more and more, we had had to hurry to avoid being cut off from dry land. As the shore by the fort of Batz was invisible we advanced by guesswork! Just after the storm, we finally saw the dyke of the Island of South Beveland. At 7 o'clock in the evening, the Dutch flag flew over the fort of Batz without a shot fired and without the loss of a man.

Despite the lack of bloodshed, or indeed of fighting, Louis created a special medal which was later awarded to nineteen officers and 125 men.

On the 5th, Dumonceau ordered the occupation of the remainder of the island, more troops being shipped across from Bergen-op-Zoom. The only event of note occurred when Cort Heyliger's advanced forces encountered a small British detachment at the village of Ellewoutsdijk; they were pursued to Borselen where they were made prisoners of war. The British soldiers informed their Dutch captors that their ships had retired to Flushing and that Walcheren had been reinforced with artillery. By the middle of the month, more than 4,000 Dutch troops occupied South Beveland. Napoleon placed the force under French leadership and Dumonceau was recalled to Amsterdam by King Louis.[3]

The French were receiving reports of low British morale. Bernadotte informed Clarke that a spy had revealed to him that the enemy were dispirited.

This agent, a pilot, has heard that the English generals and officers complain that the expedition to Antwerp has been so badly conducted that they deserve to be scorned by people in England if they attempt nothing against the coast or elsewhere before returning home.

The journals and diaries of British soldiers confirm this growing malaise. William Keep apologises to his mother for writing to her 'in such a tone of despondency'. He lived in the hope of being back in England before Christmas. Senior officers were also expressing frustration and despair; Thomas Picton thought he was employed in 'the most costly and disgraceful enterprise which the country was ever seduced into by Empirical Politicians'. Captain Henry Light believed that many of the men looked forward to falling ill. Once on the sick list, there was a chance of being sent home or being accommodated under a roof in a hospital. 'Never was an army so neglected – every person's efforts seemed paralysed – there was but one feeling, 'surely we shall soon be sent away from the charnel house'.'[4]

The fever continued its relentless harvest of men. By the end of September, there were 9,299 sick in a total force of 16,904 on Walcheren. In the week up to the 24th, the effective force of the army was reduced from 9,269 to 7,655; in just seven days, one in every six men had become unfit for duty. Death rates were approaching 300 per week. This mortality was not evenly spread. That part of the army left to garrison Walcheren suffered twice as badly as the men returning to England early in the month. The cavalry, much of which had not been landed from the transports, was relatively spared. Available sick rates confirm the differences between the ranks. The men ran more than double the chance of contracting disease than their officers and, once affected, were three times more likely to die. A similar discrepancy was seen in the Peninsula. Deputy Inspector of Hospitals Francis Burrows agreed with the popular view that the British soldier was particularly vulnerable to the fever. He was unsure whether this because he was more exposed to the causes or due to a 'peculiarity of constitution'. On 18 September, he reported from Middelburg the 'lamentable fact' that more than half the army was in hospital. This was despite good weather and the sickly season being so little advanced.[5]

Burrows complained of the shortage of medical staff and of the wretched state of the hospitals. Many of the doctors were themselves falling ill. John Webb had to return home. The correspondence of the army's senior officers contains repeated pleas for more physicians, staff surgeons and hospital mates. There were only twenty-eight medical staff doctors and forty-nine regimental surgeons on Walcheren. In England, Castlereagh was aware of the problem but there was no simple solution as he explained to Coote on 24 September.

> When you consider the number of medical assistants already sent to Walcheren and reflect upon the previous necessity of succouring the demands for aid to the wounded in Spain, you must feel how extensively difficult, if not impossible, it must be to provide an adequate supply for a calamity so sudden and so extensive.

Doctors as yet unaffected by the fever were exhausted by their duties. One medical witness claimed that the sick were 'thrice as numerous as it was possible for them to attend'. In general, the medical men, particularly the regimental surgeons and the regular officers of the staff, showed devotion and competency. Conversely, some of the temporary physicians sent out from England were hopelessly inexperienced in army medicine and many of the temporary hospital mates could barely read or write a prescription.

Visitors to the hospitals on Walcheren were horrified. William Dyott accompanied Coote on a tour of the hospitals in mid-September.

> I don't suppose it ever fell to the lot of a British officer to visit in the course of three days the sick chambers of nearly 8,000 unfortunate men in fevers; and the miserable, dirty, stinking holes some of the troops were from necessity crammed into, was more shocking than it is possible to express.

In Middelburg, where the hospital accommodation was at its best, Dyott was distressed by the state of the wards. In Flushing, large buildings were at a premium and many sick had to make do with the remains of the local dwellings: 'In one house, I found fifteen men belonging to the 5th Regiment in a room scarce twelve feet square and with twelve of the men sick, and nothing but a couple of blankets to lie down upon.' When John Green was admitted to the general hospital in the church at Ter Veere, he had to step over two corpses lying at the entrance, 'a sight that made me so sick and ill that I thought I should have fainted.'

The normal distinction between the smaller regimental hospitals and larger general hospitals was probably blurred but it seems that most of the sick were housed in the smaller facilities, often houses and farms, where they were tended by their own regimental surgeons. A return for 10–16 September shows 6,375 men in the regimental hospitals and only 769 in the general hospitals. Around 500 sick were accommodated on the two official hospital ships, the *Asia* and *Bulliver*, moored off Ramakins as convalescent vessels.

Supplying the hospitals was another headache for the military authorities. Medicines and bedding were particular problems. The resident naval commissioner stumbled upon sick men deprived of any drugs for four days and sleeping on boards in their greatcoats. Medical necessities such as wine and other comforts had not arrived from England and had to be purchased locally at exorbitant prices. Assistant Surgeon Hargrove struggled to find enough bark to treat his fever cases but it is not clear that this actually ran out.[6]

It fell to the Medical Board in London to try and bring some order to the deteriorating medical situation. At least, this was the view of senior army officers. Dundas had wanted one of the three members to visit the Scheldt as early as 8 August but this never happened. The Inspector General of Hospitals, Francis Knight, replied that he and the Surgeon General, Thomas Keate, believed that the duties required were 'purely medical' and therefore more appropriately performed by the Physician General. Keate added that he was overwhelmed by the task of providing for all the sick arriving from both Holland and Portugal. The Physician General, Lucas Pepys, also keen to remain at home, provided several reasons why he was unable to visit the army on campaign. He was busy inspecting army hospitals and examining hospital mates, he was nearly seventy years old and unwell and, most remarkably, he 'knew nothing of the investigation of Camps and Contagious diseases'. Pepys concluded that 'no possible good' could arise from his attendance and that the Inspector General of Hospitals was the proper individual to be sent to Walcheren.[7]

Frustrated by the ineptitude of the Board, the government made the fortunate decision to replace the infirm Webb with James McGrigor. The new Inspector of Hospitals took charge of the medical department at Middelburg on 9 September as his predecessor was carried to a ship delirious with fever. McGrigor, thirty-seven years old, had served his time as a regimental surgeon and had experience of active service in India and Egypt. As director of military hospitals in the southern division of England, he had managed the sick returned from the Corunna campaign. He was widely recognised as a skilful physician and able administrator and he was later to become Wellington's valued Surgeon General in the Peninsula. No previous experience could have inured him to what he now saw.

> The number of sick was immense, that of the wounded officers and men ... was considerable, and both together, most unhappily, nearly equalled that of the men in health ... the amount of sickness at Walcheren was great beyond all comparison with that which I had hitherto witnessed.

McGrigor made an inspection of the hospitals and confirmed the lack of staff and supplies. The desperate shortage of bark was fortuitously solved by the arrival of an American vessel laden with the precious drug at Flushing. To address the under-manning, McGrigor tried variously to enlist the services of captured French medical officers, navy surgeons, Dutch civilians, and British army pensioners from England. He received support from his military superiors but had a difficult relationship with the complacent Medical Board, at one point admonishing Keate, 'I unfortunately cannot give in to your opinions ... The inhumanity of this business...if there has been any, does not lie on this side of the water.'

A second highly-respected physician arrived at Walcheren on 30 September. To substitute for the stay at home members of the Board, the government appointed three medical commissioners, the foremost of whom was Sir Gilbert Blane, now a civilian but with former service in the navy. For reasons that are obscure, Blane arrived on the island a week before his physician colleagues and made his own researches on Walcheren fever, reporting to Pepys. It is possible that the Physician General encouraged Blane's enthusiasm, keen to redeem his own absenteeism by passing on this new information to the Secretary for War. When the two army doctors, Borland and Lempriere, arrived, they collaborated with Blane in writing the official report. Most of their suggestions were commonsensical and related to improvements in the soldiers' accommodation, clothing and diet. They urged that all those unfit for service should be removed immediately to

England but they stopped short of implying a full-scale evacuation.

> We presume to recommend to His Majesty's Government, in case the retention of this island should be determined on, to reinforce the garrison very early in the winter (say November) in order that the constitution of the men in some degree be habituated to the climate before the return of the sickly season.[8]

In fact, there had already been a further substantial transfer of sick from Walcheren to England during the second half of September. Forty transports were employed, the round trip taking about a fortnight. On 11 September, Keate calculated that upwards of 2,000 sick had already arrived in the Downs. Another 1,300 were embarked on Walcheren between the 14th and 29th of the month; the total number of sick and convalescents shipped to England by the end of November was probably close to 13,000.

Conditions on board the transports were often even worse than in the hospitals. Many ships carried a number of sick greater than the number of crew for which they were designed. Medical attention was uncertain, the doctors well enough to perform their duties having been left on Walcheren. The suffering was compounded by delays in departure. John Green complained that his transport lay at anchor for three days. Thomas St Clair was trapped on a 'miserable collier brig' off Ramakins for four days: 'Only half of our officers and men could be permitted to go below at the same time as there was not space sufficient to breathe in.' Such circumstances were a trial for healthy soldiers who were soon rendered 'motionless and inanimate'. It was common for the sick to die in transit. George Hargrove had eighty ill troops in his care, most of whom were brought to the ship directly from their beds. The voyage was prolonged by contrary winds and he lost four of his charges. The dead were sewn into hammocks and consigned to the sea from a wooden platform.[9]

Adverse winds delayed Chatham's departure until 2pm on 14 September. William Dyott imagined that the general must have been despondent, 'as the newspapers had been most liberal in their abuse of him'. The force left to garrison Walcheren, depleted to half its nominal strength of 16,766 men by disease, was now under the brittle command of Sir Eyre Coote. He was not helped by the government, who pestered him with endless requests for reports regarding commerce, exports, and the complaints of Flushing's citizens who remained suspicious of the British. Ministers went so far as to demand a census of the island's population and livestock. The general later claimed that when he replaced Chatham he had been given no instructions except to remain on Walcheren in command of the troops.[10]

The vital question to which Coote urgently required an answer was whether the British Army was likely to remain on the island for a significant period of time. Was there a plan to evacuate the island and, if so, when? The decision was influenced by events in Vienna. Austria's peace negotiations with France were continuing and until an agreement was reached, the government was inclined to hold on to Walcheren to use it as a bargaining tool or as a possible stepping stone for future operations on the continent. Austrian diplomats urged ministers to retain the hard-won island in the Scheldt. There was, however, some insight into the deteriorating situation on Walcheren. The Secretary for War informed the King on 19 September that 'an early decision upon the expediency and practicability of keeping that island [Walcheren] does appear to be of essential importance.'

Castlereagh also understood that the shrinking British force was under increasing threat of enemy attack, admitting this in a letter to Coote. The necessary means to defend Walcheren had already been summarised in a report prepared by Robert Brownrigg. The Quartermaster General assessed the island particularly vulnerable to attack on the coast facing North and South Beveland. Allowing for the ruined state of the fortifications and the increasing sickness, there was a need for a force of 14,000 men and for the local inhabitants to help restore the various works. Of this military force, around 10,000 would be required to garrison Flushing, Middelburg, Ramakins and Ter Haak and the remainder would be posted around the island and on St Joostland.

> We must prevent, if possible, his [the enemy] obtaining a footing in the island, for if he effects this, it will assuredly be the advanced guard to a very large force, against which it cannot reasonably be supposed that Flushing and the smaller garrisons can long hold out.

Brownrigg stressed that a defence would only be tenable with the full cooperation of the navy. Strachan was keen to keep Walcheren, regarding it as a vital naval station and trading post. He was not deterred by the disease afflicting the army, writing on 15 September:

> I do not apprehend it as more unhealthy than any of the low Parts of Kent; but the troops being at present generally infected, owing to the nature of the service to which they have been exposed, it may be proper they should be withdrawn and replaced with other Regiments.

Coote took a more cautious view. He calculated that the length of Walcheren's coast was such that it could not be guarded with less than 20,000 men. Flushing's defences were weak and would require much time and expense to be put back in a proper state. As winter set in, the ships of war would not be able to remain at sea or even in the surrounding channels. His assessment, given to Chatham just before the latter's departure, was that Walcheren was very vulnerable. Ministers would make the final decision but Coote felt obliged to point out that 'The advantages must indeed be great that can compensate the loss of lives and treasure which the retention must necessarily occasion'. Other senior officers agreed. Thomas Picton thought any attempt to hold on to Walcheren would be 'a mixture of madness and folly'. The officer of the 81st comments that 'it is the general opinion of the military that the French can retake this island whenever they may deem it advisable to send an army of thirty thousand men against it.'

In the last days of September, Coote was becoming desperate. On the 23rd, he warned Castlereagh that if the disease continued its relentless progress, then the possession of Walcheren would be 'precarious' within three weeks. He feared that the English newspapers would leak his perilous situation to the enemy and that an attack would soon follow. Individual regiments were disintegrating. The 23rd had suffered to an extent that it had been sent home and the 6th and 81st had been struck off the duty list. The 77th, 84th and several other corps were hardly any better. Six days later, the Secretary for War was informed that it was 'almost impossible to provide an adequate and immediate supply of medical assistance for the sudden and unexpected calamity which has fallen upon this army'. Coote's concerns now ran deeper than the security of the Scheldt. 'Something must be done,' he wrote to Chatham, 'or the British nation will lose the British army – far more valuable than the island of Walcheren.'[11]

Notes

1. *Correspondance de Napoléon Ier*, Vol. 19, p. 440; Fleischman, T., *L'Expedition Anglaise sur le Continent en 1809*;. pp. 86–7; De Rocca, *Campagne de Walcheren et D'Anvers en 1809*, p. 114; Fischer, A., *Napoléon et Anvers*, pp. 172–3; Pelet, Général, *Mémoires sur la Guerre de 1809*, Vol. IV, p. 319.
2. Fischer, p. 171; Bond, G., *The Grand Expedition*, p. 128; Fleischman, pp. 87–8; Rocquain, F., *Napoléon Ier et le Roi Louis*, pp. 213–6; Lecestre, L., *Lettres Inédites de Napoléon Ier*, Vol. I, pp. 364–6.
3. Wink, M., *Le Walcheren des Hollandais*, pp. 32–5; d'Hastrel, Général Baron, *Mémoires (1766–1825)*, p. 143.
4. Fleischman, p. 87; Keep, W, *In the Service of the King*, p. 62; Havard, R., *Wellington's Welsh General*, p. 107; Light, Capt H., *The Expedition to Walcheren 1809*, p. 35.

5. Blane, G., *Facts and Observations respecting Intermittent Fevers*, pp. 12–15; Marshall, H., *Contribution to Statistics of the Sickness and Mortality which occurred among the troops employed on the expedition to the Scheldt in the year 1809*, pp. 317–8; Hodge, W. B., *On the Mortality arising from Military Operations*, p. 270; Edmonds, T. R., *On the Mortality and Sickness of Soldiers engaged in War*, pp. 143–5; *A Collection of Papers Relating to the Expedition to the Scheldt*, pp. 143–4.

6. *A Collection of Papers*, pp. 143–8; Parliamentary Papers 1810, Vol. XV, pp. xlvi, liii, 6xxxi–v; ccccxv; TNA, WO 17/249; Castlereagh, Viscount, *Memoirs and Correspondence of Viscount Castlereagh*, Vol. VI, pp. 399–404; Faulkner, A. B., *Considerations respecting the expediency of establishing an hospital for Officers on Foreign Service*, p. ii; McGuffie, T. H., *The Walcheren Expedition and the Walcheren Fever*, pp. 194–9; Dyott, W., *Dyott's Diary 1781–1845*, Vol. I, pp. 285–8; Hargrove, W., *An Account of the Islands of Walcheren and South Beveland*, pp. 87–8.

7. Blanco, R. L., *Wellington's Surgeon General Sir James McGrigor*, pp. 104–5; Chaplin, A., *Medicine in England during the Reign of George III*, pp. 94–5; Cantlie, N., *A History of the Army Medical Department*, Vol. I, pp. 399–400; Crowe, K. E., *The Walcheren Expedition and the New Army Medical Board*, pp. 770–1.

8. Howard, M., *Wellington's Doctors*, pp. 84–5; McGrigor, J., *The Scalpel and the Sword*, pp. 158–60; Blanco, pp. 107–8; Borland, J., Lempriere, W, Blane, G., *Report on the Prevailing Malady among His Majesty's Forces serving in the Island of Walcheren*, pp. 185–7; Chaplin, pp. 97–8; Cantlie, Vol. I, p. 400; Blane, p. 2.

9. McGuffie, pp. 191–9; *A Collection of Papers*, pp. 61, 609–11, 629; Marshall, pp. 316–7; Parliamentary Papers, Vol. XV, p. 5lxxx; Green, W., *The Vicissitudes of a Soldier's Life*, p. 41; St Clair, Lt Col T., *A soldier's recollections of the West Indies and America with a narrative of the expedition to the Island of Walcheren*, Vol. II, pp. 354–5; Hargrove, pp. 107, 151; *The Walcheren Expedition, The Experiences of a British Officer of the 81st Regiment*, p. 133.

10. Journal of the Army, pp. 90–1, TNA, WO 1/190; Parliamentary Papers, Vol. XV, pp. xliv, ccclxix, ccccvi; McGuffie, p. 200; Dyott, Vol. I, p. 287; General Orders for the Army 10 Sept, TNA, WO 28/352.

11. Hall, C. D., *British Strategy in the Napoleonic War 1803–15*, pp. 178–9; Bond, pp. 130–6; Castlereagh, Vol. VI, pp. 325–7; Enthoven, V., *Een Haven Te Ver*, pp. 326–30; *A Collection of Papers*, pp. 659, 477–8; Parliamentary Papers, Vol. XV, pp. lii–iv, xlviii–ix, ccccvii–viii; Havard, p. 105; Fortescue, J. W., *A History of the British Army*, Vol. VII, p. 89.

CHAPTER 14

Last Act

Napoleon's spies were closely observing Bernadotte. The Emperor remained fearful of a Fouché-Bernadotte conspiracy and warned the Minister of War that Bernadotte was engaging in subversive correspondence with Paris. The Gascon's flamboyant pronouncement at Antwerp in which he had both over-flattered the troops and revealed their numbers gave Napoleon the perfect excuse to remove him. The Emperor never understated his forces, informing Clarke on 12 September:

> I am no less unhappy with his order of the day to the National Guard, when he said they had only 15,000 men when I have 60,000 of them in the Scheldt; even if he only had 10,000 it is criminal for a general to give the secret of his forces to the enemy and to Europe.

The Marshal arrived in Paris on the 27th, protesting his innocence. He had not written letters to the capital, not even to his wife, and the strength of his forces was common knowledge. Clarke thought him to be genuinely aggrieved. Napoleon was unforgiving and demanded his presence at Schönbrunn. Bernadotte made the 700 mile journey and met the Emperor on 9 October. He survived the resultant interrogation, disarming Napoleon with his charm. At the end, the Emperor allegedly patted the Marshal's forehead, 'What a head,' he exclaimed. Bernadotte, unbent, responded, 'You might add, Sire, what a heart! What a spirit!'

Marshal Jean-Baptiste Bessières, the Duke of Istria, now took command of the Armies of Antwerp and Tête de Flandre, united as the Army of the North. 'I have sent Bessières,' explained Napoleon, 'because the crisis demands a man who is confident and completely dependable.' The powers of the new commander were considerable; they extended to the control of all the French forces, the fleet and the Dutch troops. Bessières was instructed to ignore any objections from King Louis. 'Command and make yourself obeyed; even employ force as necessary in case of resistance.' Napoleon probably viewed the newly created Army of the North not only as a tool to protect a corner of his empire but also as a potentially useful corps in future wars. By mid-October, Bessières, aided by Général de Brigade Bertrand, had reduced the National Guard to 36,000 men and organised his army.[1]

Napoleon was impatient for the recapture of Walcheren. On 23 September he notified Clarke that Bessières now had more than 50,000 men under arms and it was time to concentrate the French and Dutch fleets in readiness for an attack on the island. The artillery must be prepared for the siege of Flushing. On 8 October Bessières was ordered to personally inspect the fortifications of Antwerp and to report back to the Emperor. He was to produce a map 'which will enable me to know the position as if I were there'. Napoleon's absence did not deter him from giving explicit instructions. Dutch forces on South Beveland were to be increased from 3,000 to 16,000 to support the French in their assault on the British.

Louis was sceptical. He struggled to provide the necessary men as his army was sick and he was dubious of the merits of a naval attack down the Scheldt against a British fleet waiting off Flushing. Bessières was also deterred by the powerful enemy naval force around Walcheren, believing that this made a direct attack impracticable. An increasingly frustrated Napoleon wrote again to his Minister of War in Paris on the 21st.

> I have read the observations of the Duke of Istria regarding the island of Walcheren. Make him understand that I want to retake the island of Walcheren and Flushing; that everything he has said on the impossibility of retaking Flushing is fabricated; that I want to leave the English masters of the place until the freeze, because I am persuaded they will lose an immense number of men [to sickness], but that my intention is to attack them in November and December ... .

He then methodically undermines Bessières objections. In the Emperor's opinion, the British would not be able to stay at sea indefinitely because of the winds and ice and it would then be simple to place enough batteries on South Beveland to gain control of The Slough and move forces across to Walcheren. An isolated Flushing garrison would soon fall to a bombardment. Napoleon confides to Clarke that he is starting to doubt Bessières's ability. 'He is an excellent officer of cavalry because he is experienced in this arm and he understands it well; but he has not the first notion of the art of war ... Tell him again that I believe it easy to retake the island of Walcheren.'[2]

In the middle of October, a significant event occurred away from the Scheldt. The Treaty of Schönbrunn forced Austria to give up Illyria to the French Empire, Salzburg to Bavaria, and Western Galicia to the Duchy of

Warsaw. The Austrians, crushed by Napoleon in three months, also had to pay a large indemnity and join the Continental System. In the following two weeks, rumours of the peace trickled through to London where there had been dramatic political change. The Duke of Portland had suffered a disabling stroke in early August and his ministry collapsed. The Prime Minister resigned on 6 September rather than be forced to remove Castlereagh. Canning resigned on the next day and Castlereagh left office on the 8th. The latter had learnt of Canning's plotting and after a period of brooding, he challenged his former colleague to a duel. There was no warning or demand for explanation. *The Times* reported that the insult was Canning's blame of Castlereagh for the failure of the Walcheren expedition but it was much more likely Canning's secretive attempts to remove Castlereagh from the cabinet. The two protagonists met on Putney Heath at 6am on 21 September. Castlereagh, the more expert shot, rode to the duel humming snatches of opera. Canning's second, Charles Ellis, was too nervous to properly load the pistols. Both missed with their first shot before Castlereagh insisted on a repeat and put a ball through Canning's thigh. Honour was served and Canning made a quick recovery, his injury being described by a friend as 'a very good wound, as wounds go'. There was agreement that if it had been an inch to the right, the injury could have been fatal and the news of the incident shocked even those who had originally been sympathetic to Castlereagh. 'Thank God Canning is not seriously hurt,' wrote Perceval, 'and Castlereagh is not touched. Terrible, all this, for public impression.'

On 4 October Perceval became Prime Minister and was charged with the daunting task of bringing political stability to the country in the face of the recent resignations, the unfolding Walcheren disaster, and Wellington's retreat from Talavera. The opposition refused to form a coalition government and Perceval struggled to persuade men to serve in his ministry, one stating that he had no intention of embarking in such a 'crazy vessel'. Eventually, Lord Liverpool took the role of Secretary for War with responsibility for events on Walcheren, and Richard Wellesley, Wellington's brother, accepted the offer of the Foreign Office. Few expected the new government to last long. Napoleon was aware of events in London; he revelled in his enemy's misfortunes in a letter to Alexander, Emperor of Russia, written from Schönbrunn on 10 October.

I have sent the recent English newspapers to Your Majesty; it can be seen that the ministers fight with each other, that there is a revolution in the ministry and perfect anarchy. The folly and fecklessness of this cabinet knows no name. It has just made 25 to 30,000 men die in the most horrible country in the world; it might as well have thrown them in the sea so pestilential are the marshes of the island of Walcheren.[3]

Coote handed over the Walcheren command to Lieutenant General George Don on 27 October. Don immediately made an inspection of the island's hospitals and defences. The returns for the 25th show 5,872 sick in a total force of 12,532 men. The sick rate of 47 per cent was a little less than in September but the monthly death rate among the soldiers (6.3 per cent) had actually slightly increased. Officers remained less likely to die of the disease; their monthly mortality at this time was 1.5 per cent. There was a slow fall in the number of new cases towards the end of October and through November. The threat of the fever declined with the advance of winter as had been predicted by the locals.

Most of the troops were still in a poor state. Don informed Liverpool that there was little chance of any of the sick returning to active duty on Walcheren. Among those men shown as fit on the returns, more than a third were incapable of a quick march of five miles or one night's patrolling duty. Thomas St Clair watched wagons of sick soldiers and officers entering Middelburg.

> In such numbers did they arrive, that the poor wretches were lying in thousands along the streets without the possibility of being taken under shelter so full was every part of the town. Our fine little army was by this time entirely cut up ... .

When the troops in Middelburg attended a service to mark the fiftieth year of the King's reign, it was the first parade since the onset of disease. William Dyott saw a 'melancholy and dreadful falling off in their appearance'. Most of the regiments were reduced to a handful of pale, sickly men. Burgomaster Jacob Schorer heard a rumour that the soldiers might be replaced by Germans who were better suited to the air, 'in other words, they are of lesser value than the English.'

General Don agreed with his predecessor that the state of the army demanded the early evacuation of as many sick as possible. He urged Liverpool to issue immediate orders for the sending of ships to accommodate 5,638 sick. This surprisingly exact figure was calculated from the latest returns. The general apologised for the unusually assertive tone of his letter; 'but when the lives of British soldiers are at stake it is the Duty of their General to suggest every Means to save them'. Through October, 4,536 ill and convalescent men were embarked for England. Don's military memorandum was uncompromising.

I now find that my Report on the actual state of the Island may be confined to a few words: − That the Island is almost in a defenceless state and that the Army is so much reduced as not to be able to cope with the Enemy in the field; and only capable of holding the Town of Flushing until the Enemy can open Mortars and Ricochet Batteries against it.

There was intelligence that the French forces around Antwerp amounted to around 22,600 men and that there were 7,000 Dutch troops on South Beveland. The enemy was busy constructing batteries, strengthening its flotilla and preparing fire vessels. Don concluded that to defend Walcheren with its thirty-four miles of assailable coastline, he would need to repair the fortifications of Flushing and Ter Veere, to construct new military works and communications across the island, and to have an army of 23,500 men.

The British commander asked Liverpool to augment the naval force between Walcheren and South Beveland but he was dismissive of the offer of an extra four to five thousand soldiers. He reminded the Secretary for War that the security of Walcheren relied entirely on the protection afforded by the navy. On 27 October, he had only 3,000 troops capable of active duty and it is obvious that this additional small reinforcement would still have left him well short of the force he had specified to permanently hold the island. Don remained uncertain of ministers' intentions, writing to Liverpool on 4 November:

I therefore humbly conceive, that if His Majesty's Government should deem it expedient to order the evacuation of the island, it will be better not to send the reinforcements mentioned in your Lordship's letter, provided that the evacuation takes place immediately ... .

Don also pointed out that the enemy threat was now such that if there was any weakening of the naval defence of Walcheren, he would have little choice but to flood the island between Armuyden and Ter Veere and also in front of Flushing. Only by taking this radical action, could he ensure the safe evacuation of the remaining sick, his stores, and the army.[4]

The decision to give up Walcheren appears to have been taken in the first few days of November. Ministers were very likely influenced by more definitive news of the peace between France and Austria and the despondent tone of despatches from the Scheldt. The first cryptic acknowledgement of the plan is contained in a letter of 3 November from Liverpool to Don.

Having now determined to evacuate the island of Walcheren, unless some new circumstances should occur ... .

Within a week, Don had received an unequivocal instruction.

but I am at the same Time to inform you that it is the Determination of His Majesty that previous to the Evacuation you should take such measures as you may judge most effectual for the Destruction of the Basin of Flushing, and of the Naval defences of the island.[5]

Liverpool further advised Don that he should commence these operations as soon as possible consistent with the safety of the remaining sick. The intent was that the defensive works should be left in such a condition that not even the French Emperor, with his almost unlimited command of military labour, would be able to repair them quickly. The general was given permission to flood Walcheren if he deemed this necessary for the security of the army. To facilitate the demolition of Flushing's basin, around 100 civil artificers, men used to working on canals and docks, were sent out to act under the orders of the senior engineer. A small detachment of troops was also despatched to the Scheldt to oversee proceedings, among them William Wheeler, who returned with 300 comrades of the much depleted 51st.

We marched to and embarked at Spithead, sailed for this place, dropped anchor between the islands of Walcheren and South Beveland. Since we left these islands, our people have evacuated South Beveland and the enemy has taken possession of it, the troops are so sickly in Walcheren. It is intended to destroy the works and dock yards together with every place belonging to the French Government, then leave the place; we are to remain on board to act as circumstances shall require; the enemy is throwing up works on the Island they occupy, and it is said they are meditating an attack on Walcheren. The river is full of our Gunboats, which are constantly annoying them, and they in return keep up a constant fire on our boats, so nothing is heard all night long but the clang of war, and seemingly without effecting any purpose whatever. Our situation here is not very pleasant, the weather is cold and we have not much room to exercise ourselves on deck; one comfort attending us is gin, and tobacco is cheap, so we can enjoy ourselves over a pipe and a glass; the cause of our remaining on board is the preservation of our health.

The demolition work was under the direction of Lieutenant Colonel Robert Pilkington of the Royal Engineers whose earlier report had met with ministers' approval. Pilkington's objective was to prevent Flushing's use as a naval base and depot for as long as two years. He planned to neutralise the batteries and to destroy their parapets and partially demolish the line of ramparts, especially on each side of the entrances into the harbours. The walls of the flood gates, twenty-eight feet long and thirty-six feet thick, were to be blown up with mines. Some parts of the works, for instance the retaining wall on the south side, were to be spared to avoid extensive flooding and damage to the city. Similarly destructive work was carried out at Ter Veere where, according to George Bourne, the town's defences were dismantled in three days: 'such a picture of havoc, confusion and desolation I cannot describe or can't be pointed out but to those who have witnessed it.'

In Flushing, it was agreed that once the preparations had been made, the actual destruction could be completed in a short time and it was better delayed until the fleet arrived to remove the army and its stores. There was concern that the premature disabling of the defences would both inflame the inhabitants and attract an enemy attack. Evacuation of the remaining sick was expedited and the British kept a close eye on their adversary. Lieutenant Colonel Offery, an assistant in the Quartermaster General's department, reported on 19 November that 'a gentleman from South Beveland' had revealed to him that there was little likelihood of an enemy assault for two to three weeks. Should the French and Dutch attempt to invade near Ter Veere, it was planned to land British forces from flat-bottomed boats to attack them in the flank and rear.[6]

British fears of a French offensive were increased by rumours of Napoleon's arrival at Antwerp. In fact, the Emperor was now at Fontainebleau near Paris, from where he continued to communicate with his officers in the Scheldt. In early November, he informed Clarke that the Walcheren expedition was of 'so little importance' that he intended to leave the Duke of Istria to get on with it. This was out of character and he was soon criticising his general's lack of energy, the following written to Bessières on the 20th.

> Instead of writing to the Minister of War, give orders and inform me that the Slough is purged of the enemy. The particular affection which I have for you resolved me to let you acquire this glory; show firmness, character and will.

Again, the Emperor urged Bessières to ignore Louis's opinions. The latter was in self-justificatory mood, telling his brother that he had done everything possible to help Bessières and support the recapture of the island. The French commander's reluctance to commit to an all-out assault was increased by the levels of sickness among both Dutch and French troops and a shortage of ordnance. General Seroux, commander of the artillery of the Army of the North, complained to Paris that he had only sixteen feeble companies. He asked for reinforcements to be sent to Antwerp, including the companies of the Imperial Guard at La Fère, and finished his letter with the plaintive comment that he could not use artillery that he did not have. Bessières was influenced by the counsel of those around him but not all French officers approved of his passivity. Jean Jacques Pelet thought that the Duke's advisors 'multiplied the difficulties and exaggerated the necessary means so that the attack was unnecessarily delayed'.[7]

In the first week of December, the British remained vigilant. Offery wrote to Brownrigg on the 4th that the French might attempt a last ditch attack 'if only to furnish a dashing paragraph for the Moniteur that they have driven us into the sea'. He believed the Dutch to be unenthusiastic and that there was ill feeling between Dumonceau and Bessières. The inhabitants were nervous of the consequences of a British departure. Two days later, Lieutenant Colonel Masheim wrote to the Quartermaster General from Flushing: 'we are coming near the last act.' The engineers had had some difficulty in placing the charges under the floodgates but it was expected that the demolition of the defences would proceed within a week. The intelligence of the enemy forces was contradictory: 'they are to attack every day but as yet they have not ventured the attempt'.

Bessières was not to claim the glory Napoleon intended for him. Don embarked the army on 9 December having already completed the evacuation of the ordnance and stores. Headquarters was moved to the *Caesar*. The weather was unsettled and fearing that the enemy might still make an attack on his retreating force, the British commander left a temporary rearguard in Flushing, Ter Veere, and Middelburg and in the fort of Ramakins. He embarked the divisions of the army as follows:

> The 1st Division immediately off the town of Flushing; the 2nd to the westward of that town; the 3rd between Flushing and Fort Ramakins, to act and cooperate with the naval force on the Slough passage under Captain Mason, and the 4th off Ter Veere with the naval force between the Veere Gat and the Wolversdyle under Commodore Owen.

Should the enemy attempt to invade Walcheren with British troops still on the island, these men could quickly disembark to provide reinforcements.

They were all boarded with two days' provisions ready cooked, six flints, a blanket, a pair of shoes, and a pair of socks.

The French made no attempt to molest the departing army and the rearguard was subsequently withdrawn. Don had also taken the precaution of stopping the island's freshwater sluices thus limiting to the dykes and causeway any French advance from Ter Veere through Middelburg to Flushing.

The destruction of Flushing's defences was completed on 11 December after a frigate and a brig under construction had been launched from the port. Pilkington confirmed that his objectives had been accomplished, 'the Dock Yards, Arsenal, Magazines and every building belonging to the Naval Establishment being wholly destroyed'. There was little collateral damage; the windows of nearby houses survived the detonation of the charges on the piers of the floodgates. The entrance to the harbour was blocked by sinking weighted vessels thereby preventing the passage of ships of war. The operation was witnessed by the army detained off Walcheren by adverse weather, among them James McGrigor. 'From the numerous explosions and the violence of the fire, fed by the barrels of tar and every kind of combustible, not only everything in the dockyard was doomed to destruction, but several men-of-war on the stocks.'

McGrigor's transport moved farther out to sea to avoid the explosions. He says that the wind blew so hard that it was almost a hurricane and indeed the weather blighted the expedition to its end. Strachan reported a number of 'disasters of ships' in the gales; he was uncertain of the loss of life. The enemy continued to fire from the batteries on South Beveland. As the British gunboats off Ramakins were too distant to silence their adversaries, the admiral ordered them to fall back. He assured the Admiralty that the enemy's attempts to seize naval control of The Slough had been foiled. It was 23 December before the winds weakened and allowed the departure of Don and his army from the Scheldt. The general informed Liverpool that the army had disembarked from Walcheren with excellent discipline and that he had received exemplary naval cooperation.

> I feel great satisfaction in mentioning the very able and cordial support I have uniformly received from Rear Admiral Otway and that our arrangements for the final evacuation of the island were approved of by Rear Admiral Sir Richard Strachan.

The remaining vessels in the West Scheldt under Mason and in the Veere Gat under Owen sailed for England on 26 December. Strachan arrived at the Downs the next day and hoisted his flag on the *St Domingo*.[8]

Dutch troops had been in contact with the inhabitants of Ter Veere for several weeks. The townspeople indicated the movements of the British troops by sending up smoke signals from their chimneys. Bessières had instructed Dumonceau that General Cort Heyliger's Dutch force might enter the town once the enemy had left. The Dutch were keen to occupy Walcheren before the French and when they received news of the last British vessel leaving the Scheldt, Heyliger's men advanced to the banks of The Slough. Colonel Denis Pack had earlier reached agreement with the Ter Veere locals that they would give his troops plenty of time to depart before informing their countrymen thus avoiding any bloodshed. Heyligers made the thirty-minute crossing of the channel on 25 December and occupied the town sending two companies of the *3ᵉ Régiment de Chasseurs à Pied* to Middelburg. He then replaced the tricolore flying over Ter Veere with the Dutch flag. Bessières, who had been ordered to seize the island in the name of the Emperor, was incensed.

> You will immediately order him [Heyligers] to leave the army; we have no need of rabble-rousers. The respect which I have had for the Dutch nation and army does not permit me to keep silent regarding such conduct on the part of this officer ... .

Heyligers knew that the raising of the flag was little more than a gesture. When he met with Jacob Schorer in Middelburg, he spoke of the likely annexation of Holland and Zealand to France. 'What a misfortune for this unlucky country'. Bessières and Dumonceau landed at Ter Veere on 27 December and made their way to Middelburg. Two days later, the new French governor of Walcheren, General Gilly, explained in a special order of the day that the island had been designated French territory. Walcheren was, in Bessières's words, part of the Great Empire. Schorer wrote in his journal that it was as if lightning had struck.[9]

Notes

1. *Correspondance de Napoléon Ier*, Vol. 19, pp. 478, 487, 453−5, 559; Lecestre, L, *Lettres Inédites de Napoleon Ier*, Vol. I, pp. 361−2; Fleischman, T., *L'Expedition Anglaise sur le Continent en 1809*, pp. 90−1; Wauwermans, Général, *Napoléon et Carnot*, p. 91; Palmer, A., *Bernadotte*, pp. 153−5; Pawly, R., *Le Walcheren des Français*, pp. 27−8; d'Hastrel, Général Baron, *Mémoires (1766−1825)*, pp. 140−1.

2. *Correspondance de Napoléon Ier*, Vol. 19, pp. 498, 559, Vol. 20, p. 10; Fleischman, pp. 99–100; Rocquain, F., *Napoléon Ier et Le Roi Louis*, pp. 224–5.
3. Muir, R., *Britain and the Defeat of Napoleon 1807–1815*, pp. 92, 106–9; Hall, C. D., *British Strategy in the Napoleonic War 1803–15*, pp. 55, 67; Bond, G., *The Grand Expedition*, p. 208; Gray, D., *Spencer Perceval. The Evangelical Prime Minister 1762–1812*, p. 242; *Correspondance de Napoléon Ier*, Vol. 19, p. 564.
4. Parliamentary Papers 1810, Vol. XV, pp. lxiv–v, lxx–xxv; *A Collection of Papers Relating to the Expedition to the Scheldt*, pp. 185–7, 174–5, 191–7, 715–6, 207; Marshall, H., *Contribution to Statistics of the Sickness and Mortality which occurred among the troops employed on the expedition to the Scheldt in the year 1809*, pp. 315–7; Blane, G., *Facts and Observations respecting Intermittent Fevers*, p. 15; Bond, p. 136; Dyott, W., *Dyott's Diary 1781–1845*, Vol. I, p. 289; St Clair, Lt Col, *A soldier's recollections of the West Indies and America with a narrative of the expedition to the Island of Walcheren*, Vol. II, pp. 369–70; Schorer, J. H., *Dagboek van Jacob Hendrik Schorer*, p. 24.
5. TNA, WO 6/26:97; TNA, WO 6/28:24–5; *A Collection of Papers*, pp. 51, 56; Parliamentary Papers, Vol. XV, p. xviii.
6. Parliamentary Papers, Vol. XV, pp. xix–xx, xv, 6xxxiii; *A Collection of Papers*, pp. 53–7, 201–4; Wheeler, W., *The Letters of Private Wheeler 1809–1828*, p. 39; Bourne, G, *My Military Career*, p. 64; Enthoven, V., *Een Haven Te Ver*, p. 332.
7. Parliamentary Papers, Vol. XV, p. lxxiii; *Correspondance de Napoléon Ier*, Vol. 20, p. 26; Fleischman, pp. 100–1; Rocquain, p. 226; Pawly, p. 28; Pelet, Général, *Mémoires sur la Guerre de 1809*, Vol. IV, p. 341.
8. NAS, GD364/1/1191; Parliamentary Papers, Vol. XV, pp. lxxxi–iii; General Orders for the Army Dec9, TNA, WO 28/352; *A Collection of Papers*, pp. 214–6, 518–24; Whitworth Porter, Maj Gen, *History of the Corps of Royal Engineers*, Vol. I, p. 254; McGrigor, J., *The Scalpel and the Sword*, p. 160; Brenton, E. P., *The Naval History of Great Britain*, Vol. II, p. 304.
9. Wink, M., *Le Walcheren des Hollandais*, pp. 36–7; *Correspondance de Napoléon Ier*, Vol. 20, p. 99; Schorer, pp. 59–62.

CHAPTER 15

Enquiry

T he returning British troops were demoralised and ashamed.

Nothing can be more contrary than the former and present appearance our army. Who that was to see us now would recognise the gay, gallant body of men who, under the cheering salutations of their countrymen, left Ramsgate ... Our poor fellows have learned by some means that they have not equalled the expectations of their countrymen.

Many others echoed this officer's views and expected a cold reception at home. St Clair contrasted his own feelings with those prior to his departure; their impressive army was now a mere skeleton. Men judged to be fit were incapable of much exertion. The elite unit, the 95th Rifles, struggled to make the march from Deal to the barracks at Hythe. The muster roll contains the names of many men 'left at Deal', others 'left at Dover' or 'in Regimental Hospital'.

With so many so debilitated, the transfer to the shore was perilous. Sick soldiers of the 71st were first lowered into rowboats and then carried through the heavy surf at Deal by men from a Welsh regiment. Some of the boats capsized and the unfortunates were dragged ashore 'like drowned rats' before being loaded into wagons. London medical student William Dent witnessed the disembarkation of the sick at Harwich.

Several of the men died in the landing and on the beach, and the inhabitants would not let their lodgings to the sick officers, but if they had a few of the knocks the People of Flushing have got they would be more humane to their countrymen.

Local Physician Thomas Wright comments on the distress of the local population, many of whom fled the area. Similar scenes were played out in the towns of Bexhill, Brabourne, Ashford, Canterbury, Chichester, Horsham, Chelmsford and Ipswich.[1]

As part of the medical preparations for the expedition, Surgeon General

Keate had organised general hospitals at Harwich, Deal and Portsmouth, each with 1,500 beds, and hospitals at Yarmouth and Plymouth each for 500 sick. With the 800 beds at Haslar Naval Hospital, this gave a total of 6,300 beds, enough for 15 per cent of the expeditionary force. By 1 February 1810, there were 11,000 sick receiving attention and barracks were pressed into use at Deal (where over 5,000 sick were landed), Faversham, Margate, Ramsgate, Dover and Hythe and extra hospitals used at Dover, Shorncliffe, Hythe, Ashford and Harwich. The Surgeon General made regular inspections. After an October tour of the hospitals, he stressed the need for better care of the invalids.

> The convalescents of the army from Walcheren are too thinly clothed to sustain the rigour of the approaching season ... in their feeble state they will thereby be rendered very liable to relapses ... .

When he inspected the depots in Kent in December, where the 4,000 sick were divided between general and regimental hospitals, he commented unfavourably on the temporary hospital mates and dispensers provided by his colleague, the Inspector General of Hospitals. Many were illiterate.

Eyewitness accounts suggest that the ill soldiers suffered a repeat of the miseries of Walcheren. Thomas Wright describes a typical hospital.

> Harwich became the Lazaretto to the army of Walcheren; how accurately this designation suited the reality may be learned from the Report of the Physician-General, who was present at the first landing from Transports, from which the instant they cast anchor, twenty bodies were sent ashore for interment, and of the deplorable cases landed, eighteen died in one morning in transition on the biers, nearly as many expired in the hospital, and every night after, a considerable number but perpetually decreasing; the pallid looks of the breathing spectres were so ghastly, they exhibited a type of the resurrection; and their unhappy attendants, too few to administer relief to half the number through fatigue, were marked with melancholy little calculated to communicate hope or confidence to the sick.

Journalist Cyrus Redding was taken to visit the Walcheren wards of another hospital by the officer of a cavalry regiment and was shocked, 'I have been through civil hospitals but never saw anything like it in them ... .'

The fear of the patients is well expressed by Rifleman Benjamin Harris who watched his comrades die at Hythe.

> The ward of the hospital in which I myself was, accommodated eleven men and I saw, from my bed in the corner where I lay, this

ward refilled ten times, the former patients all carried out to the grave.

Some died quietly in their beds and others in a 'shivering delirium' on the floor during the night. Harris left the ward to inspect the two lines of newly-dug graves in the churchyard. He acknowledges the kindness of the regimental surgeon, Thomas Hughes Ridgway. A soldier of the 71st received good care and solicitude from an orderly in the hospital at Deal. The two men were natives of Glasgow and had a natural bond. Others were not so fortunate. A soldier of the same regiment was admitted to the wards at Brabourne.

> All the time I was in the hospital, my soul was oppressed by the distresses of my fellow-sufferers and shocked at the conduct of the hospital men. Often I have seen them fighting over the expiring body of the patients, their eyes not yet closed in death, for articles of apparel that two had seized at once; cursing and oaths mingling with the dying groans and prayers of the poor sufferers.

Those soldiers tough enough to survive these conditions often caused a new set of problems. Ensign Robert William Dallas was given the unenviable task of overseeing the regimental sick. When the convalescents were transferred to Colchester, they were well enough to break out of the hospital every night and run into the town 'where they sold their clothes and got drunk'.[2]

The human cost of the Walcheren expedition is difficult to calculate. Most authors have concluded that the British Army lost 106 men killed in fighting and that there were 3,960 deaths from disease. These figures are taken from the Adjutant General's report of 1 February 1810. Whilst the number killed in action is close to the truth the number of disease deaths is almost certainly a gross underestimate. This return was produced at a time when there were still 11,500 sick men in the hospitals. Walcheren fever was, as we have seen, a chronic, relapsing and frequently fatal disorder. The epidemic still had to run its course. Mortality figures for the later months of 1810 are scarce but in a detailed statistical account of the fever, Inspector of Hospitals Henry Marshall states that between January and June, 36,000 men from Walcheren corps were admitted into hospital. He estimates the total loss of lives as around 8,000. It was, in the words of an eminent historian, an 'appalling catastrophe'.[3]

The British Press had gradually turned against the expedition. By August 1809, events in the Scheldt were being reported with some scepticism. Readers were informed that most of the officers were disenchanted with the climate if not the operation itself. As the military force ground to a halt, *The Times* declared that Lord Chatham had 'got to the end of his tether'. When the retreat from the Scheldt was confirmed, the paper went on to the attack, accusing the expedition's commander of callous disregard for his troops and demanding that he be court-martialled. Chatham was mercilessly portrayed in cartoons, the presence of a pet turtle or tortoise hinting of indolence. *The Star* weighed in with an attack on the government; 'If ministers had been paid and pensioned by Bonaparte; if they had been seduced by the brilliant allure of the crowns that he hands out, they could not have served him better.' *The Advertiser* agreed that only the Emperor had gained from ministers' efforts, whilst the *Morning Chronicle* concluded that the great expedition had been inspired by 'vanity, absent-mindedness, and imbecility'.

Public opinion of the period was fickle with more interest in scandals than strategy, and excessive reaction to perceived misdemeanours. Recent causes of discontent included the controversial Convention of Cintra and the allegations of corruption made by Mary Anne Clarke against the Duke of York during 1809. Now, public indignation was fuelled by the increasingly alarming accounts of fever among the troops on Walcheren, the inflammatory press reports, and the announcement of the failure of the expedition. Strachan later commented that the Admiralty believed that the public would not have been satisfied even if Walcheren had been retained. In those coastal areas where the local population came in to contact with the returning army, the opinions of the dejected soldiers added to the air of disillusionment. Most participants end their accounts of the expedition by decrying it. Typical is a soldier of the 42nd Highlanders.

> Many who had survived the race to Corunna were now gone to their long home. There was scarcely a man in our regiment who did not think the Walcheren expedition a very foolish thing.

Soldiers who had remained at home were bewildered. Captain Peter Bowlby describes the reaction of a fellow officer who had been detained at Harwich; 'on seeing the corporal of his company, he said, "Where is the company?" "I am the only man left, Sir," was the reply, "and the other companies are not much better off".' [4]

The Press demanded a formal investigation and in early December it was reported that Castlereagh had suggested that there should be a parliamentary enquiry. The King left the decision to parliament which convened on 26 January; the Whig opposition politician Lord Porchester proposed the motion that there should be 'a committee of enquiry into the policy of conduct of the late Expedition to Walcheren ...'. The enquiry was necessary, Porchester argued, because of the 'incapacity and total want of system that pervade all the military measures of his Majesty's Ministers'. He did not want an investigation conducted by 'secret committee' as this would allow the government to evade responsibility. What was needed was 'a committee of the whole House' to ensure justice. Porchester laced his speech with repeated direct attacks on the government and made more specific criticism of the slowness of the expedition (why not an immediate attack on Antwerp?), the lack of proper intelligence, the tardy evacuation of Walcheren and the shortage of transports and medical supplies. He was dismissive of the military commander.

> I do not intend to complain of the selection [of Chatham]. Although he was not one of those officers whom fame had noticed among her list of heroes – although he was not one of those who 'in camps and tented fields had bled' – although he was much more familiar with the gaieties of London or the business of office than with the annals of military experience or glory.

Opposition politicians stood up to support Porchester. William Windham argued that the expedition had achieved very little at great cost.

> We had ransacked some stores, it was true, thrown in the basin [at Flushing], and destroyed a sea-wall; but we had also entombed half of our gallant army.

Ministers, Windham added, should have been aware of the sickly nature of the Scheldt.

> They marched the British army to its grave, to be extinguished amidst the pestilential air of Walcheren, to go out like a candle in a vault.

George Ponsonby continued in similar vein and left little doubt who he believed were responsible for the disaster. It was not the French but the 'demon' of England, nurtured into a malignant influence by the unprincipled behaviour of 'a weak, divided, insincere and incapable administration'. What were ministers doing, he asked, when the 'best blood of the Empire' was putrefying in the swamps of Walcheren?

Perceval responded that the opposition's attacks were politically motivated. The course they had taken clearly demonstrated that they were less interested in investigating the conduct of ministers than in removing them from office. His government had made every effort to make the relevant papers available to the House but he thought that the enquiry should be delayed to ensure that all the evidence was assembled. This suggestion received short shrift from opposition members who pointed out that there was no need to wait for such documents 'to ascertain whether there was calamity and failure'. The vote on the motion was carried by 195 against 186 and it was agreed that the enquiry would begin the following week.[5]

Gordon Bond gives a pithy description of the proceedings which were conducted by a committee of the whole House during February and March.

> The committee was to meet in closed hearings and at regular intervals to report its progress to the Commons. The investigation was to proceed chronologically, questioning those persons concerned with the planning, execution, occupation and retreat in that order. Papers and documents relating to all phases of the expedition were also to be examined by the committee. The evidence as it was presented fell into five general categories, each pertaining to specific aspects of the expedition. The first concerned the conception of the expedition, especially the financial arrangements and other factors which prevented the troops being sent to Portugal or perhaps Germany or Italy. The committee then heard evidence relating to operational plans, medical preparations, the conduct of military and naval affairs and, finally, the retention of Walcheren.

It was intended that the enquiry focus on the wider questions such as whether the expedition should have been undertaken, rather than it being a means of attaching guilt to individuals. Canning thought that any shortcomings of senior military officers should be dealt with by a military tribunal and not by a public enquiry. Nevertheless, the men who were identified as the expedition's leaders – Castlereagh, Chatham and Strachan – were bound to be subjected to thorough cross-examination. Strachan was instructed by the Chair of the Committee, Sir John Anstruther, that he might refuse to give an answer to any question which would, in his opinion, 'inculpate or incriminate himself'.[6]

Castlereagh appeared before the committee on 13 March. There is no doubt that the former Secretary for War wanted an enquiry. Whig member Thomas Creevey describes him voting against the government.

> Castlereagh [was] in the majority with us. He sat aloof with four friends; and these five, instead of going out, decided the question in our favour. Had they gone out we should have been beat by one! ... Castlereagh bent his head from his elevated bench down almost to

the floor to catch my eye, and I gave him a sign that all was well. He could scarcely contain himself: he hid his face: but when the division was over, he was quite extravagant in the expression of his happiness.

Having attained his wish for a public debate of the Walcheren debacle, Castlereagh presented his case confidently, quoting two detailed memoranda he had sent to Chatham in June 1809. He reiterated the reasons for the expedition being undertaken, stressing the advantages of a limited operation close to home which both improved Britain's security and provided a diversion for Austria. He stated that the expedition was intended as a 'coup de main' but refused to be drawn on the make-up of the force or its slow progress which he dismissed as strictly military matters. Those who questioned the delay in launching the attack on the Scheldt were in large part silenced by the testimony of the Chairman of the Transport Board that it was not possible to obtain sufficient ships until July. Other non-military men called to give evidence included employees of the Treasury who explained the finances of the expedition. When asked the total cost, Treasury official Richard Wharton gave the remarkably precise figure of £834,275 10s 7d, of which £211,565 15s 7d was incurred after the evacuation of South Beveland. Modern comparisons are crude but the larger figure equates to around £45 million.[7]

The military testimony addressed all aspects of the expedition but focused on the defining events; the failure to land on Cadsand, the aborted attack on Antwerp, and the temporary retention of Walcheren. Army and navy officers explained their own roles and attempted to rationalise what had happened around them. The reasons for the key decisions have been discussed in earlier chapters and this testimony will not be described to avoid repetition.[8]

There was great interest in the appearance of the expedition's commanders. Chatham was anxious at the prospect of being questioned in the House. According to Thomas Creevey, the general was treating himself with 'draughts and nervous medicines'. He also sought help from senior army colleagues including Brownrigg. The Quartermaster General asked his assistant, Sir Howard Douglas, to allow him to quote from his detailed campaign journal.

The clamour that has been raised against Lord Chatham, and the extraordinary state in which the government of the country is, make it more than ever necessary that the most comprehensive and satisfactory statement of the transactions of the command should be made, and that with the least possible loss of time.

Chatham's testimony to the enquiry was brusque and evasive but he had already made a defence of his actions in a controversial report to the King. This document was begun shortly after his return to England and shown to George III in draft form before being recovered during the autumn and then resubmitted to the King and the cabinet in mid-February. His paper was thus available to the enquiry. Chatham limited himself to answering two questions; why had Antwerp not been attacked and why had the army taken so long to reach Batz?

> With respect to the former proposition, I am inclined to think that it is so clear and evident that no further operations could at that time, and in the then sickly state of the army, have been undertaken with any prospect of success, that it would be unnecessarily trespassing on Your Majesty to enter into much more detail on this point than has already been brought before Your Majesty in my dispatch of the 29th of August: and the chief object of this paper will be directed to show to Your Majesty that the second point, namely, why the army was not brought up sooner to the destination from whence its ultimate operations were to commence, is purely a naval consideration, and that the delay did in no shape rest with me ... .

Chatham's submission to the King was seized upon by opposition members of the House who insisted that it was both unconstitutional and underhand. Ponsonby accused the general of 'going into the King's closet without the knowledge of any minister and presenting His Majesty a paper justificatory of his own conduct and incriminatory of the conduct of his naval colleague'. How, Samuel Whitbread asked, could the navy defend itself against this 'private poison' instilled into the ear of their royal master? The government was rocked and it was obvious that only Chatham's resignation from his cabinet position as Master General of the Ordnance could save the administration. After a dangerous vote on 6 March, the procrastinating general was finally persuaded to step down.[9]

Upon hearing of Chatham's accusations, Strachan obtained a copy of the document and responded with his own account which was in turn submitted to the enquiry. For both men, we have their verbal testimony and their written papers. During the debate preceding the enquiry, Home Popham had pronounced that the navy would welcome a rigorous examination of their actions but Strachan viewed Chatham's statement as a personal attack. In a letter to the Admiralty of 5 March, the admiral insisted that no blame could be attached to him or the service:

I could not possibly suspect that Lord Chatham, to the irregularity of presenting immediately to His Majesty such a paper as that I have received, had added the Impropriety (to use no stronger term) of endeavouring to exculpate himself by private Insinuations against the Conduct of others.

In his own statement, Strachan methodically tackles the slow reduction of Flushing and the failure to land on Cadsand, explaining that the navy could not have done more. Strachan's exasperation with the army's commander is apparent.

When, therefore, Lord Chatham contends in his statement that the Second point, namely, 'Why the Army was not brought up sooner to the Destination from where its ulterior Operations were to commence is purely a Naval consideration,' his position is certainly true in words but is certainly incorrect in its implied Meaning. It is obvious that the Army might have marched to Batz in the course of a few days, but it is also obvious that it could not be conveyed on board a Fleet of four hundred transports, besides Frigates, Sloops and Flotilla, through a very intricate Channel, without some Delay. The Difficulty of conducting such a Fleet at all, through the mazes of such a Navigation can only be appreciated by professional men ... .

He berates Chatham for having no understanding of the significance of adverse winds. The admiral remained insistent that marching the army across South Beveland was the better plan but that he had had no choice but to acquiesce to Chatham's opinions. 'With him alone was there an option between a march of 36 hours and a Voyage of an indefinite length.'

The differences between the two men that had arisen during the expedition were replayed during the enquiry. There is no need to change the conclusion reached in earlier pages that both were to blame, neither being able and willing to understand the real problems of the other.[10]

The medical arrangements were also subjected to close scrutiny. The members of the Medical Board had been replaced at the end of February. Although the Walcheren episode can hardly have helped their cause, the Board was earmarked for reform prior to the expedition. Lucas Pepys, Thomas Keate, and Francis Knight were summoned for examination in early February and Pepys and Keate again in March after they had been superseded. The Physician General stated that he had not been consulted before the force's departure. The Board was ignorant of the destination and the duration of the expedition. He denied that there was any lack of medical assistance and rebuffed the charge of indolence.

> Why did you omit to act, why did you omit to make any representations to government?

> Because it is not our [the Board's] practice to originate anything with us, but to obey the commands we receive, we are not counsellors.

Pepys explained that he was familiar with Walcheren fever and that he had not attended the island because he did not believe himself to be competent in 'inspectatorial duties'

Keate supported Pepys's view that the Medical Board expected to receive orders and confirmed that it was not in the habit of 'voluntarily stepping forward'. The enquiry committee's vain attempts to come to terms with the tortuous workings of the Board are well captured in the following exchange with the Surgeon General.

> Of what does the medical board consist? – Of three members.
> Who are those members? – The Physician General, the Surgeon General and the Inspector General of Army Hospitals.
> Who is the head of the Board? – The Physician General.
> Are all returns made to the Physician General ultimately from all the departments included under that Board? – The returns are not made to the Physician General.
> To whom are they made? – The returns from the regiments are made to the Inspector General, the returns from foreign service are made to the Surgeon General.
> What returns are made to the Physician General? – None.
> Do the Inspector General and the Surgeon General report to the Physician General? – It is only a board on particular occasions, each member has individual duties.
> How comes the Physician General to be called head of the Board? – Whenever the three meet at the Board the Physician General presides.
> How often does that happen? – Upon very few occasions.

Keate admitted that the Board had never formally discussed Walcheren fever. He then became involved in a dysfunctional exchange regarding the amount of bark required for an average case of fever but he denied any serious shortage of medicines. He deflected questions relating to the lack of medical staff, pointing out that the vital physicians and hospital mates were the responsibility of the Physician General and Inspector General respectively, and that staff surgeons were duly provided. Francis Knight acknowledged the shortage of hospital mates but he was quick to remind the committee that, despite his title, he had no responsibility for the hospitals on Walcheren. Other doctors were called including James McGrigor who recounted the experience in his autobiography.

> I went to the Speaker's chamber at four o'clock where I found several other witnesses. Among them was the late Sir John Webb who had received a similar warrant. I did this daily for upwards of a fortnight, being every day at the Speaker's chamber by four o'clock, the warrant being renewed and sent to me every day. At length my turn came and I was in some agitation, which the appearance of the witness cited before me did not tend to diminish. This was no other than Sir Richard Strachan, as brave a man as ever trod a quarter-deck. Yet, when a messenger came to the Speaker's chamber, and two members, his friends, appeared to conduct him to the bar of the house, his appearance was anything but that of a man of courage. When his name was called, his face was as white as a sheet.

McGrigor was also affected by nerves and became temporarily confused under cross-examination.[11]

By 26 March, all the evidence had been presented and Lord Porchester opened the debate. He spoke for four hours, describing the course of the doomed expedition and placing the blame firmly upon ministers rather than the army and the navy. It was, by all accounts, a dull speech which disappointed the government's adversaries. At the end, the Lord admitted to fatigue and asked the clerk to read his two resolutions. These were, firstly, that the operation had been poorly planned with little chance of success and, secondly, that the island of Walcheren had been retained for too long, sacrificing lives with no objective.

Castlereagh then rose to defend the expedition. It was, he said, 'not only justifiable but imperiously called for by the strongest consideration of policy'. The reasons for its failure, such as the adverse weather and the fever, were outside ministers' control. Instead of rational debate, the subject had been enveloped in a 'mass of calumny and misrepresentation'. Stung by criticism of the pre-expedition plans, he defended his repeated use of the term 'coup de main'.

> It has been contended ... that an attack upon Antwerp by a coup de main was on the face of it absurd and impracticable ... if gentlemen choose to annex to the term coup de main the notion of a single attack

which is to be the effort of an hour or a day they may be borne out in their assertion but if, as I understand it, the expression may be correctly applied to a course of proceeding more extended in point of time and may properly be used to described a rapid operation of several days continument and contradistinguished from a formal siege or campaign there is no absurdity in the application which has been made of it.

Castlereagh concluded by stating that he had done his duty and that he was proud of his part in the 'important transaction'. General Charles Crauford also spoke in the government's defence, adding two resolutions of his own; that ministers were correct to advise the undertaking of the expedition, notwithstanding the difficulties, and that the delayed evacuation of Walcheren was justified by the state of negotiations between France and Austria and the possibility of renewed hostilities. The debate ground on for three more days, finally adjourning at 7am on a Saturday morning. Perceval admitted that he, the House and the discussion were all exhausted.[12]

Members voted on the four resolutions on 31 March. The first division, on Lord Porchester's resolution censuring ministers for initiating the expedition, was defeated by a vote of 275 to 227. Crauford's amendment exonerating ministers from blame for the outcome of the expedition was carried by 272 to 232. The third division, criticising ministers for temporarily retaining Walcheren, was defeated by 275 to 224 and the final division, approving the retention of Walcheren, was won by 253 to 232.

This was a crushing defeat for the Whig opposition. The voting patterns suggest that there were many members who were unwilling to approve the expedition but still more who were reluctant to condemn it. The opposition were unable to capitalise on a good case, strong allies in parliament and public sympathy. The government's survival can be attributed to three factors. Firstly, it was difficult to unreservedly attack a wartime administration without incurring the charge of being anti-patriotic. Secondly, the men most closely associated with the execution of the expedition – Castlereagh and Chatham – were already out of office. Thirdly, the Whigs were distrusted and the majority of independent members hoped that Walcheren would be a salutary lesson for a government they still preferred to a party which had neither unity nor credibility.[13]

Political expediency had won out and the government, the army and the navy were absolved. This outcome was widely considered to be a disgrace. The usually moderate Lord Holland believed that it furnished 'the strongest practical argument for the reform of parliament'. The House of Commons had spoken neither for the people it represented nor itself. The newspapers agreed. The *Edinburgh Review* asserted that the government majority acquitted itself but condemned parliament whilst the *Annual Register* described the vote as an 'insult to the people'. *The Times* asked, 'If the Walcheren expedition is to pass unmarred by the general censure, then can no calamity happen on which the British nation will deserve to be heard?' There were demands for a second investigation but this did not materialise.[14]

Notes

1. *The Walcheren Expedition. The Experiences of a British Officer of the 81st Regiment*, pp. 150–1; St Clair, Lt Col, *A soldier's recollections of the West Indies and America with a narrative of the expedition to the Island of Walcheren*, Vol. II, p. 372; Verner, W., *History and Campaigns of the Rifle Brigade*, Vol. II, p. 36; *Vicissitudes of a Scottish Soldier*, pp. 102–3; Dent, W., *A Young Surgeon in Wellington's Army*, pp. 13–4; Greenwood, Major, *British Loss of Life in the Wars of 1794–1815 and in 1914–1918*, p. 10.
2. Parliamentary Papers 1810, Vol. XV, pp. x–xi; *A Collection of Papers Relating to the Expedition to the Scheldt*, pp. 676, 727, 737; Cantlie, N., *A History of the Army Medical Department*, Vol. I, pp. 396–403; Wright, T., *History of the Walcheren Intermittent*, pp. xv–xvi; Kempthorne, G. A., *The Walcheren Expedition and the Reform of the Medical Board 1809*, p. 137; Brett-James, A., *The Walcheren Failure*, pp. 65–6; Harris, B., *Recollections of Rifleman Harris*, pp. 177–8; *Vicissitudes*, p. 103; *A Soldier of the Seventy-First*, p. 45; Dallas, R. W., *A Subaltern of the 9th in the Peninsula and Walcheren*, p. 63.
3. *A Collection of Papers*, p. 63; Marshall, H., *Contribution to Statistics of the Sickness and Mortality which occurred among the troops employed on the expedition to the Scheldt in the year 1809*, p. 319; McGuffie, T. H., *The Walcheren Expedition and the Walcheren Fever*, p. 191.
4. Bond, G., *The Grand Expedition*, pp. 140–3; Fleischman, T., *L'Expedition Anglaise sur le Continent en 1809*, pp. 97, 109–10; Muir, R., *Britain and the Defeat of Napoleon 1807–1815*, p. 13; Parliamentary Papers, Vol. XV, p. ccxliv; *The Personal Narrative of a Private Soldier in the 42nd Highlanders*, p. 108; NAM, 2002-02-729.
5. Parliamentary Debates 1810, Vol. XV, pp. 161–307; Bond, p. 143.
6. Muir, p. 109; Bond, p. 144; Christie, C. A., *The Royal Navy and the Walcheren Expedition of 1809*, p. 196; Parliamentary Debates, Vol. XV, pp. 205–7; Parliamentary Papers, Vol. XV, p. ccl.
7. Creevey, T., *Thomas Creevey's Papers 1798–1838*, p. 76; Parliamentary Papers, Vol. XV, pp. 5xlv–5xxix, ccclxxiv–ccccxxxiv, 5xii; Bond, p. 146.
8. Parliamentary Papers, Vol. XV, pp. cci–ii, cclxxxvi–iii, ccxxviii, cclxxi, cccxiv.
9. Creevey, p. 79; Christie, p. 196; *A Collection of Papers*, pp. 749–61; Parliamentary

Debates, Vol. XV, pp. 487, 490; Muir, p. 109; Parliamentary Papers, Vol. XVI, pp. 1105–1115.

10. Parliamentary Debates, Vol. XV, pp. 200–1; Parliamentary Papers, Vol. XVI, pp. 1116–1130; *A Collection of Papers*, pp. 768–89; Bond, pp. 150–5.

11. Parliamentary Papers, Vol. XV, cvii–cxxxviii, cccclxviii–cccclxxxvii; Crowe, K. E., *The Walcheren Expedition and the New Army Medical Board*, p. 771; Cantlie, Vol. I, pp. 404–5; McGrigor, J., *The Scalpel and the Sword*, pp. 161–2.

12. Parliamentary Debates, Vol. XVI, pp. 46–134, 306–72, 388–422.

13. Parliamentary Debates, Vol. XVI, pp. 421–2; Hall, C. D., *British Strategy in the Napoleonic War 1803–15*, pp. 63–4; Muir, p. 109; Roberts, M., *The Whig Party 1807–1812*, pp. 146–7.

14. Roberts, pp. 146–7; Bond, p. 158.

CHAPTER 16

The Swampy Shore

N apoleon had definite plans for Holland. At the end of 1809, he had informed Louis that the annexation of his realm to France would be best for both countries and the whole continent. It would also be the most harmful outcome for England. 'This reunion can be brought about by consent or by force. I have enough complaints against Holland to declare war on it.' The Emperor achieved his objective in two stages. On 16 March 1810, a treaty was signed in which significant areas of the country were transferred to French control. Louis, continually criticised and humiliated by his brother, finally abdicated on 1 July. An Imperial Decree written a week later stated laconically, 'Holland is reunited to the Empire'.

Napoleon now sought to secure the Scheldt against future British attack. He instructed his aide-de-camp, Count Lauriston, to undertake a tour of Cadsand, Walcheren, South Beveland, Bergen-op-Zoom and Antwerp to ascertain the state of the fortifications and the loyalty of the local population. In late January, before he had completed the political subjugation of Holland, he issued a decree from the Tuileries designed to protect the northern coasts of the Empire and particularly the docks and arsenal at Antwerp. Repairs were made to the defences and dockyards at Flushing and the fleet was strengthened. An Army of the Brabant made up of French and allied troops was to patrol the region between the Meuse, the Scheldt and the sea.[1]

The defence of the Scheldt had consumed valuable resources. In September, Napoleon had written to his brother, Eugene, complaining that his finances were in a mess and that the English attack had cost him 50 million francs. This is in stark contrast to a report in *Le Moniteur* in early 1810.

> The mischief done by the English in the Island of Walcheren is estimated at about 400,000 francs [about £16,000] but they have repaired the fortifications of Flushing on the landside and left them in the best condition. The expense thereby incurred is estimated by our engineers at 600,000 francs [£24,000]. They have left behind

balls, bombs and pieces of ordnance and suffered a great number of
their ships to be taken: several of them were laden with clothes:
fifteen thousand coats were found in one of them. On calculating the
value of these different articles and taking everything into account, it
will be found that our losses are nearly balanced by our gains: at
least, the former do not exceed the latter by 50,000 francs [£2,000].

The Emperor's private estimate is a thousand times greater than *Le
Moniteur's* figure and the truth is almost certainly between the two. A sum
of 3 million francs was paid to the inhabitants of the Scheldt to compensate
them for damage caused by bombardment and flooding. In May 1810,
Napoleon requested more information relating to the damage on Walcheren,
the local finances, and the revenues being paid to France. He was keen to
persuade his subordinates that the expedition had actually benefited the
Empire. His enemy had given him an excuse to raise an army of 100,000
men and had unlocked the navigational secrets of the Scheldt.[2]

For the British, the setback in Northern Europe meant that future military
action would be primarily in the Iberian Peninsula. This was despite low
morale in the army following a hard campaign and the retreat from Talavera.
Wellington was vulnerable and many expected the French peace pact with
Austria to lead to the recall of British troops. The government was, however,
determined to continue the conflict and Wellington was asked to undertake
the defence of Southern Spain and Portugal. This entailed a significant risk
of the destruction of Britain's main army left in the field but events turned in
Wellington's favour when Soult invaded southern Spain in early 1810.
Although this strike crippled Spain's forces and threatened Portugal, it also
meant that French armies were thinly spread over the Peninsula. There is not
space here to detail the complex events of the Peninsular War but Wellington
was able to exploit the dissimulation of the enemy's forces with a series of
tactical successes culminating in the rout of King Joseph's forces by an
Anglo-Portuguese army at Vitoria in June 1813 and the subsequent ejection
of the French across the Pyrenees.[3]

The failure in the Scheldt may have prompted the British government to
successfully support its Spanish and Portuguese allies but the expedition cast
a shadow over the British Army. Special efforts were made to rehabilitate the
regiments affected by Walcheren fever. Thousands of waistcoats with sleeves
'large enough to wrap over the breast' were issued to the men in July 1810.
Despite such laudable efforts, the Walcheren regiments in the Peninsula were
always the first to fall sick. James McGrigor noted that six of the seven
regiments composing the 6th Division had accompanied the expedition.

The most unhealthy regiment in this division, and the one which, next to the guards, suffered the greatest mortality in the army, was the 91st Highlanders. This regiment had been in Walcheren, where I observed it to suffer more than any other of the sickly corps on that service.

Wellington was aware of the problem. In September 1811, he informed Lord Liverpool that it was 'melancholy' to see the effect the Walcheren fever had had upon the constitution of both officers and soldiers. The daily loss from the Walcheren regiments was so great that it was difficult to keep up their numbers by normal reinforcement. This was despite good cantonments and food. As late as March 1812, he complained that the health of the troops had been 'so much shaken by Walcheren' that he hesitated to expose them to bad weather.

Men who travelled to the Peninsula still affected by the fever had to be patient. John Douglas of the Royals regained his health in Lisbon in March 1810; 'Here my old Walcheren companion the Ague paid me his farewell visit after intruding upon my hospitality for seven months'. William Maynard Gomm suffered from the disease he contracted on Walcheren for four years. He carried a bottle of bark in his holster pipe instead of a pistol. The fever did not depart until, as he put it, it was 'scared away' in the trenches before San Sebastian in 1813. Both soldiers probably had malaria and some were affected by relapses of the disease for even longer periods. When Surgeon Thomas Dixon of the 1st Regiment of Guards was asked by a Parliamentary Committee in 1823 why the 3rd battalion had more cases of intermittent fever than the 2nd, he replied that the 2nd battalion had never been in Walcheren but the 3rd had.

> Have you found that the relapses arising from Walcheren fever still continue to affect both officers and men? – They do; there are not a great many left now that were in the Walcheren regiment.[4]

The men who planned and led the Walcheren expedition were tainted by the association but they were able to pursue their political and military careers. Castlereagh returned to Liverpool's government as Foreign Secretary and held this post until his death. He played a crucial part on the European stage, determined to maintain a united front against Napoleon. This onerous role tested his stamina and mental health and in 1822 he committed suicide by cutting his throat. His arch-rival Canning replaced him and succeeded Liverpool as Prime Minister in 1827. Chatham and Strachan were duly promoted according to their seniority. The general later became Governor of

Gibraltar and the admiral's only return to the world stage was when Napoleon bowed to him when a prisoner on the *Bellerophon* in 1815. Most British senior officers survived the expedition, probably protected by their general health and accommodation, both likely to have been better than among the rank and file. Notable exceptions were Lieutenant General Alexander Mackenzie Fraser who died of Walcheren fever in September 1809 and Admiral Edward Otway whose death in 1815 was also ascribed to the disease. A number of those generals who fought on – men such as Hope, Picton and Graham – served with distinction in the Peninsula.[5]

Historians have debated the root cause of the Walcheren fiasco. The usual convention is that there is a division between those who assert that the plan for the expedition was too flawed to allow any possibility of success and those who believe that the operational plan was feasible but was unravelled by secondary factors. Among the former, Fortescue argues at length that even the most propitious circumstances would not have allowed Chatham to carry Antwerp by assault; 'the British force was sent upon an errand in which success was at best very precarious and practically impossible'. He is protective of Chatham, who showed 'no inactivity or want of judgement', and only mildly critical of Strachan. The expedition was dogged by undeserved adversity and misfortune but it would have needed 'extraordinary good luck' to succeed.

Most have followed Fortescue's lead, Christie claiming that 'it would have taken the greatest military and naval leaders that Britain has produced, experienced in combined operations, and mutually compatible, to have had any chance of attaining the [expedition's] objectives'. Gordon Bond makes a detailed evaluation and reaches another conclusion. He stresses the weakness of Antwerp in the first weeks of August and the potential for an early landing at Sandvliet and a quick attack on the city. He argues that the British failed primarily because of the poor choice of naval and military commanders, the bad weather and disease. These opinions are perhaps not so different. The expedition required an excellent plan and good luck and had neither; the secondary factors which contributed to its failure listed by Bond were either in ministers' hands or could have been predicted by anyone who had made a study of the British army and navy's previous campaigns in the region.[6]

Napoleon's later words on Walcheren are of interest, particularly in view of his prescience regarding the impact of disease. On St Helena, the Emperor told General Gourgaud that Antwerp was of such strength that it could have only been taken by a surprise attack and that this was impossible once the

British lost time at Flushing. In conversation with the Irish surgeon Barry O'Meara, he again expressed the view that only a true coup de main could have succeeded. Chatham was incompetent but after the delay of a few days no commander could have won through. Ministers did not understand the pestilential nature of Walcheren and the expedition was misconceived; 'You had too many and too few men; too many for a coup de main and too few for a regular siege.'[7]

In the early part of the nineteenth century, Walcheren became a byword for failure in British culture. Attitudes to the expedition are well expressed in popular epigrams, poems and folk songs. The best known of the epigrams placed the blame upon the shoulders of the two military commanders.

> The Earl of Chatham, with his sword drawn,
> Stood waiting for Sir Richard Strachan:
> Sir Richard, longing to be at 'em,
> Stood waiting for the Earl of Chatham.

Most of the opprobrium was heaped upon the hapless general. Chatham had not helped his cause by indulging in some eccentricities; for instance, he was associated with Sir William Curtis, a 'biscuit maker, banker, contractor, alderman, and Lord Mayor', who had attended the expedition's departure in a luxury yacht. A popular street song ran as follows.

> Great Chatham sailed safe from the Downs,
> With Curtis so loyal and funny;
> They both came back again safe,
> But cost John Bull twelve millions of money.

The more sombre poem by James Henry Leigh Hunt, *Walcheren Expedition or the Englishman's lamentation for the loss of his countrymen*, targeted political ineptitude and waste of life.

> Oh England! Oh my countrymen
> Ye ne'er shall thrive again,
> Till freed from Councils obstinate of Mercenary men.
> So toll for the six thousand
> Whose miseries are o'er,
> Where the deep,
> To their sleep,
> Bemoans on the swampy shore.

The British government approved a further opportunistic attack on the Scheldt in December 1813, a ragbag of an army about 8,000 strong being assembled under the command of Thomas Graham. Once again, Castlereagh was a key supporter of the aggression, writing to Lord Cathcart, 'I must beg you never to lose sight of Antwerp and its noxious contents'. Memories of 1809 were still fresh. Major Thomas Austin noted that the command to land on Walcheren was met with 'a feeling almost amounting to dismay' among those soldiers who had taken part in the previous expedition. By the time the force arrived in Holland, the French had reinforced Antwerp. Graham attacked Bergen-op-Zoom but was repulsed. The downfall of Napoleon and the restoration of the Bourbons brought hostilities to a close in the spring of 1814.[8]

There was, as ever, the danger of history repeating itself in later conflicts, a possibility eloquently expressed by Friedrich Engels in the *New York Daily Tribune* of February 10, 1855.

> When the allied expedition – late in the season, in strength too great for a coup de main, too small for a campaign or even a siege – set sail for the Crimea, and when the British and French press were revelling in the presentiment of the victories which this army was to win we pointed to the disastrous expedition of the British to Walcheren in 1809.

Allusions to the expedition became less frequent with time. The British public and the overwhelming majority of historians preferred to analyse Wellington's triumphs in the Peninsula and in the Hundred Days campaign, great victories such as Salamanca, Vitoria and Waterloo. The Walcheren expedition, the largest British force till then sent overseas, was mostly forgotten, a footnote in the history of the Napoleonic Wars.

Notes

1. Lecestre, L., *Lettres Inédites de Napoléon Ier*, Vol. I, p. 385; Fleischman, T., *L'Expedition Anglaise sur le Continent en 1809*, pp. 115–6; *Correspondance de Napoléon Ier*, Vol. 20, pp. 96, 99; Fischer, A., *Napoléon et Anvers*, pp. 188–9.
2. *Correspondance de Napoléon Ier*, Vol. 20, pp. 43, 365; Wauwermans, Général, *Napoléon et Carnot*, p. 98.
3. Muir, R., *Britain and the Defeat of Napoleon 1807–1815*, pp. 113–6; Hall, C. D., *British Strategy in the Napoleonic War 1803–15*, pp. 190–4.
4. McGuffie, T. H., *The Walcheren Expedition and the Walcheren Fever*, p. 201; McGrigor, J., *Sketch of the Medical History of the British Armies in the Peninsula*, p. 403; Blane, G., *Facts and Observations respecting Intermittent Fevers*, pp. 26–7; *The Dispatches of the Duke of Wellington*, Vol. V, pp. 270, 281–2, 554; Douglas, J.,

Douglas's Tale of the Peninsula and Waterloo 1808–1815, p. 16; Gomm, W. M., *Letters and Journals of Sir William M. Gomm*, pp. 138–; *Report from the Select Committee on the Penitentiary at Milbank*, p. 74.

5. Chandler, D. G., *Dictionary of the Napoleonic Wars*, p. 344; Haythornthwaite, P., *Who was Who in the Napoleonic Wars*, pp. 59, 62–3; McGuffie, p. 196; Burnham, R., and McGuigan, R., *The British Army against Napoleon*, pp. 42–3.

6. Muir, p. 394; Fortescue, J. W., *A History of the British Army*, Vol. VII, pp. 93–6; Christie, C. A., *The Royal Navy and the Walcheren Expedition of 1809*, p. 192, 196–7; McGuffie, pp. 191, 202; Hall, p. 179; Bond, G., *The Grand Expedition*, pp. 161–2.

7. Wauwermans, pp. 98–9; O'Meara, B., *Napoleon in Exile*, Vol. I, pp. 255–6.

8. *British Minor Expeditions 1746 to 1814*, pp. 80–8; Muir, pp. 307–; Austin, Major T., *Old Stick-Leg*, p. 41.

Appendix I

Recapitulation of the Statement of the Expedition under the Command of Lt General The Earl of Chatham. Transport Office, 27 July 1809[1]

	Infantry	Cavalry		Artillery Wagon Train[2]		Total	
	Men	Men	Horses	Men	Horses	Men	Horses
In the Downs	6825	2872	2372	1882	1137	11579	3509
To Embark at Deptford				300	18	300	18
To Embark at Ramsgate				400	690	400	690
Sailed from Portsmouth on July 25 for Downs	1023	538	533			1561	533
At Harwich	5519				64	5519	64
Embarked on HM Ships Dover						6855	
Embarked on HM Ships Portsmouth						13872	327
Embarked on HM Ships Chatham						2500	·
GRAND TOTAL						42586	5141

Transport Tonnage: 92 Troopships (19,699 tons); 160 Cavalry Ships (38,738); 60 Ordnance Store Ships (11,324); 39 Army Victuallers and Store Ships (5,797).
1. NAS, GD364/1/1188
2. Includes 387 Staff horses. The Artillery strength shown is less than that in a separate return (see Appendix III).

Appendix II

Names of the Ships of the Line and Frigates, with their Commanders, which accompanied Sir Richard Strachan to the Scheldt[1]

Ships	Guns	Commanders
Ships		
St Domingo	74	Flag – Charles Gill
Caesar	80	Rear Adm Edward Otway, Capt C. Richardson
Denmark	74	James Bisset
Victorious	74	J. Talbot
Blake	74	Rear Adm Lord Gardner, Capt E. Codrington
Audacious	74	Donald Campbell
Theseus	74	William Prowse
Repulse	74	Hon. A. K. Legge
Powerful	74	
Superb	74	R. Jackson
Centaur	74	W. H. Webley
Venerable	74	A. King acting for Sir H. Popham
Valiant	74	G. E. Hammond
Courageux	74	R. Plampin
York	74	R. Barton
Princess of Orange	74	Francis Beauman
Monarch	74	Richard Lee
Belleisle	74	George Cockburn
Orion	74	A. C. Dickson
Resolution	74	G. Burlton
Bellona	74	J. E. Douglas
Eagle	74	Charles Rowley
Impétueux	74	J. Lawford
Ganges	74	Peter Halket
Aboukir	74	G. Parker
Marlborough	74	G. Moore
Royal Oak	74	Lord Amelius Beauclerk
Alfred	74	J. R. Watson
Sceptre	74	John Ferner
Achille	74	

Namur	74	
Leyden[2]	64	
Agincourt[2]	64	
Monmouth[2]	64	
Iris[2]	50	
Adamant[2]	50	
Weymouth[2]	54	
Ulysses[2]	44	
Serapis[2]	44	
Frigates		
Impérieuse	44	T. Garth
Rota	38	P. Somerville
Perlen		
Lavinia	44	Lord William Stewart
Clyde	38	C. Owen
Amethyst	38	Sir M. Seymour
Fisgard	38	William Bolton
Statira	38	C. W. Boys
Hotspur	38	Hon. J. Percy
Euryalus	38	G. H. L. Dundas
Salcette	38	W. Bathurst
St Fiorenzo	36	
Thalia	36	
Aigle	36	– Wolfe
Nymphen	36	K. Maxwell
Dryad	36	– Galway
Heroine	32	
Bucelphus	32	
Aimable	32	Lord G. Stewart
Pallas	32	
Circe	32	
Camilla	24	

To these were attached: 33 Sloops of War of from 14 to 18 guns – 5 bomb-vessels – 23 gun-brigs– 17 hired cutters – 14 revenue cutters – 5 tenders – 82 gun-boats – 150 flat-bottomed boats – all the dockyard lighters, with anchors, cables and hawsers, for assisting ships that might get on shore – all the fast-sailing smuggling vessels which could be procured by hiring them – every rowing galley at Deal and Folkestone – transports to convey military stores and provisions, making the amount of hired shipping near 100,000 tons.

1. *A Collection of Papers Relating to the Expedition to the Scheldt*, pp. 349–52; Brenton, E. P., *The Naval History of Great Britain*, Vol. II, pp. 289–91
2. *Armées en flute* (some guns removed)

Appendix III

Memorandum for the Quartermaster General: His Majesty has been pleased to approve of the under mentioned officers being attached to the force about to proceed on a particular service [The Expedition to the Scheldt]

Horse Guards 7 July 1809[1]

Lt General The Earl of Chatham – Commander of the Forces
Lt General Sir Eyre Coote – Second in Command
Lt General Sir John Craddock KBE[2]
Lt General The Earl of Rosslyn
Lt General The Marquis of Huntley
Lt General Grosvenor
Lt General Sir John Hope KB
Lt General Mackenzie Fraser
Lt General Lord Paget
Lt General Brownrigg

Maj General Linsingen
Maj General T. Graham
Maj General Earl of Dalhousie
Maj General Dyott
Maj General Leith
Maj General Picton
Maj General William Stewart
Maj General Sir William Erskine

Brig General Houston
Brig General Disney
Brig General Montresor
Brig General Ackland
Brig General Sontag
Brig General Rottenburg
Brig General Brown

Colonel Thomas Mahon and Colonel Baron Alten as Colonels on the Staff

1. NAS, GD364/1/1187
2. Craddock remained in the Peninsula and did not accompany the expedition to the Scheldt.

Appendix IV

The Organisation and Strength of the British Army under the Earl of Chatham on 31 July 1809[1]

THE ARMY ON WALCHEREN – Lt General Sir Eyre Coote

	Officers	*NCOs*	*Men*
The Right Wing – Major General Graham			
95th Rifle Corps Detachment	1		30
68th Light infantry, 2 Companies	6	12	157
Col Hay's Brigade:			
1st Regiment, 3rd Battalion (Royals)	51	74	953
5th Regiment, 1st Battalion	44	55	936
35th Regiment, 2nd Battalion	34	58	739
Royal Staff Corps			30
TOTAL	136	199	2845
Artillery: 5 light 6-pounders, 1 5½ inch howitzer			
Centre – Lt General Lord Paget			
Brig General Rottenburg's Brigade:			
95th Rifle Corps Detachment			120
68th Light Infantry, 8 Companies	37	50	630
85th Regiment	46	59	571
TOTAL	83	109	1321
Brig General Brown's Brigade:			
23rd Regiment, 2nd Battalion	22	31	403
26th Regiment, 1st Battalion	45	62	665
32nd Regiment, 1st Battalion	37	60	565
81st Regiment, 2nd Battalion	39	60	656
TOTAL	143	213	2289
Artillery: 5 light 6-pounders, 1 5½ inch howitzer			
Reserve – Brig General Houston			
14th Regiment, 2nd Battalion	41	63	813
51st Regiment	34	46	633
82nd Regiment, 1st Battalion	36	64	971
TOTAL	111	173	971

Reserve Artillery

Left Wing – Lt General Mackenzie Fraser
Major General Picton's Brigade:

95th Rifle Corps Detachment			50
71st Regiment, 1st Battalion	42	69	955
36th Regiment, 1st Battalion	48	64	701
63rd Regiment, 2nd Battalion	22	28	393
77th Regiment	33	52	547
8th Regiment, 2nd Battalion, 2 Companies	8	11	199
Battalion of Detachments	44	51	800
Royal Staff Corps			20
TOTAL	197	275	3595

Artillery: 5 light 6-pounders, 1 5½ inch howitzer

TOTAL FOR THE ARMY ON WALCHEREN	**670**	**969**	**12467**

LIGHT DIVISION – Lt General Earl of Rosslyn

	Officers	*NCOs*	*Men*
Major General Linsingen's Brigade:			
3rd Dragoons, 6 Troops	22	40	510
12th Light Dragoons, 6 Troops	24	43	525
King's German Legion, 2nd Light Dragoons	33	50	579
TOTAL	79	133	1614
Major General Stewart's Brigade:			
43rd Regiment, 2nd Battalion	36	55	610
52nd Regiment, 2nd Battalion	29	41	429
95th Rifle, 2nd Battalion, 8 Companies	49	70	788
TOTAL	114	166	1827
Colonel Baron Alten's Brigade:			
King's German Legion, 1st Light Battalion	32	52	759
King's German Legion, 2nd Light Battalion	32	49	666
TOTAL	64	101	1425
Royal Staff Corps, 1 Company			50
TOTAL FOR THE LIGHT DIVISION	**257**	**400**	**4916**

RESERVE – Lt General Sir John Hope

	Officers	NCOs	Men
Brig General Disney's Brigade:			
1st Foot Guards, 1st Battalion	54	96	1313
1st Foot Guards, 3rd Battalion	37	74	1091
Flank Companies of Guards	18	35	482
TOTAL	109	205	2886
Major General Lord Dalhousie's Brigade:			
4th Regiment, 1st Battalion	38	71	985
4th Regiment, 2nd Battalion	39	64	919
28th Regiment, 1st Battalion	30	57	632
TOTAL	107	192	2536
Major General Erskine's Brigade:			
20th Regiment	49	68	851
92nd Regiment, 1st Battalion	42	64	977
TOTAL	91	132	1828
TOTAL FOR THE RESERVE	**307**	**529**	**7250**

2nd DIVISION – Lt General Marquis of Huntley

	Officers	NCOs	Men
Major General Dyott's Brigade:			
6th Regiment, 1st Battalion	46	73	967
50th Regiment, 1st Battalion	46	64	863
91st Regiment, 1st Battalion	41	57	638
TOTAL	133	194	2468
Brig General Montresor's Brigade:			
9th Regiment, 1st Battalion	44	67	953
38th Regiment, 1st Battalion	39	63	810
42nd Regiment, 1st Battalion	39	65	757
TOTAL	122	195	2520
TOTAL FOR THE 2nd DIVISION	**255**	**389**	**4988**

3rd DIVISION – Lt General Grosvenor

	Officers	*NCOs*	*Men*
Major General Leith's Brigade:			
59th Regiment, 2nd Battalion	42	68	795
11th Regiment, 2nd Battalion	45	60	846
79th Regiment, 1st Battalion	39	64	988
TOTAL	126	192	2629
Brig General Ackland's Brigade:			
2nd Regiment	40	60	828
76th Regiment	48	57	741
84th Regiment, 2nd Battalion	44	53	787
TOTAL	132	170	2356
TOTAL FOR THE 3rd DIVISION	**258**	**362**	**4985**

OTHER FORCE STRENGTHS: Artillery (Brig General Macleod), 126 Officers, 3108 Men; Engineers (Colonel Fyers), 29 Officers, 260 Men; Wagon Train, 21 Officers, 382 Men.

1. TNA, WO 1/190, Journal of the Army 31 July; NAS, GD364/1/1187; *Papers Ordered by the House to be printed Relating to the Expedition to the Scheldt 1810*, Vol. VII, pp. 59–63.

Appendix V

State of the French Forces on the Island of Walcheren at the time of the British landing, 30 July 1809[1]

Monnet, général de division, commandant en chef; Osten, général de brigade

Désignation de Corps	*Officiers*	*Troupes*	*Total*
1er bataillon colonial	13	716	
Bataillon de déserteurs	14	868	
1er bataillon Irlandais	15	449	
1er regiment de Prusse	49	1540	
Vétérans	1	41	
Artillerie Française	1	116	
Artillerie Hollandaise	7	150	
Canonniers vétérans	4	42	
Canonniers gardes-côtes	2	125	
			4147

Renforts reçus jusqu'au 6 août, époque où la communication a été coupée avec la France:

8e régiment provisoire	21	1112	
Bataillon de 48e de ligne	12	629	
Bataillon de 65e de ligne	16	639	
Détachement du 72e de ligne	3	206	
			2586
Total Général			6733

Depuis le débarquement de l'enemi jusqu'à le capitulation de Flessingue, nous avons perdu tant en tués que prisonniers, désertés (y compris 489 blessés ou maladies à l'hôpital):

			2960
Restant à la reddition de la place [Flushing]			
			3773

1. Osten, Général, *Rapport Circonstancé de ce qui s'est passé dans l'ile de Walcheren*, p. 285. Figures do not tally exactly but are shown as in original return.

228

Appendix VI

The Effective Strength of the Army which embarked for Service in the Scheldt according to the Late Returns
Adjutant-General's Office, 1 February 1810[1]

	Officers	*Sergeants, Trumpeters, Drummers, and Rank and File*
Embarked for Service	1738	37481
Killed	7	99
Died on Service	40	2041
Died since Sent Home	20	1859
Deserted	84	
Discharged		25
Total Officers and Men who returned and who are now borne on the strength of their respective corps:	1671	33376
Of whom are reported sick:	217	11296

1. *Papers Ordered by the House to be printed Relating to the Expedition to the Scheldt 1810*, Vol. VII, p. 61. The 59th Regiment is excluded as no returns were received.

Bibliography

Manuscripts
National Army Museum (NAM), London;
1968-07-261: Diary of the Walcheren Expedition 1809 kept by General Sir F Trench KCH
1974-01-137: Diary kept by Captain Arthur Light of the 35th Regiment, 1809–1810
1992-04-148: Memoirs of Sergeant Solomon Rich, 28th Regiment, 1803–1809
2002-02-729: Memoir of Captain Peter Bowlby 4th (or the King's Own) Regiment of Foot

The National Archives (TNA), Kew, London;
WO 1/190: Journal of the Proceedings of the Army under the command of Lt General the Earl of Chatham
WO 6/26: Walcheren Expedition. Various papers
WO 6/27: Walcheren Expedition. Various letters
WO 6/28: Walcheren Expedition. Various letters
WO 17/249: Walcheren Expedition. Various returns
WO 28/352: Walcheren Expedition. General Orders for the Army

The National Archives of Scotland (NAS), Edinburgh;
GD45/4/60: Diary of Lord Dalhousie covering the Walcheren Expedition
GD45/14/540: Letter from Lord Dalhousie describing the landing on Walcheren
GD364/1/1187: Papers relating to Walcheren Expedition
GD364/1/1188: Papers relating to Walcheren Expedition. Embarkation and early stages
GD364/1/1189: Papers relating to Walcheren Expedition. Early stages of campaign
GD364/1/1190: Walcheren Expedition. Reports and letters from James Hope
GD364/1/1191: Miscellaneous papers relating to Walcheren campaign

Zeeuws Archief (ZA), Middelburg;
De Archieven Der Gewestelijke Besturen van Zeeland 1799–1810: 647
Het Archief van de Econoom van de France militaire hospitalen in Middelburg en Veere, 1799–1814, 4–5, Registre des Morts, 1808–1809

Primary Printed Sources
A Collection of Papers Relating to the Expedition to the Scheldt presented to Parliament in 1810, London, 1811.
Anon (ed. Hibbert, C.), *A Soldier of the Seventy-First. The journal of a soldier of the Highland Light Infantry 1806–1815*, 1975.
Anon, *The Personal Narrative of a Private Soldier who served in the Forty-Second Highlanders for twelve years during the late war*, Cambridge, 1996.
Anon, *The Walcheren Expedition by a Medical Officer*, The Edinburgh Literary Journal (1831), Vol. V, pp. 111–2, 125–7, 182–3.
Anon, *The Walcheren Expedition. The Experiences of a British Officer of the 81st Regiment during the Campaign in the Low Countries of 1809* (originally *Letters from Flushing*), 2008.
Anon, *Vicissitudes of a Scottish Soldier*, London, 1827.
Archives Parlementaires de 1787 a 1860, Vol. X, Paris, 1867.
Austin, T. (ed. Austin, H. H.), *Old Stick-Leg. Extracts from the Diaries of Major Thomas Austin*, London, 1926.
Barrailier, Capt J., *Recollections of Service at Walcheren*, Colburn's United Service Magazine (1851), pp. 489–94.
Barrow, Sir J., *An Auto-Biographical Memoir of Sir John Barrow Bart*, London, 1847.
Berthezène, Lt Général, *Souvenirs Militaires par le Baron Berthezène*, Paris, 2006.

BIBLIOGRAPHY

Blakeney, R. (ed. Sturgis, J.), *A Boy in the Peninsular War*, London, 1899.

Blane, Sir G., *Facts and Observations respecting Intermittent Fevers*, Medico-Chirugical Transactions (1812), Vol. 3, pp. 1–33.

Borland, J., Lempriere, W., Blane, G., *Report on the prevailing Malady among his Majesty's Forces serving in the Island of Walcheren*, Medical and Physical Journal (1810), Vol. 23, pp. 183–7.

Bourne, G., (ed. Glover, G.), *My Military Career 1804–18*, 2006.

Browne, T. H. (ed. Buckley, R.N.), *The Napoleonic War Journal of Captain Thomas Henry Browne, 1807–1816*, London, 1987.

Byrne, M., *Memoirs of Miles Byrne edited by his widow*, Vol. II, Dublin, 1907.

Cadell, Lt Col C., *Narrative of the Campaigns of the Twenty-Eighth Regiment*, London, 1835.

Castlereagh, Viscount, *Correspondence, Despatches and other papers of Viscount Castlereagh*, Vol. VI, London, 1851.

Cooke, Lt J. (ed. Hathaway, E.), *A True Soldier Gentleman. The memoirs of Lt John Cooke 1791–1813*, Swanage, 2000.

Creevey, T. (ed. Gore, J.), *Thomas Creevey's Papers 1793–1838*, Harmondsworth, 1985.

Dallas, R. W. (ed. Atkinson, C. T.), *A Subaltern of the 9th in the Peninsula and at Walcheren*, Journal of the Society for Army Historical Research (1950), Vol. 28, pp. 59–67.

Davis, J. B., *A Scientific and Popular View of the fever of Walcheren and its Consequences as they appeared in the British Troops returned from the late Expedition*, London, 1810.

Dawson, G. P., *Observations on the Walcheren diseases which affected the British soldiers in the expedition to the Scheldt commanded by Lt Gen The Earl of Chatham*, Ipswich, 1810.

Dent, W. (ed. Woodford, L. W.), *A Young Surgeon in Wellington's Army. The letters of William Dent*, Old Woking, 1976.

Dobbs, Capt J., *Recollections of an Old 52nd Man*, Staplehurst, 2000.

Donaldson, J. *The Eventful Life of a Soldier*, Edinburgh, 1827.

Douglas, J. (ed. Monick, S.), *Douglas's Tale of the Peninsula and Waterloo*, London, 1997.

Dumonceau, Général Comte F., (ed. Puraye, J.), *Memoires du Général Comte François Dumonceau 1790–1811*, Brussels, 1958.

Dyott, W. (ed. Jeffery, R. W.), *Dyott's Diary 1781–1845*, Vol. I, London, 1907.

Eadie, R., *Recollections of Robert Eadie private of His Majesty's 79th Regiment*, London, 1987.

Facey, Sergent P. (ed.Glover, G.), *The Diary of a Veteran. The diary of Sergeant Peter Facey 28th (North Gloucester) Regiment of Foot 1803–1819*, Huntingdon, 2007.

Faulkner, A. B., *Considerations respecting the Expediency of establishing an Hospital for Officers on Foreign Service; suggested by the Writer's experience during the late Occupation of Walcheren*, London, 1810.

Fellowes, Sir J., *Reports of the Pestilential Disorder of Andalusia which appeared at Cadiz in the Years 1800, 1804, and 1813; with a detailed Account of that fatal Epidemic as it prevailed at Gibraltar during the Autumnal Months of 1804; also Observations on the Remitting and Intermitting Fever made in the Military Hospitals at Colchester after the Return of the Troops from the Expedition to Zealand in 1809*, London, 1815.

Fergusson, W., *Notes and Recollections of a Professional Life*, London, 1846.

Fernyhough, R., *Military Memoirs of Four Brothers*, Staplehurst, 2002.

First Report from the Committee of Secrecy, London, 1810.

Ford, Capt J., *Flushing*, Colburn's United Service Magazine (1844), pp. 109–11.

Fouché, J., *The Memoirs of Joseph Fouché*, Boston, 1825.

Fyers, Col W. (ed. Fyers, E. W. H.), *Journal of the Siege of Flushing 1809*, Journal of the Society for Army Historical Research (1934), Vol. 13, pp. 145–58.

Gavin, W. (ed. Oman, C.), *The Diary of William Gavin*, Glasgow, 1921.

Gomm, W. M. (ed. Carr-Gomm, F. C.), *Letters and Journals of Field Marshal Sir William Maynard Gomm GCB*, London, 1881.

Green, J., *The Vicissitudes of a Soldier's Life*, Louth, 1827.

Gunn, J. (ed. Roy, R. H.), *The Memoirs of Private James Gunn*, Journal of the Society for Army Historical Research (1971), Vol. 49, pp. 90–120.

Hale, J (ed. P Catley), *The Journal of James Hale Late Serjeant in the Ninth Regiment of Foot*, Windsor, 1998.

Hargrove, G., *An Account of the Islands of Walcheren and South Beveland against which the British Expedition proceeded in 1809*, Dublin, 1812.

Harris, B. (ed. Curling, H.), *Recollections of Rifleman Harris*, London, 1928.

Hastrel, Général Baron d', *Mémoires (1766–1825)*,Paris, 1998.

Henegan, Sir RD, *Seven Years Campaigning in the Peninsula and the Netherlands 1808–1815*, Vol. I, Stroud, 2005.

Keep, W. T. (ed. Fletcher, I.), *In the Service of the King. The letters of William Thornton Keep at home, Walcheren, and in the Peninsula, 1808–1814*, Staplehurst, 1997.

Kincaid, J., *Adventures in the Rifle Brigade and Random Shots from a Rifleman*, Glasgow, 1981.

Kinloch, Capt C. (ed. Glover, G.), *A Hellish Business. The letters of Captain Charles Kinloch 52nd Light Infantry 1806–16*, Huntingdon, 2007.

Kraijenhoff, C. R. Th., *Bijdragen tot de vaderlandsche geschiedenis van de belangrijke jaren 1809 en 1810*, Nijmegem, 1831.

Laurillard-Fallot, S-L., *Souvenirs d'un médecin Hollandais sous les aigles Françaises 1807–1833*, Paris, 1997.

Light, Capt H. (ed. Glover, G.), *The Expedition to Walcheren 1809*, Huntingdon, 2005.

Long, R. B. (ed. McGuffie, T. H.), *Peninsular Cavalry General (1811–1813). The correspondence of Lieutenant General Robert Ballard Long*, London, 1951

Macdonald, Marshal (ed. Rousset, C.), *Recollections of Marshal Macdonald Duke of Tarentum*, London, 1893.

McGrigor, Sir J. (ed. McGrigor, M.),*The Scalpel and the Sword. The autobiography of the father of army medicine*, Dalkeith, 2000.

Napoleon. *Correspondance de Napoléon Ier,* Vols. 18, 19, 20. Paris. 1865–1866.

Napoleon. Lecestre, L., *Lettres Inédites de Napoléon Ier (an VIII–1815)*, Vol. I, Paris, 1897.

Napoleon. Loyd, Lady M., *New Letters of Napoleon I*, New York, 1897.

Napoleon. *Unpublished Correspondence of Napoleon I preserved in the War Archives* (ed. Picard, E, Tuetey, L.), New York, 1913.

Nugent, Lady M. (ed. Wright, P.), *Lady Nugent's Journal of her Residence in Jamaica from 1801–1805*, Kingston, 1966.

Osten, Général de Brigade, *Rapport Circonstancié de ce qui s'est passé dans l'Isle de Walcheren depuis le debarquement des Anglais jusqu'a la capitulation*, Spectateur Militaire (1836), Vol. XXI, pp. 258–85.

Papers Ordered by the House to be Printed Relating to the Expedition to the Scheldt, Vol. VII, London, 1810.

Parliamentary Debates 1810*: The Parliamentary Debates from the year 1803 to the present time*, Vols. XV, XVI, London, 1810.

Parliamentary Papers 1810*:* in *The Parliamentary Debates for the year 1803 to the present time*, Vols. XV, XVI, London, 1810.

Pasley, C. W. (ed. Harvey, A. D.), *Captain Pasley at Walcheren August 1809*, Journal of the Society for Army Historical Research (1991), Vol. 69, pp. 16–21.

Patterson, Major J., *Camp and Quarters. Scenes and Impressions of Military Life*, Vol. I, London, 1840.

Pelet, Général, *Mémoires sur la Guerre de 1809 en Allemagne avec les opérations particulières de Corps d'Italie, de Pologne, de Saxe, de Naples et de Walcheren*, Vol. IV, Paris, 1826.

Picton, Sir T. (ed. Robinson, H. B.), *Memoirs of Lieutenant-General Sir Thomas Picton*, Vol. I, London, 1836.

Pringle, Sir J., *Observations on the Diseases of the Army*, London, 1775.

Réal, Count (ed. Hayward, A. L.), *Indiscretions of a Prefect of Police. Anecdotes of Napoleon and the Bourbons from the Papers of Count Réal*, London, 1929.

Richardson, W. (ed. Col Spencer Childers), *A Mariner of England*, London, 1908.

Robertson, D, *The Journal of Sergeant D Robertson late 92nd Foot*, London, 1982.

Rocca, Mr de, *Campagne de Walcheren et d'Anvers*, Brussels, 1816.

BIBLIOGRAPHY

Ross-Lewin, H. (ed. Wardell, J.), *With the Thirty-Second in the Peninsular and Other Campaigns*, Dublin, 1904.

St Clair, Lt Col, *A Soldier's Recollections of the West Indies and America with a narrative of the Expedition to the Island of Walcheren*, Vol. II, London, 1834.

Savary, M., *Memoirs of the Duke of Rovigo*, Vol. II, London, 1828.

Schorer, J. H., *Dagboek van Jacob Hendrik Schorer 28 Juli 1809– 6 December 1810*, Middelburg, 1963.

Scott, Capt J., *Recollections of a Naval Life*, Vol. II, London, 1834.

Steevens, C., *With the Old and Bold. The reminiscences of an officer of H.M. 20th Regiment during the Napoleonic Wars*, 2010.

Squire, J., *A Short Narrative of the Late Campaign of the British Army under the orders of the Right Honourable The Earl of Chatham*, London, 1810.

Tresal, J. B., *Essai sur la fièvre adynamique qui a régné dans l'ile de Walcheren*, Paris, 1815.

Wellington, Duke of (ed. Col Gurwood), *The Dispatches of Field Marshal The Duke of Wellington*, Vol. V, London, 1844.

Wheeler, W. (ed. Capt B. H. Liddell Hart), *The Letters of Private Wheeler 1809– 1828*, London, 1951.

Wrangle, J. P. (ed. Yarrow, D.), *Journal of the Walcheren Expedition 1809*, The Mariner's Mirror (1975), Vol. 61, pp. 183–9.

Wright, T., *History of the Walcheren remittent*, London, 1811.

Wybourne, Maj T. M. (ed. Petrides, A. and Downs, J.), *Sea Soldier. An Officer of Marines with Duncan, Nelson, Collingwood and Cockburn*, Tunbridge Wells, 2000.

Secondary Printed Sources

Abell, F., *Prisoners of War in Britain 1756 to 1815*, Oxford, 1914.

Ackroyd, M., Brocklis, L., Moss, M., Retford, K. and Stevenson, J., *Advancing with the Army. Medicine, the Professions and Social Mobility in the British Isles 1790– 1850*, Oxford, 2006.

Anglesey, The Marquess of, *One-Leg. The Life and Letters of Henry William Paget*, London, 1962.

Aspinall-Oglander, C., *Freshly Remembered. The Story of Thomas Graham Lord Lynedoch*, London, 1956.

Bamford, A., *The Corps of Embodied Detachments 1809*, Napoleon Series (2007), (www.napoleon-series.org).

Blanco, R. L., *Wellington's Surgeon General: Sir James McGrigor*, Durham, 1974.

Bond, G. C., *The Grand Expedition. The British Invasion of Holland in 1809*, Athens, 1979.

Brenton, E. P., *The Naval History of Great Britain*, Vol. II, London, 1837.

Brereton, J. M., *The British Soldier. A social history from 1661 to the present day*, London, 1986.

Brett-James, A., *The Walcheren Failure*, History Today (1963; 1964), Vol. 13, pp. 811–20; Vol. 14, pp. 60–8.

British Minor Expeditions 1746 to 1814, London, 1884.

Burnham, R. and McGuigan, R., *The British Army against Napoleon*, Barnsley, 2010.

Cantlie, Lt Gen Sir N., *A History of the Army Medical Department*, Vol. I, Edinburgh, 1974.

Chandler, D. G., *Dictionary of the Napoleonic Wars*, London, 1979.

Chaplin, A., *Medicine in England during the Reign of George III*, London, 1919.

Charrié, P., *Lettres de Guerres 1792– 1815*, Nantes, 2004.

Christie, C. A., *The Royal Navy and the Walcheren Expedition of 1809*, in Symonds, C. L. (ed.), *New Aspects of Naval History*, Annapolis, 1981.

Cresswell, Capt J., *Generals and Admirals. The Story of Amphibious Command*, London, 1952.

Crowe, K. E., *The Walcheren expedition and the new Army Medical Board: a reconsideration*, The English Historical Review (1973), Vol. 88, pp. 770–85.

Cunha, B. A., *Osler on typhoid fever: differentiating typhoid from typhus and malaria*, Infectious Disease Clinics of North America (2004), Vol. 18, pp. 111–25.

Duncan, F., *History of the Royal Regiment of Artillery compiled from original records*, Vol. II, London, 1879.

Edmonds, T. R., *On the Mortality and Sickness of Soldiers engaged in War*, The Lancet (1838), Vol. 2, pp. 143–8.

Elting, J. R., *Swords around a Throne. Napoleon's Grande Armée*, London, 1988.
Enthoven, V. (ed.), *Een Haven Te Ver. De Britse expeditie naar de Schelde van 1809*, Nijmegen, 2009.
Feibel, R. M., *What Happened at Walcheren: The Primary Medical Sources*, Bulletin of the History of Medicine (1968), Vol. 42, pp. 62–79.
Fischer, A., *Napoléon et Anvers (1810–1811)*, Anvers, 1933.
Fleischman, T., *L'Expedition Anglaise sur le Continent en 1809*, 1973.
Fortescue, J. W., *A History of the British Army*, Vol. VII, London, 1912.
Fortescue, J. W., *The County Lieutenancies and the Army 1803–1814*, London, 1909.
Fullom, S. W., *The Life of General Sir Howard Douglas*, London, 1863.
Gallaher, J. G., *Napoleon's Irish Legion*, Carbondale, 1993.
Gent, T. van, *De Engelse invasive van Walcheren in 1809*, Amsterdam, 2001.
Gillett, M. C., *The Army Medical Department 1775–1818*, Washington, 1981.
Glover, M., *Wellington's Army in the Peninsula 1808–1814*, Newton Abbot, 1977.
Glover, R., *Britain at Bay. Defence against Bonaparte 1803–14*, London, 1973.
Glover, R., *Peninsular Preparation. The Reform of the British Army 1795–1809*, Cambridge, 1963.
Graves, D. E., *Dragon Rampant. The Royal Welch Fusiliers at War 1793–1815*, London, 2010.
Gray, D., *Spencer Perceval. The Evangelical Prime Minister 1762–1812*, Manchester, 1963.
Greenwood, Major, *British Loss of Life in the Wars of 1794–1815 and in 1914–1918*, Journal of the Royal Statistical Society (1942), Vol. 105, pp. 1–16.
Hall, C. D., *British Strategy in the Napoleonic War 1803–15*, Manchester, 1999.
Havard, R., *Wellington's Welsh General. A Life of Sir Thomas Picton*, London, 1996.
Haythornthwaite, P. J., *The Armies of Wellington*, London, 1994.
Haythornthwaite, P. J., *Who Was Who in the Napoleonic Wars*, London, 1998.
Hodge, W. B., *On the Mortality arising from Military Operations*, Quarterly Journal of the Statistical Society (1856), Vol. 19, pp. 219–71.
Howard, M. E., *The Causes of Wars and Other Essays*, Cambridge, 1984.
Howard, M. R., *Medical Aspects of Sir John Moore's Corunna Campaign 1808–1809*, Journal of the Royal Society of Medicine (1991), Vol. 84, 299–302.
Howard, M. R., *Napoleon's Doctors. The Medical Services of the Grande Armée*, Stroud, 2006.
Howard, M. R., *Walcheren 1809: A Medical Catastrophe*, British Medical Journal (1999), Vol. 319, pp. 1642–5.
Howard, M. R., *Walcheren 1809. Een medische catastrophe*, De Wete (2000), Vol. 3, pp. 11–17.
Howard, M. R., *Wellington's Doctors. The British Army Medical Services in the Napoleonic Wars*, Staplehurst, 2002.
Howarth, D, *Trafalgar. The Nelson Touch*, London, 1970.
Hughes, Gen B. P., *Firepower. Weapons Effectiveness on the Battlefield 1630–1850*, London, 1974.
Jones, J. T., *Journal of Sieges carried on by the Army under the Duke of Wellington*, Vol. II, London, 1846.
Kempthorne, G. A., *The Walcheren Expedition and the Reform of the Medical Board 1809*, Journal of the Royal Army Medical Corps (1934), Vol. 62, pp. 133–40.
Lefebre, G., *Napoleon From Tilsit to Waterloo 1807–1815*, London, 1969.
Lloyd, C. and Coulter, J. S., *Medicine and the Navy 1200–1900*, Vol. III, Edinburgh, 1961.
Loo, Dr van, *Les fièvres Zélandaises et leur influence sur l'expédition Anglaise en 1809*, Gouda, 1910.
MacArthur, R., *British Army Establishments during the Napoleonic Wars: Background and Infantry*, Journal of the Society for Army Historical Research (2009), Vol. 87, pp. 150–72.
MacArthur, R., *British Army Establishments during the Napoleonic Wars: Cavalry, Artillery, Engineers and Supporting units*, Journal of the Society for Army Historical Research (2009), Vol. 87, pp. 331–56.
Marshall, H., *Contributions to Statistics of the Sickness and Mortality which occurred among the troops employed on the expedition to the Scheldt in the year 1809*, Edinburgh Medical and Surgical Journal (1837), Vol. 48, pp. 305–26.

BIBLIOGRAPHY

McGuffie T. H., *The Walcheren Expedition and the Walcheren Fever*, English Historical Review (1947), Vol. 62, pp. 191−202.

Muir, R., *Britain and the Defeat of Napoleon 1807−1815*, New Haven, 1996.

Myatt, F., *British Sieges of the Peninsular War*, Tunbridge Wells, 1987.

Oman, C. W. C., *Wellington's Army 1809−1814*, London, 1912.

O'Meara, B., *Napoleon in Exile or A Voice from St Helena*, Vol. I, London, 1834

Palmer, A., *Bernadotte. Napoleon's Marshal, Sweden's King*, London, 1990.

Pawly, R., *Le Walcheren des Français*, Soldats Napoléoniens. Les troupes françaises, alliées et coalisées (2009), Vol. 21, pp.25−8.

Pigeard, Alain, *Dictionnaire de la Grande Armée*, Paris, 2002.

Pivka, O von, *Armies of the Napoleonic Era*, Newton Abbot, 1979.

Roberts, M,, *The Whig Party 1807−1812*, London, 1965.

Robertson, I,, *A Commanding Presence. Wellington in the Peninsula 1808−1814*, Stroud, 2008.

Rocquain, F., *Napoléon Ier et le Roi Louis d'après les documents conserves aux Archives Nationales*, Paris, 1875.

Schuermans, A., *Itinéraire Général de Napoléon Ier*, Paris, 1908.

Seward, D., *Napoleon's Family*, London, 1986.

Thierry, E., *Notice sur M Le Chanteur Commissaire Principal de la Marine suivies d'actes relatives aux siéges de Flessingue et d'Anvers en 1809 et 1814*, Cherbourg, 1848.

Tondeur, J-P., *Walcheren 1809. L'Expedition Anglaise au jour le jour. Les lettres de Napoléon à ses ministres*, Brussels, 2009.

Tulard, J. (ed.), *Dictionnaire Napoléon*, Paris, 1999.

Tulard, J., *Napoleon. The Myth of the Saviour*, London, 1984.

Uffindell, A., *The National Army Museum Book of Wellington's Armies*, London, 2003.

Verner, Col W., *History and Campaigns of The Rifle Brigade*, Vol. II, London, 1919.

Wauwermans, Général, *Napoléon et Carnot. Épisode de l'histoire militaire d'Anvers (1803−1815)*, Brussels, 1888.

Whitworth Porter, R., *History of the Corps of Royal Engineers*, Chatham, 1889.

Wilkinson-Latham, R., *British Artillery on Land and Sea 1790−1820*, Newton Abbot, 1973.

Wink, M., *Le Walcheren des Hollandais: La Gloire de Hollande*, Soldats Napoléoniens. Les troupes françaises, alliées, et coalisées (2009), Vol. 21, pp. 29−38.

Woodham, R., *The Victory of Seapower. Winning the Napoleonic War 1806−1814*, London, 2005.

Index

236

INDEX

INDEX